Bridging

Bridging

How Gloria Anzaldúa's Life and Work
Transformed Our Own

EDITED BY ANALOUISE KEATING
AND GLORIA GONZÁLEZ-LÓPEZ

University of Texas Press *Austin*

Requests for permission to reproduce material from this work should be sent to:
Permissions
University of Texas Press
P.O. Box 7819
Austin, TX 78713-7819
www.utexas.edu/utpress/about/bpermission.html

⊚ The paper used in this book meets the minimum requirements of ANSI/NISO
Z39.48-1992 (R1997) (Permanence of Paper).

Library of Congress Cataloging-in-Publication Data
Bridging : how Gloria Anzaldúa's life and work transformed our own / edited by
AnaLouise Keating and Gloria González-López. — 1st ed.
  p. cm.
Includes bibliographical references and index.
ISBN 978-0-292-74395-3
  1. Anzaldúa, Gloria—Influence. 2. Anzaldúa, Gloria—Appreciation—United
States. 3. Mexican Americans in literature. 4. Ethnicity in literature. 5. So-
cial justice in literature. 6. Social change in literature. 7. Mexican Americans—
Intellectual life. 8. Women's studies. 9. Cross-cultural studies. 10. Queer
theory. I. Keating, AnaLouise, 1961– II. González-López, Gloria, 1960–
PS3551.N95Z63 2011
818'.5409—dc22   2010041700

First paperback printing, 2012

May we all become bridges
may we all become borderless
with our almas afines
and beyond

Contents

Con profunda gratitud

This book has been a collective effort spanning more than half a decade, and we have many people and organizations to thank. First and foremost, of course, we thank Gloria Anzaldúa, who has been such a source of guidance, inspiration, and brilliance to us both. We are deeply grateful to every one of the contributors of this collection. Thank you, fellow writers, for your personal and intellectual vulnerability, for "risking the personal" so thoroughly! Thank you for your outpouring of hard work and love while staying engaged from beginning to end of this (long!) process. We appreciate your prompt replies and diligent work in response to our requests for revision and your great patience as we brought this book into the world.

We're grateful to all the people who have helped to preserve Gloria Evangelina Anzaldúa's words and work. We especially thank Hilda Anzaldúa, Kit Quan, and Irene Reti for their firm commitment to making the Anzaldúa archives a reality. We express our sincere gratitude to Ann Hartness, former head librarian of the Nettie Lee Benson Latin American Collection; Margo Gutiérrez, interim head librarian at the Nettie Lee Benson Latin American Collection; Christian Kelleher, archivist at the Benson Collection; and José Limón, director of the Center for Mexican American Studies, for their various roles in the acquisition of the archive of Gloria Evangelina Anzaldúa, now housed at the Benson Latin American Collection at the University of Texas at Austin. We also thank Christian Kelleher for his ongoing support of archival research on Anzaldúa and for his assistance with our queries as we prepared this book. Thank you, Christian; your support has been priceless. Our special admiration, respect, and gratitude go to Norma E. Cantú and Sonia

Saldívar-Hull at the University of Texas at San Antonio for being hard-working maestras actively creating vibrant intellectual and spiritual communities and families committed to nurturing the priceless contributions of Gloria Anzaldúa and creating future generations of Anzaldúan scholars.

The University of Texas Press has been the ideal home for this book. Our sincere gratitude goes to Theresa May, assistant director and editor-in-chief, for her encouragement and support of this project. We are also grateful to Sarah Hudgens for her support, kindness, and help in the manuscript preparation process. We thank Lynne Chapman, manuscript editor, for her assistance in moving our manuscript through the publication process, and we thank Tana Silva for her superb copyediting skills. We're extremely grateful to the external reviewers of this manuscript, Edith Morris-Vasquez and Layli Phillips Maparyan, whose excitement for this project re-energized us and whose comments inspired us in useful and valuable ways to re-envision the introduction. We know that reading manuscripts can be a time-consuming job, and we very much appreciate the care you took with *Bridging*.

We would like to express our gratitude to Dr. Domino Perez, Acting Director, and Natasha Saldaña, Academic Advisor, of the Center for Mexican American Studies for their kindness and support as we worked on the book cover. We are also grateful to Annie Valva for allowing us to use her photograph on the cover.

The idea for this book has its source in the two-day tribute for Gloria E. Anzaldúa that took place in Austin in October 2004. With special cariño, respect, and gratitude we acknowledge all the people (students, professors, community-based activists, and artists, among other professionals) who through their affiliation with the University of Texas at Austin and ALLGO (Austin Latina/Latino Lesbian, Gay, Bisexual, & Transgender Organization) actively participated in organizing the event. Thanks to each of you for the inspiration and the original flame giving life to the idea of exploring ways to build and expand on Gloria Anzaldúa's influential scholarship.

Together, we, AnaLouise Keating and Gloria González-López, wish to acknowledge each other for mutual creativity, inspiration, and support in the process of giving birth to this book. Each of us contributed equally to the development of this collection. The order of authorship in this book and the introduction is intended to acknowledge Keating's place in the intellectual genealogy of Anzaldúan studies.

AnaLouise Keating

Co-editing a book is a big responsibility; in some ways, it's even more difficult than simply editing a book on one's own. First thanks go to my co-editor, Gloria González-López, for initiating this book, for being so touched by Gloria Evangelina Anzaldúa and her words. Comadre: When I heard your beautiful, loving, insightful discussion of nepantla/nepantleras at the October 2004 Anzaldúa tribute in Austin, I knew you would be a trustworthy co-editor and a careful interpreter of Anzaldúa's words; my faith has been entirely well placed and accurate. As you know, the academy can be an inhospitable place; it's so great to connect with other passionate, holistic scholars. To borrow Anzaldúa's words, Tú eres una nepantlera, una alma afín. I'm grateful for my job at Texas Woman's University, where Anzaldúa did her freshman year of college back in the 1960s (Is that a coincidence, or what?!); for Gail Orlando, whose time-saving office assistance is irreplaceable; and for my awesome students, whose excitement and appreciation for Anzaldúa and transformation consistently energize me. Thanks to Claire L. Sahlin, who is the best department chair I've ever encountered as well as a terrific colleague and friend. Thanks to Glenda Lehrmann and the FIRST (Faculty Information and Research Support Team) staff at Texas Woman's University for assistance with reference material. Thanks to Nadine Barrett, Kavitha Koshy, Doreen Watson, and the other mujeres of BRIDGES for encouraging me to attend the Anzaldúa tribute in Austin and for offering such helpful, nourishing feedback and support. I don't even have the words to express my profound gratitude to my family, especially Eddy Lynton and Jamitrice Keating-Lynton, for your continued patience, understanding, encouragement, generosity, and presence; you are the best parts of my life. Really. For as long as you have known me, Gloria Anzaldúa has been present in our lives, and you have had to share me—first with my friend and writing comadre, the flesh-and-blood person, and now with her work. And finally, I thank the orishas, espíritus, and ancestors for guiding me, whispering words of encouragement that nourish my body/heart/mind/spirit and inspire my vision.

Gloria González-López

Working on this book has represented a collective labor of love that has only been possible with the invaluable presence and support of many wonderful colleagues and friends. First, I am deeply grateful to AnaLouise Keating for embarking on this project with me. It has been an honor to share this journey with you. I have learned so much from you, and I am forever grateful for this priceless opportunity and privilege—gracias, comadre, de todo corazón. I express my profound respect and gratitude to Amalia Anzaldúa and Hilda Anzaldúa for their kindness and generosity while sharing and teaching me so much about Gloria Evangelina Anzaldúa's life during a visit to the Rio Grande Valley in 2004. I am especially grateful to the University of Texas at Austin for being a source of inspiration while validating the importance of Gloria Anzaldúa's intellectual legacy. I would like to express my special appreciation to Sue Heinzelman, director of the Center for Women's and Gender Studies, and Christine Williams, professor of sociology at the University of Texas at Austin, for being terrific and supportive colleagues, mentors, and friends, for always stimulating and validating the importance of my feminist thinking and intellectual curiosity within and across disciplines. Y a Pierrette Hondagneu-Sotelo expreso mi gratitud por ser la siempre presente inspiración.

A mi madre, como siempre no tengo palabras para expresar mi amor y gratitud por el regalo de la vida y amor maternal que no conoce límites, y a mi padre por estar ahora aún más presente en la ausencia; a mis hermanas y hermanos con el cariño y gratitud de toda la vida. A Jodi expreso mi más sincero amor y gratitud por su inquebrantable solidaridad y apoyo, y por su generosidad y bondad amorosa, siempre inagotables, durante este laborioso proyecto y en tiempos difíciles. Por siempre, gracias.

I express my limitless love and gratitude to my most precious and highest teachers, mis maestros y guías espirituales, Kirti Tsenshab Rinpoche and Lama Thubten Zopa Rinpoche, for their sacred presence and life-transforming blessings and teachings. May whatever contribution I have made in the process of working on this book become endlessly beneficial to others.

Bridging

Building Bridges, Transforming Loss, Shaping New Dialogues: Anzaldúan Studies for the Twenty-First Century

ANALOUISE KEATING AND
GLORIA GONZÁLEZ-LÓPEZ

By redeeming your most painful experiences, you transform them into something valuable, algo para compartir or share with others so they too may be empowered.
GLORIA ANZALDÚA, "NOW LET US SHIFT"

In this epigraph, drawn from "now let us shift . . . the path of conocimiento . . . inner work, public acts," an essay written near the end of her life, Gloria Anzaldúa emphasizes the potentially redemptive power of suffering as she enacts a movement from the personal to the communal. But what does it mean, to "redeem" our "most painful experiences"? How do we "share" pain? How do we transform pain into "something valuable," into something that empowers ourselves and others? It can be tempting to ignore such bold, optimistic statements or to dismiss them as unrealistic and overly naïve. However, to reject these visionary assertions—which occur throughout Anzaldúa's work[1]—overlooks a crucial element of her thought. Anzaldúa developed her transformative worldview in dialogue with the deeply painful situations and events she experienced throughout her life—racism, sexism, poverty, her father's death during her adolescence, early menstruation, diabetes, and numerous other health-related difficulties.[2] As a careful examination of "now let us shift" and many of her other writings indicates, Anzaldúa draws from her personal experiences to develop a sophisticated theory and praxis of transformation that posits self-reflection and self-change as the foundation for social justice work. This experientially based, holistic approach to social change—which she develops in theories like *El Mundo Zurdo, mestiza consciousness, conocimiento,* and *spiritual activism*—entails a fluid, nonlinear, synergistic combination of self-reflection and outward-directed action. For Anzaldúa, "inner work" and "public acts" are so intimately interrelated as to be inseparable.[3]

Like Anzaldúa, we believe that radical transformation begins with the personal but must move outward, linking self-change with social change. We, too, believe in the possibility of converting even our most difficult, painful situations and events into powerful lessons that can be applied to our lives, shared with others, and used to enact multilevel transformation. These lessons offer opportunities for community building and the creation of new forms of knowledge as well as pathways for additional individual and collective evolution and change.

To be sure, such transformations are neither automatic nor guaranteed. They require intense self-reflection and inner work, great determination, open-mindedness, and the willingness to risk the personal. "Risking the personal"—a phrase I (AnaLouise) coined to describe Anzaldúa's innovative use of autobiographical experience as a tool for community building, knowledge production, and social change—plays a key role in Anzaldúa's transformational process: "By incorporating her own life into her work, Anzaldúa transforms herself into a bridge and creates potential identifications with readers from diverse backgrounds. She models a process of self-disclosure which invites (and sometimes compels) us to take new risks as we reflect on our own experiences, penetrate the privacy of our own lives" (Keating, "Risking the Personal" 2). Risking the personal is central to Anzaldúa's activism and one of her key contributions to contemporary theory. As Kavitha Koshy notes in this volume, "This act, risking the personal, political, and spiritual, has been at the core of Anzaldúa's activism, where the visionary meets the pragmatist, and a spiritual activism combines with deliberate actions and physical pain to transform material realities."

Significantly, this self-disclosure and self-reflection are not (ever!) ends in themselves; they are, rather, part of a larger, recursive process. Although it sounds paradoxical, Anzaldúa's intense focus on the personal always leads outward, enabling her to develop new insights and make connections with others; with this new knowledge and these connections with others, she facilitates social change. Through her willingness to risk the personal—to disclose intimate details, provocative beliefs, and other private dimensions of herself—she challenges paradigms, creates bridges, and in other ways transforms her readers' thinking and actions.

Bridging: How Gloria Anzaldúa's Life and Work Transformed Our Own is testament to the efficacy of Anzaldúa's outward-directed, transformational process. All the contributors, in various ways, have been greatly affected by Anzaldúa's willingness to risk the personal. Inspired by Anzaldúa's bold words and acts, we take risks of our own—risks that blur boundaries, explode identity categories, and in other ways challenge status-quo thinking.[4] With this edited volume, we invite others to critically engage with Anzaldúa's theories and explore her impact on their lives and work. Our goal is not to romanticize Anzaldúa, nor are we interested in simply celebrating her life. Instead, *Bridging* does new work in the world: contributors explore and expand on Anzaldúa's intellectual, spiritual, community-building contributions while creating new bridges, knowledge, and growth across and within our respective disciplines and communities.

As we explain below, *Bridging* grew out of our own experiences of sorrow and loss, triggered by Anzaldúa's unexpected death in May 2004. However, as so often happens, the book has taken on a life of its own, representing a diversity of locations (Argentina, Canada, Chile, China, Cuba, Ecuador, India, Iran, Italy, Mexico, Puerto Rico, and the United States), professions (activists, artists, doctoral students, feminist organizers, folklorists, healers, performers, poets, professors, teachers, violence-prevention educator, and writers, among others), and academic disciplines (American Studies, Anglo-American Culture Studies, Anthropology, Chicana/o Studies, Comparative Literature, English, Ethnic Studies, Gender Studies, Latin American Studies, Latina/o Studies, Philosophy, Psychology, Rhetoric, Social Work, Sociology, Spanish, and Women's Studies) that exceeded our expectations. We represent an array of generations, ranging in age from our twenties to our seventies; though coming of age in different decades and experiencing our contrasting local and world histories and events in unique ways, we are all connected through common life histories and stories. The connection among so many differently situated people is Anzaldúa herself. Her words and presence have touched and changed each contributor. From this personal shift and transformation we move outward, calling for and attempting to enact additional transformations.

Bridging Loss, Creating Community

This book has its source in Anzaldúa's death. Five months after Anzaldúa's untimely passing, we—AnaLouise and Gloria—met at a tribute sponsored by the University of Texas at Austin and local Austin organizations to celebrate her life and honor her memory.[5] Gloria was a key organizer; she worked tirelessly with other compañeras and compañeros to create a two-day posthumous homage designed to unite a wide variety of people touched by Anzaldúa. AnaLouise gave a talk at this event, invited to speak because of her extensive working relationship and close personal friendship with Anzaldúa. We met while standing on an existential bridge of personal and professional grief, while reflecting on the multiple forms of sorrow and loss experienced by ourselves and those around us. We were deeply immersed in what Anzaldúa would describe as *nepantla*. The Náhuatl word for *in-between,* "nepantla" signals transition, uncertainty, alarming feelings of loss, pain, ambiguity, and oftentimes despair.[6] Nepantla represents a crossroads of sorts, a nexus point, a space/time of paralysis yet rich with transformational potential. Nepantla holds the promise of growth, offering multiple possibilities for movement and development . . . if we can extricate ourselves from the paralysis, if we can jump-start ourselves and move on.[7]

But when we met at that November 2004 conference, we were in a stasis of sorts, still shocked with grief as we grappled with the full implications of Anzaldúa's death. We had so many questions and concerns as we looked toward the future: She died too early, with so much work still to be done!!!! What will happen to Anzaldúa's intellectual legacy? Will scholars and other readers expand their explorations and understanding of her words? Or will they shove Anzaldúa into a box, labeling her "Chicana" and/or "lesbian" and/or "feminist" and/or "queer" and thus ignore some of the most radical dimensions of her work? Will Anzaldúa become more alive (in spirit, in our memories, in her written work)? Will she fade in significance? Is there anything we can do to ensure (and increase!) her visibility? How might we underscore and build on Anzaldúa's far-reaching, transformative intellectual legacy? How can we use her groundbreaking knowledge to continue creating intellectual bridges?

To explore these and related questions, we envisioned a collection of writings that would investigate Anzaldúa's impact on a wide range of people (the wider the range, the better!). We wanted to see how other readers have encountered, interpreted, and applied Anzaldúa's contributions, how her life and work have transformed their lives and work. We were curious about how Anzaldúa's writings have traveled within and beyond the academy: How are activists, poets, and others using her work? How have readers from different disciplinary backgrounds encountered Anzaldúa's contributions? Perhaps most importantly, we wanted to use our emergent dialogue as a foundation to build on Anzaldúa's theorizing and produce new knowledge and innovative views and perspectives with the potential to transform our inner and outer worlds—our personal lives and our local, national, and global communities.

And, of course, in addition to these joint goals, we each had personal reasons for taking on this work of anthology-making.

AnaLouise: This project offered a unique opportunity to explore and enhance Anzaldúa's transdisciplinary legacy, to connect with others passionate about her work, and to continue the politics of anthology-making—a skill I had been learning from Gloria Anzaldúa herself. As Anzaldúa taught me, drawing on her own experiences with *This Bridge Called My Back: Writings by Radical Women of Color* and *Making Face, Making Soul/Haciendo Caras,* creating an anthology can be a political act. To be sure, the politics are not automatic! The process of anthology-making as intellectual/social/spiritual activism involves careful planning and strategizing. My politics for *Bridging* have been informed by my desires to challenge contemporary academic divisions and to encourage scholars to explore Anzaldúa's theoretical contributions, particularly those in her post-*Borderlands* writings.[8] At the time of her death, Anzaldúa was fleshing out a number of bold new theories, theories that had not received the attention they deserved. I was very worried that her recent works would be underappreciated, forgotten, and perhaps even lost; I wanted them to have the broad audience I believe they deserve. What better way to ensure the duration of Anzaldúa's theories and, simultaneously, extend her influence than by co-editing an anthology? I already had co-edited one collection with Anzaldúa, and we were about halfway finished with our second collection; she taught me a lot about the artistry and skill that go into creating a powerful anthology, and I wanted to continue this mentoring process by sharing what I learned with others. I was particularly excited by the possibilities of bridging the humanities with the social sciences; my recent professional move from English to Women's Studies exposed me to the unnecessary divisions among academic fields and perspectives. And so, when Gloria González-López asked me if I would be interested in co-editing a collection on Anzaldúa, I jumped! at the chance.

Gloria: This project offered an opportunity to humbly integrate my own voice toward the development of intellectual bridges across disciplines that Gloria E. Anzaldúa and AnaLouise Keating had been building successfully in both individual and collective projects for many years. As a sociologist, I have been incorporating Anzaldúan theorizing into my more recent sociological analysis of sexuality and gender in Mexican society. I also have been striving to convey the significance of Anzaldúa's work to my fellow sociologists. My most recent project on incest in Mexican urban contexts is significantly inspired by Anzaldúan epistemologies. Anzaldúan theorizing on nepantla, mestiza consciousness, spiritual activism, la facultad, and the Coyolxauhqui imperative—all have created a methodological platform to inform empirical research on different expressions and levels of sexualized pain and nuanced experiences of consensual sex within the context of family and community in Mexico. In addition, theorizing on conocimiento has been invaluable in helping me cope with the challenges of my own academic journeys, including the tenure process.[9] These forms of intellectual bridging are one way to offer full tribute to Anzaldúan theorizing and explore creative ways to incorporate and develop her influential conceptual and paradigmatic frameworks within and across disciplines, especially while cultivating innovative research methodologies and ways of knowing and producing highly needed knowledge in the social sciences. For instance, in this volume Capetillo-Ponce, Facio and Segura, Jacobs, Koshy, and Tamdgidi offer inspirational contributions toward constructing these bridges between Anzaldúan theorizing and sociology.

As we brainstormed about this volume, we decided to create a book that would honor Anzaldúa both in content and form, building on her most innovative dimensions. We wanted our book to be (like Anzaldúa herself) grounded and visionary, simultaneously inward- and outward-looking. We created a call for papers designed to facilitate this complex, intertwined inward/outward process by requesting that potential contributors explore three interrelated topics: their first encounter with Anzaldúa and her work; the ways in which the example of Anzaldúa's life and/or writings influenced the personal, professional, political, and/or ideological dimensions of their lives; and future directions to consider as we build on Anzaldúa's intellectual inheritance. We modeled this three-part exploration on Anzaldúa herself, who begins with the personal but moves outward in looping spiral form, linking "inner work" with "public acts." In keeping with Anzaldúa's innovative, genre-breaking style, we encouraged submissions in experimental, creative forms as well as more conventional essays and scholarly work.

To our great pleasure, the book quickly took on a life of its own, becoming even more diverse—in terms of locations, professions, and disciplinary backgrounds—than we had expected. Contributors come from Argentina (Anahí Viladrich), Chile (Lorena Gajardo), China (Lei

Zhang), Cuba (Karina Céspedes), Cuba and Mexico (Jorge Capetillo-Ponce), Ecuador (EsteR Cuesta), India (Kavitha Koshy), Iran (Mohammad H. Tamdgidi), Mexico (Hector Domínguez Ruvalcaba and Gloria González-López), Puerto Rico (Sebastián José Colón-Otero), and other countries. While most now reside in the United States, some live elsewhere, in Mexico (Claire Joysmith), Canada (Lorena Gajardo), and Italy (Paola Zaccaria). We represent many academic disciplines in the social sciences and humanities, ranging from Anthropology, Comparative Literature, English, Philosophy, Psychology, Rhetoric, Sociology, and Spanish to American Studies, Anglo-American Culture Studies, Chicana/o Studies, Ethnic Studies, Gender Studies, Latino/a Studies, Latin American Studies, Social Work, and Women's Studies. We combine numerous genres: personal narrative, spoken-word poetry, haiku, ethnographic research, meditation, empirical investigation, meditative reflection, e-mail interview, "analytical testimonio" (DeGuzmán), and scholarly essay.

In keeping with Anzaldúa's willingness to "risk the personal," we requested that contributors take similar risks and incorporate their own lives into their contributions to this book. Contributors build on their personal experiences, theorizing, and intellectual creativity to develop new bridges within and beyond artistic, activist, and academic expressions. We explore many Anzaldúa-inspired lessons, including holistic epistemologies and the concurrent critique of dualistic thinking (Céspedes, Gajardo, Koshy) or what Lei Zhang describes as Anzaldúa's ability to uproot dualisms; the important roles pain, faith, and the supernatural play in Anzaldúa's mestiza politics (Bost); teaching as an exercise for liberation (Eudey, Lunsford); knowledge production as a form of individual and collective healing (DeGuzmán, Hurtado); nonoppositional explorations and critiques of Colorism (pigmentocracy) within and among communities of color and colonized nations (Joysmith, Viladrich, Zhang); the roles pain and faith play in spiritual and other technologies enabling us to survive—and even thrive—in the academy (González-López, Hurtado, Keating); thinking globally, decentering ourselves, and creating global alliances (Joysmith, Kleisath, Tamdgidi); and promoting innovative frameworks to explore global equality (Koshy, Zaytoun, Zhang) and international politics (Céspedes, Zaccaria). Contributors also offer firsthand accounts of Anzaldúa's influence on us as writers (robello, Cantú), as scholars (Facio and Segura, Hurtado), as students (González-López, Heredia), as teachers (Eudey, Lunsford), as intellectual activists (Cuesta, Lunsford, Steinem), and as spiritual activists (Bost, Céspedes, Jacobs, Tamdgidi, Viladrich). As Shelley Fisher

Fishkin notes, Anzaldúa gives us "guideposts of a new way of being in the world." Anzaldúa offers what Mariana Ortega describes as "new visions of subjectivity"; she invites us to challenge, exceed, transform academic disciplinary boundaries (Céspedes, Hurtado, Keating, Lunsford, Zaytoun).

Intimate Interconnections

You have a power bigger than this Universe and came to share it with us. La Facultad de todas nos/otras finally pouring into all our roots. You named it, Gloria Anzaldúa.
SEBASTIÁN JOSÉ COLÓN-OTERO

Not surprisingly, given this rich diversity, each contributor tells a very specific and unique story about her/his relationship to Gloria Anzaldúa and her work. Here are our stories.

AnaLouise

Like many others, I first encountered Anzaldúa through her words in *This Bridge Called My Back: Writings by Radical Women of Color,* which I found while browsing the used-book section of the Occult Bookstore on Clark Street in downtown Chicago.[10] The book jumped off the shelf, and I bought it. Anzaldúa's introduction to *This Bridge*'s final section, which she titled "El Mundo Zurdo: The Vision," swept me away. I was especially struck by this bold assertion:

> We, the women here, take a trip back into the self, travel to the deep core of our roots to discover and reclaim our colored souls, our rituals, our religion. We reach a spirituality that has been hidden in the hearts of oppressed people under layers of centuries of traditional god-worship. It emerges from under the veils of La Virgen de Guadalupe and unrolls from Yemaya's ocean waves whenever we need to be uplifted or need the courage to face the tribulations of a racist patriarchal world where there is no relief. Our spirituality does not come from outside ourselves. It emerges when we listen to the "small still voice" (Teish) within us which can empower us to create actual change in the world.
> The vision of our spirituality provides us with no trap door solution, no escape hatch tempting us to "transcend" our struggle. We must act in the everyday world. Words are not enough. We must perform visible and

public acts that might make us more vulnerable to the very oppressions we are fighting against. But, our vulnerability *can* be the source of our power—**if we use it.**" (195, her emphasis)

I was amazed to read—in print—my most private beliefs; I was so impressed and inspired by Anzaldúa's courage. Her defiant words affirmed my own deeply personal (that is, extremely closeted) practices and confirmed my belief in a politics of spirit, a spirituality that offers a transformative tool for social change. Distinguishing her activist spirituality from organized religion (or what she calls "traditional god-worship"), Anzaldúa challenges the commonly held belief that spirituality is, by definition, escapist. Her theories offered me a way to live out and, indeed, to extend my own passionate beliefs about spirituality for social change, which she began theorizing and describing as spiritual activism.[11]

I was hooked! As quickly as possible, I tracked down and read everything Anzaldúa had published, and I began incorporating her work into my own scholarship. About a year later, through a series of serendipitous events, I was fortunate to participate in a Rockefeller Humanities project at the University of Arizona, where Anzaldúa was the resident artist for a week. Because she promised me an interview, I tagged after her each day as she went from one meeting to another. I followed her around for the entire week until finally, the afternoon before we were to depart, I was able to have a long conversation with her. After Arizona we kept in touch, and a few years later (through another series of serendipitous events) I offered to edit a volume of her interviews for her and she agreed. For about two or three years, we worked on *Interviews/Entrevistas*. As this book neared publication, we decided to take on another project, *this bridge we call home: radical visions for transformation*—a collection of personal narratives, theoretical essays, textual collage, poetry, letters, artwork, and fiction designed to examine and extend the discussion of issues at the center of the first *Bridge*. At the time of her death, we were in the midst of our third book project. Working with Anzaldúa has been one of the greatest privileges and brightest highlights of my life. Because I appreciated (and shared!) her obsessions about writing, language, spirituality, and transformation, we worked well together. In addition to being my most significant mentor, she was a close friend.

Gloria

I first encountered Anzaldúa's work through a feminist theory graduate seminar I took as part of my academic training. Although her work was discussed very briefly in this class and other required courses I took, I developed an intimate relationship with her provoking, refreshing, and stimulating ideas. As a shy graduate student who usually got lost in silence in class discussions, *Borderlands/La Frontera* gave unexpected answers to many questions I had. As a Mexican immigrant woman, I often felt isolated and lonely within the higher education system in the United States. Anzaldúa became the imaginary feminist who would answer the questions I was either too shy or modest to pose to my otherwise generous mentors. Secretly, I was developing a fond relationship with the woman I would visit in my private imagination. In these silent conversations, I would pose questions to Anzaldúa about why I felt so marginalized in graduate school and why I was so hesitant to pursue an academic career. Anzaldúa gave a language while validating a sense of feeling uprooted, displaced, and marginalized that had accompanied my journey as a well-educated immigrant coming to this country in her mid-twenties. She validated the sense of not belonging anywhere and belonging everywhere. Anzaldúan concepts and paradigms (nepantla, conocimiento, and la facultad, among others) eventually became soothing caresses as I discovered the borderlands inside my heart and in everyday life. In fall 2002, my first year as an assistant professor, I finally met Anzaldúa. I attended a workshop she gave in San Antonio. By then, not only *Borderlands/La Frontera* but also *This Bridge Called My Back* and *this bridge we call home: radical visions for transformation* had become bestsellers in my heart.

We give you this information neither to impress you with our Anzaldúan encounters nor to suggest that we have some type of superior access (an epistemic privilege of sorts) to "all things Anzaldúa" because we personally knew her. Indeed, we resist any type of hierarchical ranking or intellectual competition. While our relationships with Anzaldúa and her writings have been quite different from each other's, these differences do not make one person's encounter superior to those of another. Instead, these differences (along with the many different relationships described in this book) enrich us all, deepen our collective understanding of Anzaldúa and her work, and create numerous pathways for social change. Our stories have parallels and intersections with those of other contributors to this volume, who learned about Anzaldúa's life and work through many venues: chance encounters at bookstores; assigned readings in Women's Studies, Chicana/o Studies, and English classrooms; workshops at grassroots and community-based organizing events; instruction from mentors; gifts from friends, relatives, and lovers; and articles by womanist/feminist and critical race theorists. While some met Anzaldúa in face-to-face situations, many did not. While some have been familiar with Anzaldúa and her writings for decades, others did not encounter her words until after her death. While some contributors grew up practically in Anzaldúa's backyard (if we define *backyard* broadly, as South Texas), others grew up more than halfway around the world.

We intentionally include a broad range of contributors, and we resist the temptation to judge or in any way rank the differences among our encounters. Anzaldúa's words resonate deeply with many different readers, giving them a sense of intimate connection with her. These intimate connections do not depend on shared identity categories or personal, face-to-face encounters with Anzaldúa. As this collection evolved, our contributors have demonstrated, again and again, a priceless lesson: Anzaldúan thought is borderless; Gloria Anzaldúa, the human being and the producer of knowledge, goes far beyond any fixed identities and cultural boundaries.

The rejection of simplistic identity categories was one of Anzaldúa's most enduring lessons and an important component in her willingness to risk the personal and, through this risk, make connections with people from diverse backgrounds. Look, for instance, at "now let us shift" (published in 2002), in which Anzaldúa explores, critiques, and moves beyond social identity categories—including those treasured identities she previously embraced. In the opening pages of this lengthy essay, before she narrates her personal-collective journey of conocimiento, she exposes the ways conventional social thinking—with its rigid binary-oppositional identity categories, separatist intentions, and institutionally imposed labels—has mobilized and controlled contemporary human beings. Describing these early years of the twenty-first century as a crucial time/space of nepantla, she calls for radical change:

> We stand at a major threshold in the extension of consciousness, caught in the remolinos (vortices) of systemic change across all fields of knowledge. The binaries of colored/white, female/male, mind/body are collapsing. Living in nepantla, the overlapping space between different perceptions and belief systems, you are aware of the changeability of racial, gender, sexual, and other categories rendering the conventional labelings obsolete. Though these markings are outworn and inaccurate, those in power continue using them to single out and negate those who are

"different" because of color, language, notions of reality, or other diversity. You know that the new paradigm must come from outside as well as within the system. (541)

At this point in her career, Anzaldúa is fully aware of the dangerous ways that institutional identity categories are used to organize, separate, and otherwise disempower people of color, queers, and others whose identities fall outside the "norm."

Although in some of her earlier writings Anzaldúa redefined and reclaimed these institutionally imposed identity categories—celebrating her identity as a woman, as a Chicana, as a lesbian, and so on—in this essay she eschews the temporary pleasures of these previously celebrated "home" identities by exposing their limitations:

> Being Chicana (indigenous, Mexican, Basque, Spanish, Berber-Arab, Gypsy) is no longer enough, being female, woman of color, patlache (queer) no longer suffices. Your resistance to identity boxes leads you to a different tribe, a different story (of mestizaje) enabling you to rethink yourself in more global-spiritual terms instead of conventional categories of color, class, career. It calls you to retribalize your identity to a more inclusive one, redefining what it means to be una mexicana de este lado, an American in the U.S., a citizen of the world, classifications reflecting an emerging planetary culture. In this narrative national boundaries dividing us from the "others" (nos/otras) are porous and the cracks between worlds serve as gateways. (561)

We want to underscore the radical nature of Anzaldúa's call for innovative, difference-inflected models of planetary citizenship. She moves beyond—without denying—conventional "identity boxes" and calls for a more expansive approach to identity formation that includes "global-spiritual" dimensions. While most feminist and social justice theorists rely on various intersectional frameworks structured according to race, gender, and other social identities, Anzaldúa replaces these segmented identity models with a relational approach. By so doing, she enacts a politics of interconnectivity.[12]

Whether she theorizes this new politics as *nos/otras, the new tribalism, El Mundo Zurdo*, or *nepantleras*, Anzaldúa insists on the relational nature of all human beings. Focusing on our radical interconnectedness, she develops holistic models for identity formation and coalition building. These models do not ignore difference; instead, they enable us to develop new forms of complex commonalities. Look, for instance, at her post-*Borderlands* theory of nos/otras. The word "nosotras" is Spanish for the feminine "we" and represents a collectivity, a type of group identity or consciousness. By partially dividing this word into two, Anzaldúa simultaneously affirms this collectivity and acknowledges the divisiveness so often experienced in contemporary life: "nos" implying community, "otras" implying otherness. Joined together, nos + otras holds the promise of healing: We contain the others; the others contain us. Significantly, nos/otras does not represent sameness; the differences among "us" still exist, but they function dialogically, generating previously unrecognized commonalities and connections, or what Anzaldúa describes in "now let us shift" as "an unmapped common ground" (570). Drawing "us" and "them" closer together, Anzaldúa's theory of nos/otras offers an alternative to binary self/other constellations, a philosophy and praxis enabling us to acknowledge, bridge, and sometimes transform the distances between self and other.[13]

This radical Anzaldúan resistance to conventional identity categories is a recurring theme in *Bridging*. Indeed, working on this edited collection enabled us to see the historical and theoretical evolution of Anzaldúan thought in this area. Contributors demonstrate that we can no longer hide behind conventional identity categories and labels; risking the personal demands that we acknowledge this fact. In the words of Karina Céspedes, "our desire to be 'safe' within identity categories, is in fact killing us."

Forging El Mundo Zurdo

I dream of more inclusive spaces.
KAVITHA KOSHY

Bridging honors Gloria Anzaldúa's radically inclusionary stance, her desire to make connections with wildly disparate peoples and groups. We follow Anzaldúa's lead, shifting our emphasis from conventional forms of intersectionality, which employ a "race/class/gender/sexuality/religion" interpretive framework, toward the less frequently emphasized (and more innovative) "cosmic consciousness/cosmic citizenship" frame.[14] We are not replacing one paradigm with another but rather expanding our vision and inviting others to engage in this conversation. We hope that the reflections we all offer in this volume will enhance

Anzaldúa's innovative contributions to theorizing and research across disciplines as we work to cultivate a deeper, increasingly nuanced, and more sophisticated understanding of diversity and inequality beyond rigid divisions, categories, and rankings. We hope these essays will build on while stimulating innovative possibilities for interconnectedness, social justice, and change locally and globally.

The kaleidoscopic collage of perspectives and voices illustrates and enacts one form that El Mundo Zurdo might take. El Mundo Zurdo is one of Anzaldúa's earliest and most important theories. She began creating it in the late 1970s and was still expanding upon it in her final writings.[15] El Mundo Zurdo represents a visionary approach to community building in which people from varied backgrounds and with different needs and concerns coexist and work together to bring about revolutionary change. El Mundo Zurdo defines difference relationally (rather than hierarchically) and thus makes it possible to develop communities based on commonalities (not sameness). Anzaldúa insists that the inhabitants of El Mundo Zurdo are not all alike; our specific oppressions, politics, solutions, and beliefs can be different. Significantly, however, these different affinities are not opposed to each other but instead function as catalysts, facilitating new, potentially transformative alliances.[16] As she explains in "La Prieta,"

> We are the queer groups, the people that don't belong anywhere, not in the dominant world nor completely within our own respective cultures. Combined we cover so many oppressions. But the overwhelming oppression is the collective fact that we do not fit, and because we do not fit *we are a threat*. Not all of us have the same oppressions, but we empathize and identify with each other's oppressions. We do not have the same ideology, nor do we derive similar solutions. Some of us are leftists, some of us practitioners of magic. Some of us are both. But these different affinities are not opposed to each other. In El Mundo Zurdo I with my own affinities and my people with theirs can live together and transform the planet. (209, her italics)

By shifting the focus from identity to affinity, Anzaldúa's theory of El Mundo Zurdo offers a refreshing, potentially transformational alternative to conventional forms of coalition-building and oppositional politics. Unlike identity-based alliances—which often rely on externally imposed social identity labels and thus seem to be shaped by fate, not personal agency—affinity is more open-ended and volitional; it implies choice, desire, and movement.

Bridging

Unlike a conventional academic book, which would focus primarily (if not exclusively) on analyzing Anzaldúa's words, *Bridging* does not stop with analysis but also includes excavation and application. Contributors do not simply investigate Anzaldúa's writings; rather, we apply them— to our own lives, to our work, and to our visions for the future. We look inward, to discuss how encountering Anzaldúa transformed us, and we take our transformations outward to explore how her theories and the lessons we have learned from her work could alter other areas of the world, ranging from the "postcolonial inferiority complex" that Lei Zhang develops and applies to "white"-supremacist beauty standards in China to Elisa Facio and Denise Segura's exploration of a "borderlands community praxis" to demonstrate how Anzaldúa's concepts can usefully expand the sociological imagination.

Throughout this introduction we have consistently referred to Gloria Anzaldúa by her last name, as "Anzaldúa" rather than as "Gloria." This usage is intentional—in our introduction and throughout the book. Unless contributors are enacting a dialogue with Anzaldúa herself, they, too, refer to Anzaldúa by her last name rather than her first. Given *Bridging*'s emphasis on risking the personal, why have we adopted this policy? While our references to "Anzaldúa" might seem to lose a certain intimacy, we base our decision on our intention to promote respect toward her intellectual significance and transformative contributions. We are concerned that the tendency to refer to Anzaldúa exclusively by her first name (as "Gloria") diminishes her intellectual stature in ways that could have negative long-term implications—especially as a new generation of students and scholars becomes familiar with her work. For instance, influential theorists from the nineteenth and twentieth centuries are traditionally referred to and cited by their last names ("Marx," "Einstein," "Freud," "Lacan," and "Foucault," among others). While male authors are generally referenced by their last names (Walt Whitman, for instance, is called "Whitman"), female authors are often cited by their first names alone ("Emily," say, rather than "Emily Dickinson"). In this collection, we also have intentionally kept all Spanish text in regular font. We do so for several reasons. First, the non-italicized format is our political and theoretical attempt to avoid the "othering" of non-English language. And second, we follow Anzaldúa's own beliefs and practice. In her later works, she strongly preferred not to italicize Spanish or other non-English words.

Finally, this book is not a hagiography—our attempt to elevate Anzaldúa into some kind of intellectual sainthood. Our goals are rooted in the here and now, the material reality of contemporary academic life and its interconnectedness with different and complex dimensions of our humanity. With this book, the contributors and editors risk the personal, humbly becoming bridges ourselves, so that we can engage with others in what we believe to be a vital conversation within academic and activist communities. We hope that this edited collection will nurture and build on the development of Anzaldúan studies for the twenty-first century within, across, and beyond the disciplines, fields, and ways of embracing life that each of us represents. We share with our readers our heartfelt desire to explore the many ways we can implement and expand on Anzaldúa's theories, from intellectual development and innovation within and across disciplines and fields to personal, institutional, and collective evolution and change—locally and globally. *Bridging* demonstrates that the willingness to risk the personal can lead to additional risks—risks that blur boundaries, explode identity categories, and in other ways challenge status-quo thinking. With this edited volume, we invite others to participate in and expand on our speculations, to critically engage with Anzaldúa's theories and explore her impact on their lives, their work, and the world.

We invite you to engage in these open, ongoing collective conversations within our communities, within and beyond academic walls.

I

THE NEW MESTIZAS:
"TRANSITIONS AND TRANSFORMATIONS"

CHAPTER 1

Bridges of conocimiento: Una conversación con Gloria Anzaldúa

LORENA M. P. GAJARDO

Part One: Learning from a Compañera

Gloria: We have come to realize that we are not alone in our struggles nor separate nor autonomous but that we . . . are connected and inter-dependent. We are each accountable for what is happening down the street, south of the border or across the sea. (*This Bridge Called My Back* foreword)

Beyond and more powerful than marginalization is solidarity, and I have found a place of rewarding fruition en tus palabras y conocimiento; your approach of autohistoria-teoría speaks to me as an alternative path to conocimiento. It crosses the divide between "intellectual" activity and our inner knowledge, making us look at the actual effects, the emotional consequences of being subjected to processes of inferiorized subjectiva-tion. For you, Gloria, there is no divide, no contradiction between writing history and speaking about the effects of that history upon our bodies, our souls. You taught me that the soul knows and that the intellect feels, a lesson forgotten by those who would fracture the experience of knowing. Moving beyond this dichotomy toward an embodied and holistic perspective enables the emergence of a new consciousness, a new understanding of our identity as a complicated process of permanent change related to personal and collective past and present experiences of becoming. Who we were, who we are, and who we are becoming articulates with the possibilities and impossibilities offered up by power, choice, and ways of seeing/sensing.

Gloria: Breaking out of your mental and emotional prison and deepening the range of perception enables you to link inner reflection and vision—the mental, emotional, instinctive, imaginal, spiritual, subtle bodily awareness—with social, political action and lived experiences to generate subversive knowledges. ("now let us shift" 542)

The function of autohistoria, of writing from the body, the intellect, and the imagination is neither a naïve flight nor a romantic turn away from rationality. On the contrary, it is an act of conocimiento, a way of knowing that deepens our range of perception, engaging not only our intellect but our whole self, making our teeth capable of biting into awareness and in so doing acting and transforming the world ("now let us shift" 543). Conocimiento is about acting in the world because it is about me/we and about me/we in the world as is and in the one I/we want. So, unlike positivist objectivity, which demands fragmentation, of the intellect from the body, to achieve knowing, holistic conocimiento encourages inner exploration—embodied knowledge—to find sites of transformation that may open up the possibility of collective transformation through compassion and solidarity. Facing our inner wounds and our shadow-beast is a potentially transformative act because it forces us to build bridges that can take us beyond anger and victimhood to a place of compassion and solidarity where our empowered selves may listen to others without feeling always threatened ("now let us shift" 566). This difficult dialogue is entered into not out of misplaced idealism but out of the imperative to create a new way of seeing, one born out of the necessity to stop the madness of destruction enveloping our worlds. The old way has not worked, so our task remains to build bridges to cross toward one another.

Part Two: Autohistorias and Paths of Possibilities

Understanding Our History

> *Gloria:* Con el destierro y el exilio fuimos desuñados, destroneados, destripados—we were jerked out by the roots, truncated, disemboweled, dispossessed, and separated from our identity and our history. (*Borderlands/La Frontera* 29–30)

Que duro es el desarraigo, el sentirse siempre como huérfana, mujer sin tierra. Yo/nosotros también fuimos desuñados, destroneados, destripados, jerked out by the roots and dispossessed. It's the story of all

Latin America; it is the his/herstory of all her peoples. Since the conquest, men have come in search of her riches, taking lives and stealing the vitality of the people who take care of Pacha Mama. El pueblo, sí, el pueblo—la gente digna y trabajadora, siempre paga por las barbaridades de los conquistadores. They changed their ways, but the conquistadors kept on coming—sometimes they spoke Spanish, and sometimes they speak English, but regardless of the language they always speak the language of greed, justifying theft and plunder with the law of the powerful, that is, with the law of guns and armies.

And so, I ask myself, how can they continue looking into our eyes and telling us that we "chose" to come here, that we are lucky to be accepted inside the walled cities of the North and that we can be turned back if we don't fulfill contracts of servile labor? Is immigration really a choice? Did I/we "choose" to immigrate? What would you do if you could not feed your family? What would you do if you had to live the quotidian violence of persecution and poverty? How would you react if you knew that poverty or the development of underdevelopment is not a choice lazy or stupid people make but a project of domination? What would you say if I told you that white Europeans and their descendants are no more intelligent or hard-working than the rest of humanity and that it's not their God-given right to decide the fate of all of us? Tell me, are the descendants and survivors of the conquista and of the neo-conquista "immigrants by choice" or "illegals"? Can a human being ever be illegal? During the neo-conquest, Latin Americans suffered the imposition of antidemocratic, brutal military regimes whose draconian neoliberal projects created the desperation we see on our TV screens where people will risk death while climbing walls of barbed wire. The South is not exporting poverty; it is the North in collaboration with Southern elites that has created the poverty—yes, that same poverty that now allows the rich within the walled cities to get even richer by exploiting the labor of vulnerable Latina/o populations. And so, we come; we are here because the neo-conquest has not stopped.

Living in the Borderlands

Gloria:
In the Borderlands
  you are the battleground
  where enemies are kin to each other;
  you are at home, a stranger,

the border disputes have been settled
the volley of shots have shattered the truce
you are wounded, lost in action
dead, fighting back
(*Borderlands/La Frontera* 216)

Viviendo en el desarraigo, to live deracinated means to live continuously with the burden/opportunity of carrying and building our own roots. Hogar, home, can be defined and redefined. I have found that the process of labeling myself a Latina, a Latina Canadian, a Chilena, a Chilean Latina is a contingent act related to many other factors, including the way in which nationalist discourses construct me/us as "authentic" or "inauthentic" citizens. Who we are or who we imagine ourselves to be is related to but not fully determined by the manner in which the nation is imagined. And this imagining is not an intellectual abstraction—the answers to the questions of who is the nation imagined for and whose imagining is given primacy determines to a large extent the location that will be given to "otherness." And it is this relation that we have to deal with as Latinas/os in Canada—our subaltern positioning within the Canadian nation, related to racialized processes of nation building along with capitalist processes of accumulation, is our struggle, for it is here that we now have to build our hogar.

Becoming Latina in Canada

> *Gloria:* Now that we had a name, some of the fragmented pieces began to fall together—who we were, how we had evolved. We began to get glimpses of what we might eventually become. (*Borderlands/La Frontera* 63)

They called me chilena in the beginning; my belonging to that land and to those people was a given because of the accident that was my birth in the nationalist project called Chile. But here, in Canada, I don't think I will ever be considered a Canadian. You see, here, "authentic" Canadians are of white French or English descent, and the rest of us are called immigrants. So, I/we must negotiate our Latin American identities within racialized definitions of Canadian identity that discursively construct us as "inauthentic" Canadians.

And so, to fit the pieces of the puzzle together and to get glimpses of what we might become I have begun a conversation with young Latinas/os. I want to know if second-generation Latinas/os born here feel safe to be Latinas/os and Canadians or if there is always a prize to be exacted and demanded because of our "difference." This work, my lived experience, and my conversations with Latinas/os here en el Norte have provided me with valuable glimpses into our Latina/o Canadian reality. Many of us feel—materially, intellectually, and emotionally—that the privileged space of citizenship continues to be a carefully guarded border that excludes many of us. We find that First World nations like Canada prefer to temporarily import Latina/o labor power, as migrant workers, for example, to do work that is badly paid and highly exploitive. And even when we have official status as either landed immigrants or even as legal citizens we exist at the margins of society—with no economic, political, or cultural power.

We, as Latinas/os, therefore, are almost always starting from a location of material exploitation, insecurity, and emotional anxiety. These feelings are compounded by the manner in which we are represented in the popular media. Canada's own cultural dependence on the United States means that for Latinas/os in Canada what passes for Latina/o culture is for the most part made in the USA. Reduced en el Norte to racialized portrayals of us as hypersexualized señoritas or as dangerous illegals and criminals, our "difference" is constructed as an original cultural/genetic trait of a degeneracy to be feared and contained. As one of the characters in Carmen Aguirre's play *Qué pasa con la raza, eh?* says: "I don't feel like I'm part of this cultural mosaic when I'm surrounded by bleeding hearts who suffer from amnesia about the history of their country. . . . We are living together in Vancouver, a place where white supremacists beat an old Sikh brother to death, where they chase black brothers out of the Ivanhoe with baseball bats, where they beat the crap out of Filipino brothers in Squamish, where everywhere I look I'm portrayed as a fuckin' dealer 'cause I'm Latino" (in Habell-Pallán 182). This graphic statement points out that we Latinas/os, as "immigrants" and therefore as "inauthentic" citizens, are located in the quicksand of national belonging.

Paths of Possibility

> *Gloria:* It's not enough to denounce the culture's old account—you must provide new narratives embodying alternative potentials. ("now let us shift" 560)

We must not surrender accounts of our latinidad; we need to generate counternarratives that provide for us new versions/visions of who we are and who we can become. And so the question of who we are as Latinas/os in Canada remains open, for we are multiple and heterogeneous. But in telling our own stories, we could consider options that, although respecting our identity and our struggles, are able to, when necessary, push us through our identifications ("now let us shift" 556). That is, we could choose to not confine our latinidad to a category of identification limited by reactive scripts that reduce our realities to marginality and victimhood. We are after all people of great creativity and great solidarity. We have helped each other, sometimes not too eagerly, for we also sometimes measure each other according to hegemonic categories of nationality, sexuality, race, class, and ability. But here in Canada, we are not so many that we can afford to carry divisions based on oppressive constructs. If we want positive transformation we need to meet halfway, not only and maybe not even as Latinas/os but as people with valid awareness willing to use la facultad del conocimiento. A conocimiento that, as you tell us, Gloria, is capable of bringing different pulses of knowledge together where I/we can create a tempo that rhythmically, spiritually, and intimately creates bridges within and among us. With this conocimiento I/we can step outside imposed identifications and reshape myself/ourselves and our communities out of divisive categories and with this facultad of solidarity reinterpret the past and the future so I/we can create a more just present ("now let us shift" 568).

> *Gloria:* Through the act of writing you call, like the ancient chamana, the scattered pieces of your soul back to your body. You commence the arduous task of rebuilding yourself, composing a story that more accurately expresses your new identity. You seek out allies and, together, begin building spiritual/political communities that struggle for personal growth and social justice. ("now let us shift" 573–74)

Sí Gloria, gracias por recordarme que este conocimiento no es en vano; it has the job of transforming through respect and solidarity our fragmented selves into the strength of a pueblo ("now let us shift" 568). As you say, this job is not easy. Thinking and acting holistically—in conocimiento—does not mean adopting a naïve relativism incapable of understanding the functions and effects of power and oppression in ourselves and our world. Some things are indeed unforgivable and as such almost impossible to bridge ("now let us shift" 573). What conocimiento offers is the possibility of beginning a dialogue under different terms because it demands mutual awareness where I/we see not only ourselves but also others as not being limited/caged by imposed identifications. The objective is to enable the difficult task of finding the common ground upon which we must stand if we are to achieve solidarity, if we are to achieve transformation. This becomes the required condition to help subvert the dichotomy of winners/losers upon which much hegemonic knowledge (religious, scientific, political, historical) is based. Solidarity not as an abstraction but as a practice is the work of conocimiento. Y como tú nos recuerdas, Gloria, este puente/this bridge can always be built, even today when violence, fear, and bombs threaten to become the only alternatives.

Gracias, Gloria,
gracias compañera pensadora y soñadora
que con tus palabras me enseñaste que no se necesitan
    alas para volar.

CHAPTER 2

A Letter to Gloria Anzaldúa Written from 30,000 Feet and 25 Years after Her "Speaking In Tongues: A Letter to 3rd-World Women Writers"

ARIEL ROBELLO

Querida Gloria,
From 30,000 feet sunset is a nuclear kiss.
It takes five hours to cross the continent,
five hours to jettison from my home in Florida
where I am merely a daughter caring for her parents
to Los Angeles where I am poet—refined and adorned with feathers.

When we most need them, the words—find us.
They marry our ears to the sonic boom of Mother Earth's heart.
It is a revelry to be this high—a dense plastic
panel between the hope of swollen clouds and the will of the seat
holding the poet erect.
In this condensed modern world with its toilets flushing blue,
I notice a cross-eyed baby boy gnawing his fist,
a sweaty man drowning in his plaid overcoat,
a dozen Brazilian tourists in matching sun-bright T-shirts
and you—Gloria,
floating up here like a bolt of lightning,
a phosphorescent bookmark in the middle of these journal pages.

Tomorrow I will present my "expertise" on the poet's life—not just any poet's life but the *womanofcolor* poet's life—to *womenofcolor* who want to believe that writing is not in vain. I have been invited by *Miss* Kristina Wong, the bravest performance artist I know. It is an honor to be called to this community center in the Valley (a place I avoided due to my fear of the 405 while I lived in L.A.). I have planned everything, the time I will spend commuting, my opening remarks, the warm-up exercises, my outfit, and most of all the hope I will try to feign. You see, when your days are spent watching orange chemo drip from hovering medicine bags into your mother's bruised arms, it can be hard to see the beauty in life, but that is exactly what a poet must do.

Gloria,
In the night sky you shine and dart like a silver dagger,
still, your tenderness makes me outstretch my hands,
eager to (caress) the soft layers of feathers,
reds and greens worked through a darkest green.
You fly alongside me,
dancing on the airstreams,
the longest of your quetzal feathers streaming behind you.

When presenting workshops I like to carry at least two bags of texts written by *womenofcolor*. I like to carry them as a woman in the marketplace might carry two bags of rice or maíz, one in each hand to balance her walk, or both balanced on her head. Like her, I deliver my family's diet. These books serve as proof that publishing is possible. They serve as reinforcement when I feel too weary or uncertain to speak. They serve as markers from where we have been to where we might go. But most of all they serve as inspiration.

On this trip, however, I have to carry back the last remains of my life in L.A., and so there is no room to bring two bags full of books. The only one with me on this red-eye flight is *This Bridge Called My Back* published in 1981 by you and Cherríe Moraga, both Libras with a Virgo Cusp. The spine of the book gives way naturally to the essay that first tapped my Chicana consciousness. I have not looked back over the "bridge" that this book became for me since my freshman year of college when I sat on the floor of the student bookstore counting the financial aid money as if it would magically double in front of my eyes. There were so many books I *had* to buy for classes I *had* to attend, but I wanted a book that my fingertips chose, so I traced the spines of the masses of books and ended up with a used copy of *This Bridge.* I sat in that bookstore until closing, reading the essays. I would have swallowed the pages to take them home with me, but in the end I decided that the art history book I *had* to buy would have to wait, and I went home with the sum of your sweat, your tears, and your love tucked in my backpack.

Gloria,
I want to break through the oval window,
through to the other side where daughters and mothers,
lovers and tías, feministas y hocicona warriors are taking turns
doing pirouettes in the sky,
stirring the night's ink and laughing as they lose their balance and
  fall into
each other's arms.
I am on my way again.
Barreling westward to Los Angeles—the city that taught me to speak up,
the city that took away my addiction to saccharine love
and replaced it with ambition.
Manifest.
How many times?
That word married to Destiny.
How many times?
Their excuses for how this country was born,
how it lives and how it goes on.

Below the clouds tickling the wings of this 747 are quadrants of land—
some rusty octagons, some lazy gray squares. I try to imagine a time
when the land was unhinged, but for *womenofcolor* there seems to be an
endless supply of borders that break the limbs of our lives. Tomorrow
I will say to them, this work, this writer's work, is to reset the broken
bones. Only like the land below, the natural seams of things undone
never fully mend.
Tomorrow this diadem of the Diaspora that is *womenofcolor* will look
into my tired eyes and at my newborn book and decide whether or not
to believe a *womanofcolor* can succeed in the publishing industry. They
will share their poems, their prose, their laughter, and their sorrows with
me in an intimate circle, and I will convey as best I can what little I have
learned of the literary world. The truth, I will tell them, is that the literary world is the same as every other world; it can be unjust, imbalanced,
tedious, finicky, and harsh. Some will sigh, some will roll their eyes, and
some will laugh because we all know there is a greater reward. To be
heard. To be heard. What greater reward is there?

Gloria,
I was two when you wrote this letter,
I was born brown but there were no fields,

no work picking tomatoes.
I clung to my white mother's breast,
in a suburban house
just blocks from good schools.
I'd never heard the word Chicana,
never looked at my father and mother and seen anything
but their love.
I had not been bruised yet,
knocked to the ground,
laughed at or made to feel "other"
but you did not write it for the baby that was
you wrote it for the lost girl—
and the woman she would become.
"I write because I'm scared of writing but I'm more scared of not writing"
("Speaking in Tongues" 169).
I'd never heard a brown woman admit to being scared before reading your
letter.
Some days I am still scared, you know?
What if the world decides not to listen? What if I give in to the why and let
go my embrace of the why not?
What if I turn to stone again to survive the cruelty of these cities, these
hallowed halls, these school yards, these concrete fields—then crumble
under the weight of the obligations that I crave, those same obligations I
run from?
There is always this dream that while I sleep my heart will burst and a flood
of black ink will rise up and choke what was left to say.
Did you dream these things? Did you fear yourself, your lovers, your own
brown fist and what you could make it do—worse yet what it could
make you do?

I know the cracks in the desert below are always stretching and closing to accommodate the lack of rain. I know how to accommodate men, deadlines, bosses, and family demands. I know that the wind outside my window would pull my arm off if I stuck my hand out. I know that the pages of this journal would scatter like moths and shred on their way down. But I don't know what guarantee I can give these *womenofcolor* writers that writing is not in vain. They have children to feed and bills to pay and partners to care for and ailing parents with no health insurance and no wills; they will not be inheriting freedom, they will be inheriting struggle, as is the way of the world.

Gloria,
it was you who dared to take
the bulimic, biracial, gangstergirl
with malt liquor and cinnamon on her breath to task.
Like the slaves building Monte Albán
the weight of a thousand-pound stone rested on my back
my eyes and my tongue always daring the world
to prove to me that it was worth
any effort to fit in, to be heard,
to say what I no longer wanted to carry in my heart,
on my shoulders,
behind my teeth,
in my lungs.
It was you who took that daredevil bruja by her shoulders and shook her,
shut up and listen,
and I did: At first all I heard was wind
then the wind took shape—it had face, and flesh, and breath
and I could no longer swing blind.

Tomorrow, after the words have been shared, at the close of the workshop I will sit with the *womenofcolor* writers and say to them that the only guarantee I can provide that their writing is not in vain is that proof which Gloria Evangelina Anzaldúa, Tejana-Chicana poet, hija de Amalia, Hecate, y Yemayá, Fortune Teller and Radical Lover, gave me at eighteen years of age. I will read them your essay, and I will say Gloria did not live or die a martyr. She molted and danced in both public and private. She painted death with the same colors as she painted life. She made white feminists trying to make their place in the world understand that no good could come without us. She quoted her comrades, their mothers, the Dalai Lama, and Zapata. And when it came to excuses for why *womenofcolor* writers were not writing, she said, "forget the room of one's own—write in the kitchen, lock yourself up in the bathroom."

The sweaty man in his plaid coat decides
to shift in his seat
the thin atmosphere of the plane
reeks with what still smells like rape to me
sweaty white men—taking up too many seats.
Although it is as black as coalminers' lungs outside I sense we are over the
    Grand Canyon because I can feel its hunger.

How it opens its beautiful bloody sores
asking for its wounds to be admired and attended by all who come near.
Gloria, I see you dive into this canyon and sail just above its narrow rivers
and I know you know true freedom.

Yes, tomorrow I will remind these *womenofcolor* writers as Gloria continues to remind me that to thrive you can never live as a victim. Gloria Anzaldúa gave us the nerve to be RADICAL, LIBERAL, and, yes, FREE. She did the unthinkable when she gave the breath of life to this movement for *womenofcolor* to write, and it no longer seems forced or muddled with doubt—it seems OURS, undeniably and irrevocably OURS.

Gloria,
mi hermana quit her job
they wouldn't give the ten days off
she needed to attend a writing workshop
we cheer her,
we lift her on our shoulders,
parade her through the streets
chanting her poems
and singing her songs.
And when my sister told her poetman
it was her turn in the spotlight
his ego died and he gave her back her key.
That night while she embraced her standing ovation,
we collected the flowers
flooding the stage.
And when my little sister wrote a poem to the world
saying "war is no good"
we held the megaphone to her lips.

Tomorrow, when I am parched from saying what has to be said and when I am sure I believed and they believed every word I will confess that I saw you at the end of the right wing, flying, your emerald plumes waving behind you, a silver streak under your eye.
I will tell them that you sang to me at 3 a.m. while flying over the Grand Canyon and then again as the plane made its U-turn over the Pacific. I will tell them that you reminded me that not even death can rescind our right to write, to speak and be heard, to sing, to love, to roam this earth with child, without breast, with lover, with spouse, with teeth,

with whistle, with shoes, with work, with rested feet, with degrees, with GEDs, without having known a single day of school, with mothers, with fathers, with brothers who kicked our asses, with coffee, with unnatural highs, with sex between hours, with impatient bosses, without crosses, with forty-pound bags of rice on our heads, with stained sheets, with burning beds, with braids, bald, and with nappy dreads, with painted toes, without pantyhose, without a single cent, with pens, with ink, with bold black markers, with tape, with sheets of eager blank pages, without knowing how to spell our name, with tattoos claiming who we have to beat—we are to be, we are to be, we are to be, the she in you is the you in me.

Tomorrow a beautiful sister with harvest arms and amber eyes will cry when I read your essay. When she hears what she has unheard all her life, she will thank me for being a link on the Bridge that calls us all back. This beauty and I will lie side by side with Lan, Yen, Ashanti, Khadijah, Maria, Natasha, Lorena, Dolores, Cristina, Jasmine, Wendy, Lourdes, Josselyn, Alma, Imani, V, Juniper, Monessa, Jaha, Raquel, Lady Pink, and we will breathe until our breaths become one. And when the silence has built up like hot flames on our tongues we will speak from our hands, from our guts, from our feet, and from our words our children will eat.

From 30,000 feet high.
In remembrance of you and with profound gratitude.
En paz y poesía,

ariel robello
poeta

CHAPTER 3

Deconstructing the Immigrant Self: The Day I Discovered I Am a Latina

ANAHÍ VILADRICH

Learning to Live between Two Worlds

Early on during the beginnings of my academic career in the United States, about twelve years ago, I became interested in Anzaldúa's work, as I was struck by her original thinking, her compassionate understanding of Latinas' struggles, and her work toward proposing bridges between our different political and personal "selves."

My arrival to U.S. soil in the mid-1990s brought exciting discoveries and unexpected misperceptions about my individual persona. A single Argentine woman in my late twenties, I suddenly found myself living in the "most exciting" city in the world, secretly believing that unseen opportunities would be waiting for me just around the corner. I had entered the United States as a graduate student of the then-called New School for Social Research, thanks to a student visa and a generous fellowship, which assured my adscription to a deserving international "intelligentsia." In the fall of 1994, I decided to take an anthropology course on feminist theory and practice that was brilliantly taught by Kamala Visweswaran. Selecting the seminar on this topic was not fortuitous. With a long-term background of research in medical sociology and extensive publications on reproductive health and women's struggles in Argentina, I had assumed that the class's readings would be easy for me to master.

I was also coming of age as a mature woman in need of redefining myself, from internal to external boundaries, in a country that could not have been more different from my former protective environment. A descendant of northern Italians and Spaniards from Catalonia, I had mostly grown up in Argentina under an ethnocentric middle-class spell

that considered me the genuine stem, both phenotypically and culturally, of a well-represented European heritage. My parents and grandpar-
ents belonged to the lineage of those who had arrived at Latin America's
Southern Cone by the end of the nineteenth century to populate a modern nation created under the motto of a civilizatory national project,
which, as in the case of the United States, had relegated native indigenous groups to both physical and symbolic internal borderlands.

Traveling alone to study in a new country pushed my own frontiers
to discover new selves within myself, now deprived of their protective shield. In the months that followed my arrival in New York City, I
learned much more than about women's struggles toward building up
coalitions in this country. Slowly, I began to feel lonely and vulnerable
to a new language, English, which exposed my new identity as *the other*.
As I had a light complexion, fair skin, long dark hair, and big brown
eyes, along with a heavy Spanish accent and expressive manners, I was
early on identified as an *exotic* Latina. While moving from the safe place
as a white, privileged woman in Argentina to my new ethnic adscription
in the United States, all the Pandora's boxes of my inner personas began
to emerge in confusion and rebellion against the novel, unshaped forms
of a shifting ego.

Reading Gloria Anzaldúa's work during that time became a gate-
way to new inner representations that continued unfolding for years. As
Anzaldúa suggests in "(Un)natural bridges," I had to leave my home in
order to find a *self* that differed from the comforting one that had been
imposed upon me based on racial and class privilege. No longer a member of the mainstream white majority, I was now confronted with my
sudden belonging to an ethnic minority about which I knew little. Soon
I felt like an excluída—excluded from a white majority, befuddled about
who I was, and unsure about how I should fit in. Away from home, my
feelings of inadequacy, uncertainty, and insecurity were all on the surface. For the first time in my life, I could not find a place where I could
camouflage as one of them, the "others" in academia, and soon felt like
an impostor or an intellectual hoax who, sooner or later, would be exposed. Who was I, a seemingly "white" Latina struggling to speak broken English while painfully trying to achieve a successful academic path?
Was I an immigrant deprived of public representations? Would I be able
to find others like myself, part-time nationals of a foreign land, performing as unwilling members of a diasporic ethnic community? These questions secretly haunted me.

During my first three years in the United States, I felt pulled by a synergistic roller coaster of mixed emotions: puzzlement about finding a supportive niche, resentment for not being recognized for who I was, and remorse for trying to put inner distance from my Latino self. My initial excitement about living in the United States was gone and replaced with a marked sense of injustice and guilt, as I was no longer treated as a member of the "privileged majority," while I was hesitant to join the Latino aggregate. Through time, my conflicting feelings would become part of an existential portfolio that would accompany me throughout the difficult path that was still waiting to unfold.

Uncovering My Own Nepantla: Becoming a Latina after All

If while living in Argentina a condescending faux consciousness had allowed me to neither become aware of nor experience racism in my daily life, my new immigrant journey had made it harshly evident. My own biases against joining an ethnic minority in the United States emerged from my new ascriptions as a Latina. In the end, I had to embrace my own status depreciation and felt it in mi propia carne; in my own skin I experienced what it was to be placed into an ethnic minority in the United States. I had originally resisted this possibility because deep inside I still secretly identified with the white majority of my home country. My pain also emerged from my awareness of the struggles that other Latinas, darker and less privileged, endured both in their countries of origin and after migrating to the United States.

By the time I became a graduate student at Columbia University, in 1996, Anzaldúa's writings were already placed by my bedside. I particularly remember the day I met another graduate student, a woman from Guatemala of indigenous heritage, with whom I eventually bonded through our mutual feelings of not "fitting into" mainstream academia. Excluded and deprived of support, we felt like impostors trying to achieve academic respect in a foreign milieu. I can still sense the "hermandad," the sense of sisterhood I experienced with my new friend. Yet I was haunted by remorse and shame while thinking that I probably would have been alienated from her in other contexts where I had been identified as white.

"Nepantla" (the Náhuatl word for the space in between) is the term Anzaldúa chose to describe a theoretical and empirical field of ambiguous belonging and dynamic transformation. Indeed, this concept best describes the materialization of my inner changes. My own nepantla

helped me reconcile my identities as a European—white—and an immigrant—Latina. Thinking about my Guatemalan friend, I felt relieved
and comforted, knowing that I was not alone in the battle of making
sense of my own contradictions. Anzaldúa had spread her wings and
embraced both of us. She conceived la conciencia de la mestiza as a
transformative tool that allowed her to surpass the dialectic oppositions
between being white and colored, female and male, heterosexual and
queer toward achieving a holistic collective consciousness while accepting, rather than rejecting, her internal borderlands. By enmeshing myself
into Anzaldúa's new mestiza, I was able to hold the mixed-race woman
within myself, an awareness that subtly impinged upon my becoming
"a recovered Latina" or a Latina "in the making" while accepting my
contradictory selves (Pérez, "Gloria Anzaldúa"). When feeling lost, an-
guished, or insecure, I would now seek other Latinas, similar to and
different from me, with whom I could bond both emotionally and intellectually. I learned to let my soul flow, either by writing poetry or by
daydreaming, always trying to find a quiet, spiritual space where my inner wounded pieces, as in a puzzle, would finally find their own place.

   I finally *encountered* Anzaldúa in her *Interviews/Entrevistas,* writings
that revealed to me the mosaic of her own individual struggles while
navigating the overlapping territories of the political, the academic, and
the personal. Being labeled, and learning to be identified as, the "other"
became my inner way of confronting mainstream attempts to categorize
myself. If being a Latina was going to be one of my main outsider/in-
sider markers in the United States, I should start learning how to acknowledge myself as both similar to and different from my Latina sisters
as part of my coming-of-age. In the end, I realized that my voyage had
not started with my entry to this nation but with my new awareness of
my own contradictory personas, revealed through a theoretical practice
of oppositional consciousness (Sandoval, "U.S. Third World Feminism"),
embraced via a prolific production of overlapping selves. The journey
had been painful but worthwhile. By continuing to read Anzaldúa's
work, I finally learned to deal with my eurocentric paradigmatic ego and
began leaving room for a growing awareness of my Latinidad, which,
since then, has been blossoming in joyful and still unexplored ways.

An Unfinished Path

My evolving work in the field of migration studies was finally formalized
in a dissertation project on Argentine immigrants and access to health

care in New York City that I began in the late 1990s. In this study I further explored how racist ideologies of white superiority in Argentina had been reproduced under a national project. The more I worked on my own ethnic community, the more I was able to deconstruct Argentine ethnocentric discourses, and the more I found myself embracing my own Latin American roots.

As noted above, my Latina adscription brought up dialectic feelings between being empowered on the one hand and being marginalized on the other. This dialectic awareness ultimately strengthened my commitment to work with others toward genuinely identifying the common struggles that feed our endeavors for social justice. As a full-time professor of urban public health at Hunter College, City University of New York, for the past three years I have been working on immigrants' health rights. I give workshops, seminars, and presentations—both in academia and for nonprofit and immigrants' organizations—in which I address racial inequalities, quite often hidden amid colorblind discourses for social justice. As in Gloria González-López's case, Anzaldúa's work has been by my side, almost silent but ever present.[1]

While reflecting on the future, I believe that the paths toward creating enduring coalitions should be based on sensitively accepting our ascriptions to overlapping sisterhoods, which will lead us to a newer consciousness that will be more than the sum of our parts. Rather than minimizing our contradictions, it is precisely in their acknowledgment that we will be able to challenge mainstream ideologies while proposing innovative theories and enduring alliances. *Spiritual activism* is the term that Anzaldúa chose to identify the emotional interconnectedness that gives us strength in communion with others, albeit acknowledging the differences between us (González-López, "Epistemologies"). Anzaldúa taught us well: our most striking contributions to theory come from the deepest passionate experiences of the self eager to join others' spirits. She also insisted that we cannot free ourselves without acknowledging the multilayered oppressions that shape women's experiences.

The conflicting construction of a latinidad has a long way to go, a path that ought be nurtured by an ongoing critical analysis of the traces of privilege and oppression that separate us, Latinas and Latinos, in terms of class, sexuality, and religion, among others. Being in between cultural identities is not only possible but also necessary for the sake of our passage throughout hermeneutic frontiers of class, sexuality, and race/ethnicity (Anzaldúa, *this bridge we call home*). Reclaiming our willingness to rewrite and re-inscribe ourselves and the official history (Anzaldúa, *Interviews/Entrevistas*) is part of the most enduring legacy of Gloria Anzaldúa's work. As one step toward fulfilling Anzaldúa's bequest, I hope to continue bringing together the academic and the community-based worlds toward building new alliances in the defense of immigrants' human rights. Rather than working in separate domains, I propose encompassing collaborations such as the Immigration and Health Initiative that I direct at Hunter College, which supports coalitions of diverse groups (scholars, professionals, and community activists) toward working on the solution of immigrants' diverse health needs.

Coalitional politics will not blossom without decolonizing ourselves first while searching for innovative frameworks that propose global equity. Anzaldúa did just that by uncovering the deceptive paths through which well-intended standpoint feminist agendas supported the mainstream status quo of class, race, and sexism (*This Bridge Called My Back; Making Face, Making Soul*). To that end, I have committed myself to exposing the politics of racism and white essentialism, a practice that has let my mestiza consciousness emerge from her lethargic state. In addition, by teaching my students about the sociopolitical construction of racial and ethnic differences and by continuing to examine immigrants' overt and hidden inequalities (such as the nuances of color even within the same national groups), I have humbly committed myself to continuing Anzaldúa's unfinished, and still rising, legacy.

CHAPTER 4

My Path of Conocimiento: How Graduate School Transformed Me into a Nepantlera

JESSICA HEREDIA

It took me three days to read Gloria Anzaldúa's essay "now let us shift . . . the path of conocimiento . . . inner work, public acts" in *this bridge we call home: radical visions for transformation*. The essay was assigned in a graduate-level Women's Studies course titled Latinas in the Americas that I enrolled in because it was with my mentor, Dr. Irene Lara, and I wanted to read Anzaldúa's *Borderlands/La Frontera: The New Mestiza*. When I read "La conciencia de la mestiza/Towards a New Consciousness" I knew I *needed* to read Anzaldúa. I am a mixed-race woman of color who exists in that "state of perpetual transition" while "simultaneously straddling . . . two or more cultures" (*Borderlands/La Frontera* 100, 102). I am *PerMex*, a handy label my brother came up with to describe our Persian and Mexican heritage. PerMex is my mestiza identity, and Anzaldúa seemed to be one of the only voices I read who understood this. Before reading "now let us shift," I thought my mixed heritage was the only reason I lived in constant transition. I didn't expect what was coming.

I sat outside by our community pool because the sun was finally out and I was going to enjoy it. I took my book and expected to fly through the essay. Instead, I found myself rereading sentences and paragraphs because I wasn't sure if I understood everything. There was so much here; it seemed to be the capstone essay of all her theories and beliefs. Frustrated with my own inability to "catch on," I decided to take a step back from the reading and think about why the essay was affecting me in such a drastic way. Putting it aside, I returned to it a day later. The frustration continued. The third day, I finished reading the essay and imagined myself telling Anzaldúa, "Every time that I think I understand you, I read something else and I'm thrown for a loop." This isn't terrible, but for someone who likes to understand everything, it is difficult to admit. I thought: if I were to ask Anzaldúa to summarize the message of this reading into one word or phrase, what would it be? *Transformation/Transition*. *Trans—across, beyond, through, change*. I imagined her writing this transformative piece during a period in her life full of transitions. Rooted in Anzaldúa's theory of conocimiento, "now let us shift" encourages us to use the transitions in our own lives as catalysts to transform the world into a better place. I hadn't planned on writing about this essay, but I could not get it out of my mind. Three weeks after reading it, I wrote the following.

What is my path of conocimiento? Where am I on this path? How will my path make the world a better place? To answer these questions, Anzaldúa asserts, "Tu camino de conocimiento requires that you encounter your shadow side and confront what you've programmed yourself (and have been programmed by your cultures) to avoid (desconocer), to confront the traits and habits distorting how you see reality and inhibiting the full use of your facultades" ("now let us shift" 540–41). In "The Historian as Curandera," Aurora Levins Morales similarly argues that we have to do a little curandera work on ourselves before we can practice curandera work when writing history. As I approach the end of my first year of graduate school, I reflect on how this transition in my life has allowed me to experience the seven stages of conocimiento. Here is my attempt at healing . . .

Stage One: "el arrebato . . . rupture, fragmentation . . . an ending, a beginning"

I am in the middle of my first semester of graduate school and all of a sudden it hits me—there is violence (it may not be physical, but it is spiritual and emotional), "betrayal, systematic racism and marginalization" (546). I can't even point to an isolated experience because so much has happened. The tokenization is insulting, the hierarchy is exaggerated, and I can't escape comments like "You won't have problems with the language requirement because you speak Spanish of course" (How do you know I speak Spanish?) or "My maid from Tee-yah-juana teaches me Spanish" (I don't want to go to your damn party because I'll feel guilty the whole time knowing she has to clean up after us). All at once my utopian vision of Women's Studies is turned upside down. . . . I see the "cracks [in] the walls" that I thought made up my reality (546). I am sad because in my mind this vision has died. My dreams, hopes, and goals start to fade. . . . I question my purpose in this program/discipline/movement. . . . I am "confused and conflicted." . . . I am fragmented (547). What the hell am I doing here? Did I make a mistake? I suffer un susto that is so obvious in one of my final papers that I look at it and don't even remember writing the words on the paper . . . that was not me sitting there; I did not write this. Someone else wrote this to please somebody. I don't do that, remember?

Stage Two: "nepantla . . . torn between ways"

School is difficult right now, and I try to leave it there and not bring it home. I don't want to be upset at home. I try to make school work for me by making friends/allies. I share my joys from home with my "friends" at school. "Hey, we bought a home!" They laugh and dismiss me and say "You're so old . . . you're such a homebody." I realize I need to keep them separate—school/home. I am not doing a very good job. I can't sleep. I feel like I am on the verge of a panic attack every night. I don't want my love to think that the sacrifices he made to move here with me were all in vain. I keep everything inside, but eventually I am physically forced to let it all out. I hit my knee on the nightstand and can't stop crying for thirty minutes. I cry for the pain of the actual injury, and eventually I begin to sob when los arrebatos from the semester come crashing down on me. I cannot perpetuate this dichotomy, these two "opposing realities"—school versus home (548). I question over and over again, wouldn't it be easier to give one up? But I can't do that. I love to learn, I love to be challenged, I love my family, I love my partner. If I can't negotiate this transitional space now, I will never be able to "honor the space/time between [the] transitions" of my future (549).

Stage Three: "the Coatlicue state . . . desconocimiento and the cost of knowing"

My friend left. I tried everything to keep her here, and then I realized that maybe a part of me was holding on because I needed her for myself. She made me laugh, she understood my jokes, and she didn't make me feel bad about having someone to love in my life. I had a mentor in undergrad who said that as a Latina in academia you could look forward to gaining academic comadres. I am hoping we stay in touch because I know that she would be one of these. But I am upset and depression hits—I delve more fully into my "pain, anger, despair" (553). Why her?

Of all the people to be attacked and to leave, why my friend? She asked a lot of questions that many people didn't like. She was convinced that she just didn't "understand" and that maybe she wasn't fit for academia. She was basically told, "You're lucky we even accepted you." I wanted to protect her and tell everyone who hurt her to fuck off. Lesson one of graduate school becomes very clear: Just because you are studying feminism doesn't mean you're in a feminist environment; this is still the ACADEMY! This was a painful realization, but now I know what to expect. My anger makes me refocus. I know what I need to do in order to prevent myself or any other potential comadres from leaving.

Stage Four: "the call . . . el compromiso . . . the crossing and conversion"

Clarity has arrived. I know it is temporary because states of awareness don't last, but I plan on taking full advantage of this moment (556). I realize I can't do it all. My Nana is sick, and suddenly death becomes much scarier than a B on a paper. As someone trained to value A's, this shift is a major crossroads in my life. School is not first anymore. Life and all of its possibilities become a priority. I need to do the things that make me happy. My inner voice begins to speak to me: You have a purpose . . . you can become "a fully functioning human being, a contributing member of all your communities . . . [you are] worthy of self-respect and love" (557). What is fully functioning to me, and how can I contribute to my communities? I know that I want to write and teach to make a difference, but I also realize that I want to raise children who make a difference. The academic feminist in me says, "Ph.D. first and then babies," but that's not what I want. I'm scared that I've sold out somehow. For so long, I've internalized this notion that "real feminists" and "real academics" can't have both. This is a change for me, admitting to myself that these are equal priorities. I have crossed over into a new belief system in which I know I can have both (557). This potential compromise between my two worlds helps me sleep again.

Stage Five: "putting Coyolxauhqui together . . . new personal and collective 'stories'"

I make it to the second semester, and Coyolxauhqui comes to me in the form of my mentor because she too "personifies the wish to repair and heal" (563). She has supported me throughout the year; I would have left if it weren't for her. I meet with her one afternoon and we discuss why there isn't an anthology where women of color creatively address their sexuality. Guided by "the light of the moon (Coyolxauhqui consciousness)" (562), I decide to make my own anthology, and suddenly I have a thesis topic! Women of color writing about sexuality . . . together we will make a group narrative . . . a "group/cultural story." We will resist, we will fight, we will subvert assumptions made about us and our bodies. We will create and circulate narratives that embody "alternative potentials" (560). We will shatter myths and create our own autohistorias. We are not exotic belly dancers, veiled virgins, Hottentots, savage beauties, lotus blossoms, or hot tamales. We want to create visions and representations of our own sexualities, sexualities we control (560). Watch out world, here we come!

Stage Six: "the blow-up . . . a clash of realities"

I am moving along quite well and then another arrebato occurs. This time, I blow up right away and drive home from class crying. A woman-of-color professor told one of my white peers in so many words, "You're screwed; white women are not getting into Ph.D. programs. If you aren't a woman of color or an international feminist, then you don't have a chance." All at once this professor managed to shoot down the hopes of my white friend while insinuating that the only reason women of color or international women get into Ph.D. programs is because of our race/ethnicity. One woman-of-color peer said that this professor definitely wasn't trying to insinuate that; instead, she was just "speaking the truth and warning the white women." The professor and my peer "fall into the trap of claiming moral higher ground, [and] using skin color as a license for judging a whole category of people" (565). I can't accept this mentality. It implies that women of color are "taking away" spots from white women who "deserve" the positions. It also diminishes our own accomplishments. I thought this was an isolated experience until a woman-of-color peer informed me that I received a teaching position because "they *had* to give it to you—you're a woman of color!" It was so painful to hear her words. I am angry that these thoughts are so prevalent in this community. I began to question my previous views in light of these unsettling statements. Did I only get the position because I am a woman of color? Do they have substandards for me? I go all the way back to my acceptance into this program. Was I accepted because of white guilt? I doubt my own skills, knowledge, and experiences. I can't accept praise about my work because now I think everyone is full of shit. It wasn't until I told someone about these incidents that I was given the language to describe it—yes, it is internalized racism. A woman of color who encounters a racist mentality from other women of color indeed experiences a clash of realities.

Stage Seven: "shifting realities . . . acting out the vision or spiritual activism"

Am I here yet? Honestly, I don't know. Even if I did know, it wouldn't be the end. Ends are just new beginnings to Anzaldúa anyway, right? We would eventually arrive at another stage of conocimiento as we develop new ways of thinking based on different transitions and transformations in our lives. But maybe this autohistoria of my first year of graduate school is my stage seven? What are the conocimientos that I have gained over this past year? I have perpetuated a body/mind/spirit split all of my life, and now I acknowledge this division. My body reacted when my spirit was damaged. Without spirit, my mind spit out words that weren't my own. I want my bodymindspirit to come together so that I can be that fully functioning human being. Reality has shifted and I know that living life in fragments will not work. Healing the split between bodymindspirit, school/home, career/children will take continuous work . . . it is the work of a nepantlera. Change is necessary, and since "nepantla is the only space where change happens" I must open myself to embracing the in-between spaces and living life in a state of "constant transition" (574). With Anzaldúa, it is always about change: "Change requires more than words on a page—it takes perseverance, creative in- genuity, and acts of love" (574). I think of Anzaldúa, my mother, my Nana, my mentors, my friends, my love when I attempt to build spiri- tual/political communities that struggle for personal growth and social justice (574). With these voices guiding my own path to conocimiento, I feel more sure of myself and ready for the transformations and transi- tions to come.

CHAPTER 5

Aprendiendo a Vivir/Aprendiendo a Morir

NORMA ELIA CANTÚ

As a mestiza I have no country . . .
GLORIA ANZALDÚA, *BORDERLANDS/LA FRONTERA*

Although we grew up only a few miles from each other along the U.S.-Mexico border, she in the Valley and I in Laredo, I didn't hear of Gloria Anzaldúa until the 1980s at a conference in Michigan where she was scheduled to speak and had problems with the patriarchal structure of the organization and the conference. It was the National Association of Chicano Studies (NACS) meeting in East Lansing, and her scheduled talk was in a room where there was nothing going on. I searched for the session and never found it. In 1980 I had returned to my border community and was teaching at what was then Laredo State University, and, desperately seeking like-minded Chicanas, I had attended my first NACS conference. Dismayed at the dearth of women speakers, I was excited about meeting her, a Chicana from Tejas.

But I didn't meet Anzaldúa until years later, when I again sought her out at a NACS meeting, this time in Albuquerque. We walked the streets of Old Town and shopped, as we talked and discussed who we were, what we believed. I knew I had found a paisana, a compañera in the struggle, someone who understood and articulated the border condition, who cared and wanted things to change, someone who like me had known the terrorism of the linguistic and social torment of the educational system, who like me wanted a better world for everyone. We remained friends and sought each other out whenever we were in the same city, attending the same conference, or just visiting. That is how I got to know her as a person, through long talks over meals or on walks in Washington, D.C., at the zoo, or in Austin; driving around lost looking for Liliana Wilson's house, where she was staying; at women's conferences where she and I coincided, like at the small women-of-color literature conference in Salisbury, Maryland; and of course, en Tejas, in San Antonio, or in Austin. Her presence in my life made me a stronger Tejana, taught me to acknowledge the spiritual in my life and to seek balance between the academic and spiritual, what Barbara Renaud González calls "el Corazón" that we academics and intellectuals tend to forget when we favor the mind, the left brain.

Anzaldúa's work shattered much of the earlier scholarship on the border, such as Madsden's narrow and skewed sociological work, and set Border Studies at a different plane. Her ideas and philosophies, shaped by life and learning (for she truly had la facultad to understand life), made her work indispensable for those of us working in Border Studies and related disciplinary fields. Reading *Borderlands* empowered my own writing and freed me to think beyond the borders of my life on the geophysical borderlands in Laredo. Her analysis of our language(s) confirmed what I had been teaching in my introductory linguistics classes, classes required for future bilingual educators who feared and were often still enslaved by the master's languages—both the Spanish and the English. I saw how liberating it was for them to read Anzaldúa's work, and teaching her work has given me insight into my own work. I knew only too well the linguistic terrorism she spoke of, where we were not only devalued for speaking Spanish but punished. And it wasn't only the monolingual English-speaking teachers who were guilty of such torture; no, it was our own. Don Tomás Sánchez Elementary School had at least three Spanish-speaking teachers, Mexican Americans like the student body, but they were as feared as the Anglo teachers, for some also punished us for speaking Spanish.

Over the years, as I have ventured forth writing my own creative autobioethnography, I know that Anzaldúa's influence has hovered like a patient and kind guide. I often use her work as epigraphs for my essays and for my creative work, not only because the phrases may encapsulate what the piece is about but because her words allow readers to prepare for the work that follows. Her work has always bridged thoughts, beliefs, ways of looking at the world. The images and the words set the tone for my own words and images. I thank Anzaldúa for the pathbreaking work that allowed so many of us to break with genres and with expected modes and tones. She is the warrior forging new paths for the rest of us, breaking ground for the buildings and constructing and deconstructing even her own work.

My favorite dicho is "Cada cabeza es un mundo," and Gloria Anzaldúa's mundo intersects with mine in many ways. Her work has influenced my own writing and thinking in innumerable ways. When I practice tolerance or think beyond the borders of my life, I am being influenced by Anzaldúa's work. I practice meditation and feel connected spiritually to many mujeres in my life because I learned from her to look for the connections. Whenever I had to weather some difficult personal or professional crisis she offered solace and perspective. "Look at it as potential for growth," she told me once when I was despairing about the racism in a particular academic situation. Another friend of ours, Mirtha Quintanales, told me how she and Gloria Anzaldúa had visited with the guru who had given them their "names," and I became more interested in Siddha yoga as a result, although Anzaldúa was not affiliated with it.

We had ideological differences, and we often had long conversations during which I would refute some claim or introduce my perspective on a particular event or philosophy. She always listened, and we sometimes agreed to disagree. For instance, I preferred to focus on local indigenous groups of the border, not the conqueror tribes of central Mexico. One of the theoretically and ideologically challenging premises lies at the heart of her latest work: the idea of the cenote and of plunging into the depths in order to emerge changed and transformed; I told her that this idea was not "new," that many western psychological premises relied on this metaphor for transformation. Again, she listened and we discussed the differences between the western view of the process and the ways that we as mestizas and mestizos come to the change that is inherent in our lives, the many transformations that we individually and collectively experience. In typical Anzaldúan fashion, she then threw it up into a much wider sphere, and before it was all over we were discussing cosmic change especially as reflected in global warming and the climate change that the earth is experiencing. I am convinced that one of the future directions we should consider is to continue building on the many areas for thinking about our condition as Chicanas, as women, as human beings on this earth, and for making the radical change necessary to ensure that we all achieve our full potential as human beings.

The passing of a loved one always spurs us to think of our own mortality, reminds us of how transitory our stint in this realm is and of what we seek to leave behind. Anzaldúa's spirit still lives in her words and in the minds of all who knew her. But her legacy is greater than any text or any memory of her voice or her laughter. It is a challenge, un reto, to all of us to continue her work. Our work. Sara Estela Ramírez, South Texas poet and teacher, wrote a hundred years ago, "la vida es acción," and indeed our life is action and in right action will we honor Gloria Anzaldúa's memory.

We must put her ideas and her thinking to work as we seek to eradicate social injustice, to ensure a world free of racism, where economic and ecological justice reigns. I believe our actions speak louder than our words; our work is the best way to remember Gloria Anzaldúa, to honor her memory. I cannot stand idly by while my hermanas are being destroyed in academic wars; I will not remain silent when one of ours is killed or maimed, physically or emotionally, because she or he didn't conform. My way is not hers; I do not write as she did—only she did that. But I have my path, my way, and that is what I believe we must all find, our individual way within the larger struggle. It is after all one struggle, la lucha. And it is not just local, although it begins at that level. The struggle is regional; it is national. The struggle is beyond all borders and connects globally with all who are engaged in the struggle to bring light, peace, love to the hearts and minds of those who will destroy, who will annihilate, who deny human beings their rights to live peacefully, to lead their lives. Writing letters, marching with others in the street, doing research, bringing to life buried lessons, teaching someone to read, listening to someone who needs comforting, forgiving those who have wronged us, speaking out, thinking and speaking our thoughts, educating and standing firm. Not easy to do. Not always possible. But it is in trying to do our best that we succeed.

The lessons are many; the paths are many. We must choose and take them all. They are all valid and all attainable. Radical shifts occur through incremental change. We must stand united and alone. All at once speak as one voice and in a cacophony of many voices and languages. If there are indigenous languages dying with the last speaker of that language, we must not forget the ones that have already been silenced forever and how the ways of looking at the world that those languages conveyed has also died. The Coahuiltecan tribes of South Texas whose words lie silent in the past, buried in the Texas brush that Gloria so loved, along with their bones and the bones of her and my ancestors, demand that we not forget, that we not give up, but that we persist and continue on the path for the generations to come. Gloria Anzaldúa taught us how to live and how to die. We must not forget.

CHAPTER 6

Making Face, Rompiendo Barreras:
The Activist Legacy of Gloria E. Anzaldúa

AÍDA HURTADO

Late in the day on May 16, 2004, many of us who were familiar with Gloria Anzaldúa's work received an e-mail from Profesora Norma Alarcón from the University of California, Berkeley, with the following message:

> Dear Friends:
> With great sorrow I pass on the news of Gloria Anzaldúa's death. She was found dead in her house by a friend who came by on Thursday of last week. Her family is taking her back to Texas. . . . She was finishing a book for Routledge. She is a great loss to us. A woman of great spirit— the Chicanita from Texas, as she said of herself.[1]

Not long after the first message, we received an e-mail from Edén Torres with the following short poem:

> I go to the bookshelf
> and press the ragged spine of a well read book
> as if written in Braille
> I feel your name through my flesh
> and I begin the long slow wail
> of enormous mourning.[2]

This brief statement expresses the collective wail of mourning heard through the Internet as e-mails flew back and forth announcing the untimely death, at the age of sixty-one, of our beloved Gloria Anzaldúa. During the next couple of weeks the e-mails poured in almost nonstop as we commiserated over our collective loss. Messages came from mujeres of all ages, ethnicities, races, generations, countries, social classes, and sexualities. The scope and reach of Gloria Anzaldúa's work and life knew no boundaries; her greatness and contributions were appreciated by many.

With the outpouring of grief came the testimonials of what Anzaldúa had left behind through her writing, her art, and her life. As if by spontaneous combustion, people across the country left their daily routines to seek out others who were also mourning the loss of Gloria Anzaldúa. We gathered in university department hallways, Chicano Studies libraries, Women's Studies lounges, Ethnic Studies classrooms, city parks, people's homes, all in an effort to share our grief, which seemed too great for one to bear. In my own institution, there were at least ten altars erected at various campus sites only hours after the e-mails announcing Gloria's death started to arrive.

Why did Gloria Anzaldúa's work and life have such an enormous impact? ¿Qué herencia nos dejó esta pequeña gigante? What lessons did this small giant leave behind that so many of us feel bereft now that she is gone? In this essay I outline a few key lessons, not only as they apply to individuals from different communities but also as they affected my own life. I want to illustrate "in the flesh," as Gloria Anzaldúa and Cherríe Moraga would say, why Gloria's passing caused a national and international earthquake of grieving and what her life and work can teach us.

I use three sources to illustrate the lessons Anzaldúa left us to inherit. One source is the archives of the e-mails individuals wrote dando testimonio to the extent and meaning of their loss. Second, I use the interviews I conducted for my book *Voicing Chicana Feminisms: Young Women Speak Out on Sexuality and Identity*, in which 101 young Chicanas in higher education participated. Most of these young women had read or knew of Gloria's work, as well as the work of other Chicana feminist writers. They represent the future of Chicana feminisms—an area of study that many feel Anzaldúa created in collaboration with other scholars. Third, I use the art of Chicanas to illustrate Anzaldúa's lessons further. Perhaps in this cacophony of voice and art we can find clues to the immense impact Gloria Anzaldúa had on so many of us.

Personal Theorizing, Personal History—Theories in the Flesh

Remarkably Gloria Anzaldúa and I have common histories. We both grew up in poverty in the Rio Grande Valley in South Texas, otherwise known as El Valle. We lived in barrios without paved streets or running

Colonia, El Valle, South Texas, 2010.

water, places where you can still find cases of tuberculosis and malaria and where curanderos and parteras are the only sources of health care. El Valle is a beautiful and haunting place where indeed many realities collide, where people like us are not expected to succeed, much less become writers and thinkers. In these colonias de calles polvorientas, neighborhoods of dusty roads with massive cacti and open skies, we both fed our fantasies of having the right to think, read, and write.

We came from this region that Anzaldúa later labeled "the borderlands," the "in-between" place where families live on both sides of the river and the boundary between the two countries is nothing more than an imaginary line controlled and enforced by the Border Patrol. We were both from Hidalgo County, where anthropologists like William Madsen arrived in 1964 to study us, objectify our families, and derogate our communities. We were supposed to be subjects of study—calladitas and deferential—not human beings with voice and agency. We came from a long line of border crossers—las mujeres of the interstices of two countries, two worlds, and two cultures and, as Anzaldúa *might* say, chingadas—women who are screwed by everyone around them. We were not supposed to leave our beloved valley or get an education (both of us at

Pan American, the local university, often referred to as "Taco Tech" because nearly 80 percent of its 10,000 students are of Mexican descent). I earned my bachelor's degree in sociology and psychology, she in English and art.

Although we had similar backgrounds and ages, we never met in the Valley. Nor did our paths cross in our respective sojourns to the East Coast. Indeed I had not even read Anzaldúa's work until I arrived in Santa Cruz, California, in 1983. But I distinctly remember the first time I met this woman. We smile as our eyes meet across the room at a gathering of women of color at the Women's Center at the University of California, Santa Cruz. After speaking a few words we identify the singsong accent of South Texas and spontaneously begin code switching into Spanglish, as fellow Tejanas so often do. ¿Gloria, eres de Tejas? ¿Del valle? ¿No me digas? Wow, mujer, whatcha doin' acá con los hippies? We laugh, we talk, we reminisce about professors at Pan American University, and we gaze at each other like rare birds of the same exotic species. We also chuckle because we recognize the strength and humor it has taken to get this far. She writes in my newly acquired copy of *This Bridge Called My Back:* "Para Aída, Te deseo lo mejor de la vida, Tejanita, y chingos de honores. Contigo, Gloria, August 12, 1990, Santa Cruz."

In spite of our similar backgrounds, our lives had taken very different caminos: Gloria became an artist, poet, and writer; I became a social scientist, trained in empirical work based on "objectivity" and the "gathering of data." Yet our paths converged in the most unlikely of places—in Santa Cruz, California, home of the counterculture hippy movement.

Lesson One: Disclosure of Self

I discovered Anzaldúa's work in Santa Cruz, and ultimately the lessons that I learned from her have been the most significant in my professional life. She believed deeply that one could not have access to knowledge, much less produce it, without disclosing oneself in one's work.

Self-exposure, I believe, is one lesson and perhaps *the* lesson derived from Anzaldúa's legacy. In her words:

> In our daily lives, we women of color strip off the *máscaras* others have imposed on us, see through the disguises we hide behind and drop our *personas* so that we may become subjects in our own discourses. We rip out the stitches, expose the multilayered "inner faces," attempting to confront and oust the internalized oppression embedded in them, and

Gloria Anzaldúa altar at her grave site. Photograph by Karina Cervantez, 2009.

remake anew both inner and outer faces. . . . We begin to acquire the agency of making our own *caras*. "Making faces" is my metaphor for constructing one's identity. ("Haciendo caras" xxvi, her italics)

With unsure steps, I applied Anzaldúa's words about disrobing the self in one's work for the first time in my book *Voicing Chicana Feminisms*. I was elated with the results, never before feeling so at home with my work. With naïve assurance, I sent the manuscript to my editors, believing that they too would appreciate how much better it was not to hide behind academic jargon. To my surprise, I received a skeptical letter back, disagreeing with the personal tone I had taken. I was in despair until later that same week, by coincidence, I began reading AnaLouise Keating's new book *Interviews/Entrevistas,* a compilation of interviews with Gloria Anzaldúa.

Anzaldúa had urged AnaLouise Keating to leave the protection of academic writing behind. Keating's fears in reaction to Anzaldúa's suggestion were not unlike my own. Keating writes:

I am a product of the U.S. university system. I have learned to mask my own agenda—my own desires for social justice, spiritual transformation, and cultural change—in academic language. . . . Because it seems to hide private feelings, desires, and deeply held beliefs behind rational, objective discourse and abstract thought, theory can be more persuasive for some readers. . . . My academic training, coupled with my love of privacy, make me fear self-disclosure. If I incorporate the personal into my words, perhaps I won't be respected as a scholar. Or maybe you'll think that I'm vain, egocentric, and selfish. . . . Or maybe I'll sound stupid, unsophisticated, naïve. ("Risking the Personal" 1–3)

Returning to Anzaldúa's writings, Keating finds the answer to her dilemma:

But one of the most important things I've learned from reading and teaching Anzaldúa's works is the importance of risking the personal. Throughout her writings, Anzaldúa draws extensively on her own life— her early menstruation; her campesino background; her childhood in the Rio Grande Valley of South Texas; her experiences as a brown-skinned, Spanish-speaking girl in a dominant culture that values light-skinned, English-speaking boys; and her sexual and spiritual desires. ("Risking the Personal" 2)

After encountering this work, I wrote in the preface of *Voicing Chicana Feminisms*:

So I, too, take Anzaldúa's challenge to disclose at the risk of sounding biased, unsophisticated, unscholarly, and lacking in objectivity. I have chosen a style of writing that communicates to the reader that I admire my respondents, that I do not take their struggles for granted, and that I do not feel I have the authority to judge them. I let them speak for themselves rather than only analyzing their words to make theoretical points. I have chosen to follow Gloria's advice to "put myself into it more," not to glorify myself or to decenter my respondents. I do so in spite of the fact that this may lead some readers to exactly those conclusions, when, in fact, I am trying to enhance my respondents' life stories by not denying my own.

Lesson Two: The Crossing of Borders, Regardless of Risks

Society puts us into neat little compartments to label us and keep us in our places. India, mestiza, naca, vieja, Latin spitfire, Chicana-dyke-

La Muerte (Present), Transformation Triptych Series. Photograph by Mica Valdez
© 2003.

feminist, tortillera, sexy, burro, maid, stupid, prieta, hocicona, bocona, cabrona, loser, whore, malinche, bad writer, worse thinker, undeserving, affirmative-action hire—you name it, we've heard it.

When injured, Anzaldúa advises the use of "spiritual tools to cope with racial and gender oppression and other modern *maldades*." She advocates "the spiritual practice of *conocimiento* by dropping down into yourself, through the skin and muscles and tendons, down deep into the bones' marrow, where your soul is ballast . . . [enabling] you to defuse the negative energy of putdowns, complaints, excessive talk, verbal attacks, and other killers of the spirit" ("now let us shift" 572). Anzaldúa encourages us to dive under the insult, swim across the accusation, sail above the torment, go deep, deep, into the ocean of love that others like us can provide. She reminds us that we are not alone, that we can form alliances with others similarly injured, that we can fight the objectification and, through spirituality, deflect the injury through the sheer power of kindness.

To paraphrase Anzaldúa: Don't let them confine you, define you, debase you—you are more than their insults. Speak up against the gringo, the mexicanos, your brother, even your mother. Love them but don't let their love give them power over you. Or, as she writes so poignantly:

> I will not glorify those aspects of my culture which have injured me and which injured me in the name of protecting me.
>
> So, don't give me your tenets and your laws. Don't give me your lukewarm gods. What I want is an accounting with all three cultures— white, Mexican, Indian. I want the freedom to carve and chisel my own face, to staunch the bleeding with ashes, to fashion my own gods out of my entrails. And if going home is denied me then I will have to stand and claim my space, making a new culture—*una cultura mestiza*—with my own lumber, my own bricks and mortar and my own feminist architecture. (*Borderlands/La Frontera* 44, her italics)

Anzaldúa taught us all to cross borders, including disciplinary ones, to find our true voice. Velma Perez, a doctoral student from San Antonio, Texas, writes in an e-mail:

> Me siento muy triste. I guess I just couldn't come to terms with Gloria's death. I never met her, but saw her once at a conference. Gloria's writing inspired me to finish my dissertation. She was referred to me by Dr. Scheurich, one of my committee members. I was about ready to quit the academic BS. The way I wrote wasn't acceptable, it wasn't academic. Dr. Scheurich told me that I had compassion in my writing and that it was ok to write how I felt. I still didn't believe him until I picked up her book. Wow! Finally, someone had put in words what I was feeling. To Gloria I owe you my Ph.D. It was because of her that I decided that I had to finish my dissertation and tell my story. I wish I could have met her, but I plan to continue telling our "herstory." Con amor.[3]

Lesson Three: Living in Kindness through Commitment to Social Justice

Anzaldúa had a kind and generous spirit. Stories abound about the care she took to listen to people, especially women, regardless of their stature

Soy Xicana. Mixed-media collage by Mica Valdez © 2000.

in life. Whenever she would do a guest lecture or a conference keynote, she thanked the organizers, the students conducting registration, and the service workers alike. At book signings, she spoke individually to each buyer, staying hours after events to speak to everyone waiting. As she had done in her writing, Anzaldúa was able and eager to connect with others through her honesty and self-disclosure.

Anzaldúa's legacy of human connectedness, humanity, and caring was often echoed in the interviews I conducted with young Chicanas for my book. These young women too wanted to go beyond obtaining individual privilege through education, imagining their life's work to be connected to the communities they left to attend institutions of higher education. Sofía, a twenty-six-year-old respondent who was working on her master's degree in education at Harvard University, responded when asked, "Do you think you will work on behalf of Latino issues in the future?"

Yes, I will be politically involved with the Latino community. . . . That's my choice. I know that no matter how long I live, our community, my community is always going to have issues and challenges and struggles and I have to be a part of that. I couldn't just sit here and say, "Oh well, now I have my nice paying job and my nice little house. I don't need to worry about those things." I want to continue to work in education, I want to have my own school and I would want it to be based on true parent involvement. (*Voicing Chicana Feminisms* 247)

Anzaldúa's work is multifaceted and relational. Her writings are like lagartijas, little lizards with multilayered skins that peel off under different conditions. Every time one reads them, new and surprising meanings emerge. Therefore, there are many lessons in her work that are beyond what I could possibly cover in this essay. In many ways Anzaldúa will never be gone because she will live through her legacy of words in the hearts, minds, and lives of future generations. As Marcos Andrés Flores, a young man, wrote in his poem in response to her passing:[4]

In dark corners
we huddle en masse
holding each other
mourning the loss
of yet another elder
as we sit in circle
singing songs
of remembrance
asking questions like
where do we go from here
who will be left
will life ever be the same
but tearstained letters
and storied words and deeds
indeed
sustain the flame of flickering candles
velas of freedom
as la Gloria shouts out
at shadows
reflecting our own bodies

smashed against the wall of liberation
beaten and battered
we are still whole
forever healing
as we put pieces
of memory together
collectively
fighting the real enemy
and what it means to forget
on this day and everyday
we remember you Gloria
Mother
Grandmother
To us all.
AUSTIN, TEXAS, MAY 2004

¿Y Ahora Qué? What Now That You Are Gone?

"now let us shift" is one of Anzaldúa's most painful pieces to read/re-read. In it is the fulfillment and promise of her talents and visions. With her usual bravery and lack of guile, Anzaldúa articulates the pain and confusion of facing her illness and mortality.

> Three weeks after the doctor confirms your own diagnosis you cross the trestle bridge near the wharf, your shortcut to downtown Santa Cruz. As you listen to your footsteps echoing on the timber, the reality of having a disease that could cost you your feet . . . your eyes . . . your creativity . . . the life of the writer you've worked so hard to build . . . life itself . . . finally penetrates, arresting you in the middle del puente (bridge). You're furious with your body for limiting your artistic activities, for its slow crawl toward the grave. You're infuriated with yourself for not living up to your expectations, not living your life fully. You realize that you use the whip of your ideals to flagellate yourself, and the masochist in you gets pleasure from your suffering.
> . . . De este lugar de muerte viva the promise of sunlight is unreachable. Though you want deliverance you cling to your misery. (550)

The piece is a gripping story because, as many of her writings are, it is also a prescient tale of what will befall her only a few years later. However, the essay also communicates the vision of a less divisive world where the separation between "I" and "we" is connected to form a more perfect union. Every paragraph allows the exploration of a new way of being in the world that is more kind and connected than what we currently experience. "now let us shift" makes most obvious what we would lose in the future when Anzaldúa was no longer with us. The reader can fully understand her depression over the possibility of not having the physical strength and time to fully document what she had learned in the flesh. Each insight begs for further elaboration. Each sentence/paragraph/section holds a universe of wisdom—a universe we sorely need. Yet this piece is also complete and encapsulates the technologies and methodologies that many young scholars will explore for years as they unravel their own visions for the future. Coming full circle, my initial sorrow at reading/rereading this piece dissipates like the fog over the ocean when the sun appears over Anzaldúa's favorite walk on West Cliff Drive, because I now understand that she made peace with her initial desconocimiento when she discovered her illness—everything is temporary, our bodies, our minds, even our words. Like the circle she used to draw in the sand during her daily walks on the beach in Santa Cruz, the important thing is that the circle was drawn, the earth honored, the elements acknowledged, that our work came from a place of kindness and connection—that's all that matters. Others will take it up if you have lived right.

Hasta Luego, Gloria

Anzaldúa built a life of love, community, and words in Santa Cruz. She could feed the "writing monster," as she called it, in the wee hours of the night, sleeping during the day. She lived only blocks away from the ocean, where she would take daily walks.

One of my favorite pictures of Anzaldúa was taken by former Santa Cruzan Annie Valva. When I saw this picture I recalled the words of Eugene O'Neill:

> I lay on the bowsprit facing astern with the water foaming into spume under me, the masts with every sail white in the moonlight, towering high above me. I became drunk with the beauty and singing rhythm of it, and for a moment I lost myself—actually lost my life. I was set free! I dissolved in the sea, became white sails and flying spray, became beauty

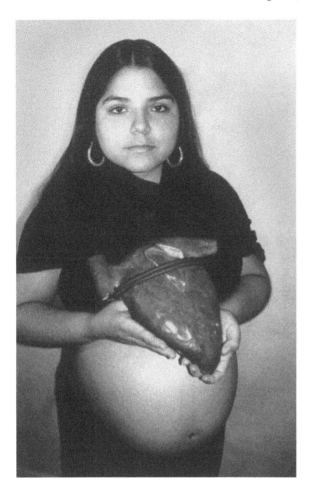

Expectant Mother with Heart. Photograph by Mica Valdez © 2004.

and rhythm, became moonlight and the high dim-starred sky! I belonged . . . within a peace and unity and a wild joy . . . to life itself. (3)

Not surprisingly, Anzaldúa did not see herself as someday dying but
as being able to, in her words, "one day . . . walk through the walls,
grow wings and fly." In the hearts and minds of this and future generations, Gloria Anzaldúa did not die. She flew away but left behind a
legacy of kindness, truth, and inspiration.

Gloria E. Anzaldúa in the ocean, Santa Cruz, California. Photograph by Annie Valva, circa 1991.

II

EXPOSING THE WOUNDS: "YOU GAVE ME PERMISSION TO FLY INTO THE DARK"

CHAPTER 7

Anzaldúa, Maestra

SEBASTIÁN JOSÉ COLÓN-OTERO

I have been searching and searching and searching. I have been looking through every window. Following every pathway. I have cried to every god and goddess on this earth.

My tongue got dry from asking. My eyes burned out from reading. My mom cansada de tantos huesos milenarios arrastrados. My mom looked at me: "I don't know what you are, mi'ja." "I don't know what you are, mi'jo." I've been looking and looking for my mirror. I've gazed at every little crystal, every broken reflection. I found nothing. I found nothing.

I swallowed all the papers looking for my race, my wholeness. This multiple spirit, I was spitting contradictions from every single one of my million mouths. Gloria, I found you. You found me, Maestra. Not in the bookstore, not on the website. No. I found you, Gloria, during a regular day at work.

"Who's that writer?" I asked. "Who's that spirit calling? I can feel it." Surprised by the energy, I asked: "She is not Puerto Rican, ha?" In a last attempt at making something mine. And there I found you—Gloria Evangelina.

No dissertation, no case study, no deconstruction.

You name my name: Borderlands—Gloria. You came to me as survival.

My skin is erupting. A million bumps, something from within, my inside is making its way out:

Borderlands.

I've been seeking and seeking and seeking. Seeking for my monsters reflected in black and red, looking for a sense of humanity.

Gloria, guerrera que me llenaste los ojos con agua bendita. You came through my eyes.

I swallowed my reflection page after page. My ancient legs, el macho in me, grounded on a false floor . . . now being validated by the words of my people for the first time. There, in *Borderlands*. In the Fronteras, Gloria Anzaldúa MAESTRA, there I Exist.

There for the first time in Spanglish. With serpientes de plumas que yo también llevaba por dentro. Page 41—Gloria . . . I have a page of my own now.

I've been searching and scrutinizing, looking for my name within and beyond this skin/border/sex/gender. For something to tell me and tell the others about this monster mágico que vive en mi: hombre/mujer, yo soy. Y tú, Maestra, le das vida. You saw me inside yourself, in your own gender. There in the Borderlands: the gender of us all. The Whole.

Yemayá me está llamando y Ochún celebra este encuentro. This is my Coatlicue state, Gloria (I was in the Coatlicue and you knew it!) walking into nepantla, that eternal place where I live.

You attached yourself to my tongue and gave me names for the calling!

En Borderlands, Gloria Anzaldúa, mis tetas grandes, mis manos pequeñas, mi ser otra cosa EXISTE!

Shamán en convulsión. Me das de la poción del reflejo aire pa' seguir viviendo.

¿Por qué te nos fuiste, guerrera emplumada? Yo te necesito . . . y te suelto. Your magic power is all over. It came through me, from my eyes to my tongue, traveled down to my chest de hombre. Soy un hombre con tetas grandes. My gender is not forced to be in a room without air any more. Mitá y mitá, half and half, Gloria Evangelina.

Después de devorarme a Borges, a Cortazar, y a Luisa. Después de tra-garme a Feinberg, a Butler, y a Derrida. Después de hacer de los Ben-jamin Guidelines a fire to warm the dogs. There I found you, Maestra. You draw the Borderlands for me so I can see myself. You draw the Bor-derlands for me with the Whole included: my mom at the sweatshop, my absent father, my obsession with reading los libros gordos and memoriz-ing la encyclopedia. You gave a name to me and to all my contradictions. You have a power bigger than this Universe and came to share it with us. La Facultad de todas nos/otras finally pouring into all our roots. You named it, Gloria Anzaldúa.

You gave me a new reference for living and being. You didn't question my humanity, me being everything: muchacho, caballero, macho en el buen sentido, en guayabera, y en calzoncillos. You named us beyond the duality. You gave me permission to fly into the dark, not having to be one or the other any more.

THANK YOU—GLORIA ANZALDÚA—MAESTRA

I honor you!

In front of you, I ask for your blessings. Humildemente vengo a ti, musa . . .

You knew your place in the Universe. Your clear brújula guided by vi-sions of another world. I honor you. I am blessed by your presence . . . eternal energy breaking through all the chains and restrictions, burning ancient powers, emerging from the earth and going back to it.

I HONOR YOU and I hold this NEW TRUTH

Between my lengua y mis dientes . . . y te suelto . . .

Yo le canto a mis Santos y a la Virgen María en una alabanza a tu nom-bre, Gloria.

Gloria Evangelina Anzaldúa, Maestra. I honor You and I let you go. . . . I honor you and I let you go, I honor you and I let you go.

In honor of Gloria Evangelina Anzaldúa 2004

CHAPTER 8

"May We Do Work That Matters":
Bridging Gloria Anzaldúa across Borders

CLAIRE JOYSMITH

I think of you quietly, Gloria, as I sit here today, in a conference room, about to give a talk titled "Sueños, pesadillas y heridas: Mexicanidades y chicanidades en transición" in a symposium: La cultura contemporánea en Estados Unidos. Panelists talk about U.S. culture from a Mexican perspective—más bien dicho, a Central Mexico, Mexico City, La Capital perspective, where chilango-centrism prevails. And I wonder once again which margins can be reached by speaking out at the Universidad Nacional Autónoma de México (UNAM), the largest public university in Mexico, the oldest on the continent.[1] Panelists talk about Manifest Destiny, the American dream, Starbucks, the Simpsons; nobody talks about anything non-mainstream, nonwhite. This does not surprise me.

My turn. I talk about dreams turned nightmares, heridas abiertas, post–11 September 2001 margins, chicanidades, lo chicanofemenino, lo fronterizo, borderlands; I talk about how much we in Mexico can learn from Chican@ and Latin@ writings, the imperative to create more conciencia de este lado, (c)overt racism-classism in Mexico, and the need to address multiple mexicanidades. I hope to reach a few members of the audience, convey con espíritu una pizquita of what I've learned from you, Gloria. I quote from your post–11 September 2001 testimonio "Let us be the healing of the wound: The Coyolxauhqui imperative—la sombra y el sueño." My intention is to bridge back—using your own words—a gift of ancient Mesoamerican lore to the all-Mexican audience, an admixture of skin colors, social and class differences, such as one is bound to encounter at the UNAM:

In terms of evolutionary stages, the world is presently between el quinto sol y el sexto. According to Maya knowledge, the sixth world starts December 2012. It is this Nuevo Mundo, this new order, we need to create with the choices we make, the acts we perform, and the futures we dream. . . . We are the song that sings us. It begins with "Let us fight no more but heal the wounds of nations. Let us be the healing of the wound." (99, 103)

I language-bridge your words across linguistic-cultural borders by offering a translated version in Spanish, un regalito:

En términos de etapas evolutivas, el mundo se encuentra en estos momentos entre el quinto y sexto sol. De acuerdo con el conocimiento maya, el sexto mundo se inicia en diciembre de 2012. Es este Nuevo Mundo, este nuevo orden, el que debemos crear con las elecciones que hacemos, los actos que realizamos y los futuros que soñamos. Somos el canto que nos canta. Y éste comienza con: "Que no se libren más batallas, que sanemos las heridas de las naciones. Que seamos la sanación de la herida."

As I utter your words, I think of how you would enjoy this tongue-bridging that gifts back to your hermandad mexicana de este lado. I feel grateful for your selflessly cultivated lengua—gifts, your simple, painful, hard work, the true healing love of continued creativity and sharing. I also ponder the fact that most in the audience are unfamiliar with your writings, probably because these are mostly in English, although you interlingually scatter them with Spanish like corn on fertile land.

Suddenly, me doy cuenta: I have uttered your words today in the very same UNAM conference room where, in 1992, I heard you read from your work, saw you for the first time, standing up—not sitting like the other panelists—to your fullest height, talking con tanta fuerza, con espíritu, mesmerizing me. You were part of a multicultural U.S. panel. I don't even remember how I first knew about your writings; I had only read fragments and a few poems from *Borderlands/La Frontera;* I do remember, though, seeing your name and knowing I had to go hear you read. Maybe it was pure intuition. I understand now: a good karma is a good karma is a good karma . . .

We later had lunch at La Fonda de Santa Anita en la Zona Rosa. You had recently been diagnosed with diabetes. During the interview after lunch, you were generous with your time and energy, speaking mostly in Spanish, using more English as you tired (Joysmith, "Ya se me quitó la vergüenza"). We talked y hasta chismeamos. We laughed about the ironies: here we were, yo una güera, Mexicana-born, conversing in Mexico City in an admixture of English and Spanish, with "la prieta," una chicana fronteriza, considerada de este lado—particularly in Central Mexico—como estadounidense, gringa, pocha, but no way mexicana. I continued to be mesmerized. The afternoon grew into the evening; still we talked; still you were patient enough to open so many windows for me. I later had to find the doors.

Sure, I had read feminist writings: eurocentric, white. How to make sense of these, though, how to integrate them to daily life while experiencing myriad criss-crossing realities in México as una gringa-looking mexicana, alien-seeming yet legal Mexico national with a cultural and linguistic British, Mexican, American, French, Oaxacan upbringing (my parents immigrated crossing charco-borders on a spiritual quest, reaching Mexico City via Cuba in the early '50s). In Mexico I experienced multiple forms of racism, classism, sexism. Out of sheer intuitive necessity, I spoke a form of Spanglish or Engliñol. I continuously experienced being different, gazed at with curiosity, hatred, envy, anger, disdain, awe, lust, por ser güerita, "descolorida," blanquita, la Claire, clarita, and for being mujercita. Even though I was proud of being mexicana, even though I spoke impeccable Spanish y me hacía mis trenzas apretadas, apretadas—para que mi cabello no ondeara libre y brillara bajo el sol. Although I knew desde niña México was where I had to be, I wanted "to dye my hair black," como escribí en un poema.[2]

When you gave me a signed a copy of *Borderlands/La Frontera*, I had no idea what this would mean, how it would change my life. I began to seriously read Chicana literature, theory, feminist nonwhite writings; I discovered new meanings, more puentes, new challenges: how the crossings could take place, how to pragmatize your propuestas within the patriarcado machista mexicano, within the specificity of chilango-centrism. I began finding ways to open up mexicanidades in everyday life, in my academic work, in the classroom, at home, every time I wrote poetry, wrote for academia, crossed over to the United States, regresaba a casa. I began finding ways to cross and build bridges desde acá, seeking ways to understand what chicanidades and Chicana feminisms could contribute to cambios de este lado.

Crossing over into new discursive and experiential territories, within and outside academia, I was christened a reverse chicana. I found myself quoting you in most of my academic and creative writings. I translated some of your poems into Spanish, using nontranslation strategies by leaving in English words, an attempt to espejear some resonance of your intent. I wrote about how in a single poem you problematize racial, ethnic, cultural issues, female-gendering English-language gender-erased words by subversively using Spanish, a language that overprivileges male-gendered markers.[3]

Needless to say, I encountered "resistance reactions" (Joysmith, "(Re)Mapping mexicanidades") on the way, ranging from being snubbed and targeted as anti-academic for teaching dubious literary subjects such as Chicana literature, to near-erasure of the initial postgraduate comparative Chicana-Mexicana literature course, to being questioned by highly intelligent people about the literary merits of Chicana texts, to a rosario de siete+ años to get a bilingual Chicana poetry anthology, *Cantar de espejos/Singing Mirrors,* published (with two of your poems included).[4]

In my experience in Central Mexico, Chican@s are generally considered "malinchistas" who have betrayed their motherland, their raza, pa' irse "al otro lado." Son "poch@s" que no hablan bien el español. Historically, it is a complex phenomenon. Emotionally, even more so. I perceive entrenched cultural, religious, nationalistic prejudices, perhaps a collective consciousness, a fear of transgression, of being singled out; also, I sense deep undercurrents of insecurity, mistrust, aversion, and envy toward what simultaneously embodies the familiar and the alien: hybridity can become threatening. Moreover, Chican@s are mostly descendants of campesinos, como tú, Gloria; and in academia, as within the context of chilango-centrism, eso es tabú, as are issues of race, class, ethnicity, more so when gender-related. This is changing gradually. An increase in colleges and institutions integrating transdisciplinary, transcultural, and gender studies outside chilango-centric constraints is cracking open new doors. Yet a key figure in this process is, ironically, the very globalization that brings knife-edged consequences for Mexico, pushing the poverty line further.

Today, I speak up, quote you once again in this conference room, Gloria, this same space where the first Coloquio de Escritoras Chicanas and the Encuentro de Escritoras Chicanas y Mexicanas I organized at the CISAN/UNAM (Centro de Investigaciones sobre América del Norte/UNAM) took place. This coloquio offered the first time in Mexico City, heart of chilango-centrism, that Chicanas and Mexicanas attempted a dialogue focused on their experiences as women writers in the margins, addressing issues of race, class, ethnicity, sexuality, language.[5] Gloria, you were unable to join us, but you had sown the now-sprouting seeds. Yes, this is the very same conference room where shortly afterward Elena Poniatowska became literary madrina to "Las formas de nuestras voces: Chicana and Mexicana Writers in Mexico."

Eleven years later, in this same space, I hear myself echo from your *Borderlands/La Frontera*: "The U.S.-Mexican border *es una herida abierta* where the Third World grates against the first and bleeds. And before a scab forms it hemorrhages again, the lifeblood of two worlds merging to form a third country—a border culture" (25, her italics).

And I remember being struck by the resonance of this, what you wrote in 1987, and your compassionate vision of new healing possibilities in your 2002 testimonio "Let us be the healing of the wound": "We are all wounded but we can connect through the wound that's alienated us from others. When the wound forms a cicatrize, the scar can become a bridge linking people split apart" (102).

Me acuerdo when I invited you to contribute a cyber-testimonio, later published in *One Wound for Another/Una herida por otra. Testimonios de Latin@s in the U.S. through Cyberspace (11 de septiembre de 2001–11 de marzo de 2002)*, a cross-border Mexico-U.S. edition. Posthumously dedicated to your memory, our book owes much to you; the title "one wound for another" is borrowed from your testimonio. You almost didn't write your essay, almost pulled out, arguing that it needed reworking, that you had no time to do the revisions you felt necessary. I am so glad I persisted, that you agreed to let it go.

I did not realize that this piece would be one of the last you would write or publish, but I did recognize immediately its power: in gathering the quintessential filaments of your theoretical-critical discursivity-iconography you responded con corazón, wisely, strongly, intelligently, compassionately, as a true curandera cultural to 9-11-01.[6]

A momentous event such as that of 9/11 . . . shifts us to nepantla, a psychological, liminal space between the way things had been and an unknown future. Nepantla is the space-in-between, the locus and sign of transition. . . . En este lugar we fall into chaos, fear of the unknown, and are forced to take up the task of self-redefinition. . . . Conocimiento urges us to respond not just with the traditional practice of spirituality (contemplation, meditation, and private rituals) or with the technologies of political activism (protests, demonstrations, and speakouts), but with the amalgam of the two—spiritual activism, which we've also inherited along with la sombra. Conocimiento pushes us into engaging the spirit in confronting our social sickness with new tools and practices whose goal it is to effect a shift. . . . The healing of our wounds results in trans-formation and transformation results in the healing of our wounds ("Let us be the healing" 99–100)

I realized your essay's value for future readers, future generations who will also have to "be a crossroads," "live sin fronteras," "survive the Borderlands" of their own, on both sides of la frontera, survivors of this new history-border: pre– and post–September 11, 2001. As I see it, this wound-scar-bridge is a kind of bruja-potion for harsh post–9-11-01 nepantla times.

As the symposium concludes, a former student of mine comes up, now teaching Chicana literature, whose Ph.D. dissertation on Chicana narratives was the first of its kind at the UNAM. Students approach me wanting to do research on, asking about chicanidades y mexicanidades: algo de tí, Gloria, sí, ha cruzado la frontera.

Yet, la verdad es que, as far as I know, *Borderlands/La Frontera* is taught in only a few courses, is available in a few libraries, unavailable in bookstores in Mexico City.[7] Why? Because it is mainly in English, has not yet been translated, only fragments here and there. No publisher is interested. Were it available, though, would it be more widely read, included on more syllabi? Possibly, but my guess is that it is too radi-cal, even today. Of course, most Chican@ texts would also be suspect. Hay otro tipo de malinchismo that makes white eurocentric texts more acceptable.

True, you are a self-declared patlache amid the realities of lesbofobia, homophobia.[8] Yet other realities are prominent: gender study programs are scarce; colleges and alternative groups do not proliferate as in the States; only 6 percent of women in Mexico get to college. My own corazonada signals in red: class-race-linguistic issues. Your use of class-branded archaic oral-rooted Spanish, your daring iconographic-mythic-linguistic hybridity que llega del otro lado and touches other heridas that are externalized as "resistance reactions."

As I leave the conference room, I think of you, Gloria la nepantlera, curandera cultural, que has cruzado al reino de los muertos, pero sigues atendiendo las heridas de otr@s, compartiendo múltiples sanaciones.

May we all find inspiration, as you urged, to continue en la lucha and to "do work that matters" ("Let us be the healing" 102).

Mexico City, 11 September 2006

CHAPTER 9

A Call to Action: Spiritual Activism . . . an Inevitable Unfolding

KARINA L. CÉSPEDES

Caught between the sudden contraction, the breath sucked in and the endless space, the brown woman stands still, looks at the sky. She decides to go down, digging her way along the roots of trees. Sifting through the bones, she shakes them to see if there is any marrow in them. Then, touching the dirt to her forehead, to her tongue, she takes a few bones, leaves the rest in their burial place.

She goes through her backpack, keeps her journal and address book, throws away the muni-bart metromaps. The coins are heavy and they go next, then the greenbacks flutter through the air. She keeps her knife, can opener and eyebrow pencil. She puts bones, pieces of bark, hierbas, *eagle feather, snakeskin, tape recorder, the rattle and drum in her pack and she sets out to become the complete* tolteca.

GLORIA ANZALDÚA, *BORDERLANDS/LA FRONTERA*

When I read Gloria Anzaldúa's *Borderlands/La Frontera* during my junior year in college I immediately responded to her mapping of a "border consciousness"; it gave me a way to express the deep disconnection I felt as a daughter not of the Cuban middle class but of the seldom-acknowledged racially mixed Cuban working-poor immigrants who came to the United States in the 1980s to the open disdain of more established Cubans and non-Cubans alike. Although I hailed from a different generation and cultural background, Anzaldúa's writing inspired and guided me through graduate school and then while teaching my own undergraduate classes.

As a teacher, I frequently found her work useful in getting at the heart of racism, sexism, classism, homophobia, and other prejudices that run as rampant in the classroom as they do in most of our daily interactions. As in my own undergraduate classes, Anzaldúa's writing produced wildly different reactions in my students, ranging from great admiration to great discomfort. These emotions facilitated students' ability to grapple with the internalized prejudices they carried with them into the classroom. Right before my eyes, across decades and geographical locations, Anzaldúa's work challenged the socially mobile aspirations of students who would prefer not to encounter the confusion invoked by her multiple languages and anticolonial, feminist position. Yet for others, Anzaldúa's challenge to racism, classism, and colonial languages permitted deep belly sighs of relief: it was not they who were somehow deficient. Within their broken, mal hablado languages, within their otherwise "abnormal" bodies, sat a powerful truth: the inability to "dominate" any colonial language is to be able to enter a space where most of humanity resides, a space that is in between worlds.

After celebrating more than a decade of rereading Anzaldúa's work, most recently I have turned to her writing in my search for insights concerning the global violence that has redefined how most of the world lives, travels, works, and interacts. My overwhelming need to access an approach capable of envisioning a shift in consciousness, a way of moving toward meaningful social change and toward peace at this particular historical moment, has provoked a different (re)reading of Anzaldúa's work. I have discovered that Anzaldúa's recommendations for effecting profound social change go well beyond the usual combative "call to action" that requires a clearly defined enemy. Anzaldúa calls for a huge epistemological shift: a "massive uprooting of dualistic thinking in the individual and the collective consciousness" (*Borderlands/La Frontera* 102). For Anzaldúa, this "uprooting" requires that we forgo our oppositional approach: "On our way to a new consciousness, we will have to leave the opposite bank, the split between the two mortal combatants somehow healed so that we are on both shores at once and, at once see through serpent and eagle eyes. Or perhaps we will decide to disengage from the dominant culture . . . and cross . . . into a wholly new and separate territory. The possibilities are numerous once we decide to act and not react" (100–01).

Anzaldúa's "way to a new consciousness" offers an alternative to postmodern solutions that interrogate the dualistic thinking at the root of existing power structures (man/woman, black/white, identity/difference, stance/counterstance) but don't connect this interrogation to alternative forms of transformation.

Anzaldúa takes this challenge to dualistic thinking well beyond the interrogation of discourse. Rather than stand on one side or the other of the paired opposites (or of merely recognizing that such positioning is the problem), she insists that we "leave the opposite bank," the spaces that may feel safe; doing so will end a life filled with preemptive strikes followed by endless violence. In order to heal "the split between the two mortal combatants" we must disengage from our personal and collective stance/counterstance, move beyond our story, beyond the social identities that feed a sense of belonging to "our" particular groups (race, nationality, class, ethnicity, sexuality, caste, gender, religious and political affiliations) to which we desperately cling while shouting at one another from the opposite side of the river bank (or conference table, issue, border, and so on).

Although such shouting matches feel important, as if they are a matter of life or death—inescapable, as an addiction feels inescapable—we must move away from imagining ourselves, and others, as either heroes or villains. We need a more honest assessment: on whose back are we gaining our fictitious sense of "self"? Anzaldúa's call for disidentification requires facing up to the real effects such identities produce, the personal privileges one may gain from them alongside the tragic limitations these categories create. To disidentify from either side is to question the privileges we take for granted and the power, which is carelessly given away in order to stand on one side or the other.

As part of a community split politically (one half on the island of Cuba and the other dispersed throughout the United States), I know firsthand the vicious power of the self-righteous indignation that has divided families, violently pitted a people against themselves, kept the majority of a population—whether "here" or "there"—in states of seldom-acknowledged economic and psychic destitution. Standing on either shore has defined "being Cuban" as reacting to the latest posturing of one side or the other.

Yet this disidentification from social identity categories is but a way station to a deeper, transformative politics that synthesizes social activism with spiritual vision, thereby creating a unique form of "spiritual activism."[1] Spiritual activism, unlike conventional religion's and activism's hurried and frantic pace, has its source within the individual and, as Anzaldúa explains, "emerges when we listen to the 'small still voice' (Teish) within us which can empower us to create actual change in the world" ("El Mundo Zurdo" 195). It requires a slowing down in order to permit an expansive awareness "that finds the best instead of the worst in the other" ("now let us shift" 572). Those who enact spiritual

activism simultaneously engage in a movement for complete social, economic, and political justice *and* a profound spiritual journey toward a
consciousness that will bring about an end to internal and external wars.
Much like the process of disidentification, spiritual activism is neither
escapism nor an easy universalism that says "identity doesn't matter" in
order to avoid confronting privilege (Fernandes). Spiritual activism does
not celebrate a directionless denial of the very real material effects of the
identities that structure our lives; nor is it simply an exercise in imagining
a different, better, stronger kind of self. Spiritual activism is "a two-way
movement—a going deep into the self and an expanding out into the
world, a simultaneous recreation of the self and a reconstruction of society" ("La Prieta" 208). As such, it challenges the very root of the ego-
driven identifications that shape our aspirations for recognition, success,
and superiority (Fernandes) and begins to fill the immense need to be in
relation. This process compels the individual committed to social justice
to question who truly are "my/our enemies" or "the population 'I/we'
wish to help." These questions in turn challenge our engagement with
those on either side of the table, issue, or border because they boldly
acknowledge that our need to stay on either side, our desire to be "safe"
within identity categories, is in fact killing us.[2]

This process is crucial, particularly in this post-9/11 era with its emphasis on personal and geographic borders and the crisis in national and
international immigration. In these times of individual and collective
panic, those committed to social change must slowly but surely access a
mode of perception capable of bringing forth peace.

spiritual mestizaje . . . "an inevitable unfolding" . . .

> We are the people who leap in the dark, we are the people on the knees
> of the gods. In our very flesh, (r)evolution works out the clash of cul-
> tures. It makes us crazy constantly, but if the center holds, we've made
> some kind of evolutionary step forward . . . the opus, the great alchemi-
> cal work; spiritual *mestizaje,* a "morphogenesis," an inevitable unfolding.
> (*Borderlands/La Frontera* 103)

Anzaldúa's work tells us that resistance to identity boxes leads to a different tribe, a different story enabling a rethinking of oneself "in more
global-spiritual terms instead of conventional categories of color, class,
career," and furthermore changes the ways we perceive reality, the way

we see ourselves, and the ways we behave ("now let us shift" 561). The spiritual activist's role is to extend herself—in small ways and in big, flamboyant (even obnoxious) ways—toward ending the internal conflict that is mirrored in the external turmoil of the two sides and to do so with the understanding that it is not only the "right" thing to do but also the only thing to do. Social change requires that we love, care for, and wish well upon those occupying what otherwise we would find to be a deplorable position. Applied to immigrant rights, for example, the spiritual-activist approach includes loving those who risk their lives to enter U.S. boundaries as well as those who create painful borders in the name of securing their own sense of safety. We must love both extremes, understanding that they are one and the same, as they face national economies' failures, basic health care's exorbitant costs, reduced labor options, and the belief that personal safety requires either fleeing from home or pushing people out of a home that is also their birthright to inhabit (as it is the right of all to inhabit their desired space on the planet).

For the activist and scholar looking to Anzaldúa's work for encouragement, she offers a simple, but nonetheless challenging, recommendation: "Change requires more than words on a page—it takes perseverance, creative ingenuity, and acts of love" ("now let us shift" 575). We must focus less on our respective counterstance (including our specific disciplines or academic fields) and instead talk and listen to one another with connection as our agenda, daring to ask at all times, *How would the world we inhabit be better if our work centered a consciousness that would allow "problematic populations" to survive the abandonment of (his)tory; and what would our life's work look like if we were to tap into the consciousness that bestows upon us the right to live and work toward possibility? What if, instead of creating heroes and victims within the global violence we all witness, we saw a people divided against themselves needlessly shouting across a divide? What if this vision moved us toward teaching, working, writing, and loving guided by the conviction that to end the suffering we must reduce our contribution to the chaos?*

For me, this spiritual-activist approach encourages intellectual creativity as I remain immersed in the collective healing and evolution of Cuban communities beyond fictitious borders. It means that I cannot stand self-righteously on either side of the Cuban political divide, nor can I ignore it. It means I must act with the understanding that we, on all sides, are hurting, but we all also hold in our hands the ability to forgive. I bring this perspective to the table when sitting either in Miami or Havana across from people whom I love very much and with whom I have disagreed very much.

As we make our way toward peace, the fact that we are living in a place/time of nepantla—"exiting from the old world view . . . not yet entered or created a new one" (Keating, "Forging El Mundo Zurdo" 529)—indicates that the space between violence and peace, counterstance and disidentification, discomfort and deep belly sighs, "the place where different perspectives come into conflict and . . . where you struggle to find equilibrium" (Anzaldúa, "now let us shift" 548–49) is itself a site of transformation. Anzaldua's spiritual-activist approach offers an intellectual foundation as we continue to be innovative in our inner and personal evolutions, as we remain open to forgiving and creating bridges within our families, communities, and larger political conversations. The prayer and the intellectual hypothesis, which are one and the same, is that by operating from the belief that this population can heal, and must heal, we can indeed end these wars.

CHAPTER 10

Gloria Anzaldúa and the Meaning of Queer

HÉCTOR DOMÍNGUEZ-RUVALCABA

In the fall of 1993, during my first semester as a master of arts student in Hispanic literature at New Mexico State University, one of my professors recommended I read *Borderlands/La Frontera: The New Mestiza* by Gloria Anzaldúa.[1] The book got my attention in more than one way with its amalgam of poetry, political statements, intimate diary entries of resentment, essays of mythological interpretation, and colloquial word games. I talked to my professor about the inaccuracy of some data referring to pre-Columbian religion. He observed that in my reading I was only looking for mistakes and that I did not get the point. "What's the point?" I asked. "Identity," he said, without knowing that he was opening the way to several questions that in the future would be the core of my intellectual preoccupations. Since then, this concept has become unavoidable, mysterious, and somehow a multipurpose instrument. After years of discussions and reconsiderations, this hybrid text became one of my keystones as I learned about hegemonic identity politics in both racial and gender realms.[2] That is, *Borderlands* expanded my understanding of why dominant culture establishes the ways identities are expected to be, restricting the legitimacy of practices that are not prescribed in the models already adopted by society.

Challenging definitions of sex and ethnicity has been the most important lesson I have received from Anzaldúa. This challenge is rooted in the discomfort that identity norms generate in queer people. This discomfort leads to a radical intervention into normativity, precisely the one that rules those notions considered liberating against colonialism but that become oppressive for dissident sexualities. Being queer is a starting point to undermine those identity definitions. Based on this premise, I offer a critical reflection on Anzaldúa's arguments concerning hegemonic notions of identity. I revisit the concepts of queer and identity, exploring how they transformed my personal, intellectual, and professional positions as an academic in the fields of gender studies of Mexican literature and culture and U.S.-Mexico border issues. Finally, I reflect on the future directions I believe we must use following Anzaldúa's groundbreaking contributions to queer theory and its intersection with race, ethnicity, nationality, globalization, gender, and sexuality.

My first encounter with Anzaldúa became the catalyst of an academic project exploring my own subjectivity. Knowledge cannot be performed without reflecting on oneself; my subjectivity, like hers, has been produced by overlapping, contradictory identity features. Anzaldúa conveys a complex racial and sex-gender definition: woman, Chicana, mestiza, and lesbian. Being immigrant, gay, mestizo, and bilingual, I found myself positioned in a symbolic and real border where, as in Anzaldúa, the uniqueness of this sum of marginalities determined a queer point of view. This juxtaposed identity is suggested in the title *Borderlands/La Frontera,* which rests on a slash that I read not as a graphic representation of bilingualism and hybridization but as a wound: the metaphor of subject fragmentation where the text itself is also constructed.[3] To inquire into the paradoxes produced in these overlapping identities implies an archeology of the fragmented subject. My work on the formation of masculinity and homophobia in Mexican culture is, in this way, an archeology of my own subjectivity, or what Anzaldúa calls "autohistoria-teoría": writing not only about abstract ideas but also bringing the personal history into the history of the community (*Interviews/Entrevistas* 242).

When Anzaldúa focuses on a human landscape to depict her view of the borderland, I feel myself in the procession: "The prohibited and forbidden are its inhabitants. *Los atravesados* live here: the squint-eyed, the perverse, the queer, the troublesome, the mongrel, the mulato, the half-breed, the half dead; in short, those who cross over, pass over, or go through the confines of the 'normal'" (*Borderlands/La Frontera* 25). It was not easy to find myself reflected in the Border. Becoming its inhabitant rather than a detached observer required not only that I complete the readings proposed by the professor who introduced me to *Borderlands/La Frontera* but also that I question my own subjectivity. I was a migrant and not a visitor in this country. My encounter with the United Stated involved a new life project rather than a tourist's curiosity and admiration. This migrant status started to be evident when my habits and values proved to be impertinent, deficient, or even forbidden. Like Anzaldúa, I experienced intolerance from those I should call my people.

Homophobia seemed to be a way of ethnic self-affirmation for Mexicans in the United States. My diary entries of those years show the difficulties of being rejected by my people and how I escaped that hostile atmosphere in my weekly trips to Ciudad Juárez.

I had just moved to the United States; my future wasn't clear yet, but I was starting to conceive of my homosexuality not as a stigma but as a privileged position from which I was impelled to exercise a critical perspective. I can say that being queer, atravesado, or forbidden was a point of departure for an intellectual project to understand subjectivity in a migratory situation. To migrate is a process of losing identity: "we were jerked out by the roots, truncated, disemboweled, disposed, and separated from our identity" (*Borderlands/La Frontera* 30). One can only be concerned with identity when it becomes problematic. Anzaldúa brought me to understand the awareness of being expelled from the constituted (privileged) identities. I do not mean that Anzaldúa induced victimization; rather, she opened a path of empowerment through queerness, or what I think of as queer imagination. Anzaldúa asserts in a 1982 interview with Linda Smuckler: "I want to write from the body; that's why we're in a body" (*Interviews/Entrevistas* 63). She makes a distinction between writing from the mind and speaking from the body, where fantasies flow out (66). To be queer is not just to be different because the body overcomes, with its relentless imagination, heteronormative identity limitations. Queerness is a power that stems from difference and prevails over homogeneous and uniform definitions. Queer imagination can be defined as the process of escaping heterosexual norms, which implies the search for alternative forms of desire and aesthetic values.

Unity (like that called for by conventional forms of identity) is challenged by multiplicity. The Aztec goddess Coatlicue provides Anzaldúa with a suggestive mythological source of that queer imagination. "[Coatlicue] represents: duality in life, a synthesis of duality, and a third perspective—something more than mere duality or a synthesis of duality" (*Borderlands/La Frontera* 68). Embodying a duality, Coatlicue is composed of a dialectical contradiction enabling a third element—the synthesis of masculine and feminine. It is a reluctance to be ruled by binary logic, abolishing the hegemonic discourse of gender. This desire for the discursive collapse recalls Theodor Adorno's negative dialectics. For this philosopher, the coexistence of heterogeneous concepts defines an entity that resists generalization (Buck-Mors 203). Anzaldúa's ambition is to get to the unspeakable point of gender—that is, the point at which gender identity does not make sense—by turning Coatlicue's ambivalence into "something else" (*Borderlands/La Frontera* 101). Anzaldúa does not clearly define that "something else"; its promise stays unresolved because it cannot have a fixed definition. Attaining any definition would stop the relentless promise of the "something else," which is the sense of queer imagination.

Coatlicue enacts queer imagination. Anzaldúa embodies the goddess and, like her, evades any stable definition. When Coatlicue "makes 'sense,'" she immediately escapes the boundaries of meaning and crosses over, "dragging the old skin along" (*Borderlands/La Frontera* 71). By painfully shedding her "old skin," Coatlicue drives us through the sense of queerness, enabling us to flee from the given identity.[4] Coatlicue's queerness conveys a sliding meaning of subject toward its lack of identity—that is, the subject experiences a continuous replacement of self-definition; then, a queer deconstructive perspective is confirmed. I cannot conceive of Queer and Border Studies without this constant slide of meaning. The experience of escaping one's identities results in a cognitive position that dismisses definitive terms. This notion of migration and queerness conceived as a permanent crossing over is one of Anzaldúa's most important contributions. This image connotes a ceaseless journey from one condition to another, an open subjectivity that never finds its definite meaning, to the point of abolishing oppressive differences: the conception of human relationships in terms of the asymmetry of male/female, heterosexual/homosexual, white people/people of color, and other such binary distinctions.

By concentrating a number of marks of marginalization, Anzaldúa locates herself in the position of radical difference: the other of every other. This labyrinth of marginalization conveys what Jorge Moreiras calls *relational subalternism,* an "abyssal ground for a critique of the social able to see beyond some crucial narratives of the present" (267). In *Borderlands/La Frontera,* exacerbating differences becomes a path to neutralize identities' segregating network. Whereas segregation consists of excluding and contrasting identities, Anzaldúa's radical difference is more than a sum of many differences. The crossroad of queerness takes gender and racial differences into the inclusiveness: "As a lesbian I have no race, my own people disclaim me; but I am all races because there is the queer of me in all races" (102).

Race difference for Anzaldúa is overcome by the queerness that is in all races; queerness shows an intersubjective inside where differences are redefined as human value rather than a mark of segregation. Queerness brings hegemonic notions of race and gender into question by transforming the significance of difference. In her preface to *this bridge we call home* Anzaldúa calls for bridges that cross race and gender classifications (2–3). In *Borderlands/La Frontera,* she introduces a political statement that breaks the barriers of identity: "The new *mestiza* copes by developing a tolerance for contradictions, a tolerance for ambiguity" (101, her italics).[5] In other words, developing this tolerance for contradictions and ambiguity enables her not only to redefine oppositional differences but also to state that contradictions and ambiguities are desirable as liberating conditions of humanness and sources of creativity.

The notion of queer as ethnic and gender multiplicity delineates a politics of difference that subverts the segregating order. Anti-homophobic interventions, as Eve K. Sedgwick proposes (9–10), should target a binary system of exclusion: heterosexual versus homosexual, masculine versus feminine, white versus all other races, demonstrating that such a binary distribution is asymmetrical. In fact, most social categorization is based on uneven relationships. Queer deconstruction focuses that system of differences, making visible the binary-asymmetrical order's obsolescence and emphasizing the importance of building bridges in order to neutralize exclusionary practices. This perspective posits an enveloping community that overcomes interethnic and international segregation. Queer perspective blurs oppositional categorization, precisely confronting "the traits and habits distorting how you see reality and inhibiting the full use of your facultades" ("now let us shift" 541).

The utopian horizon of queer perspective must be articulated with an inclusive notion of identity and citizenship, canceling the oppositional to allow what Anzaldúa calls "the new tribalism" ("(Un)natural bridges" 3). In other words, this project involves deconstructing heterosexual hegemony in a manner that focuses on and calls into question the exclusion and prejudices of the modern state, exploring ways to build a transnational coalition of queer bridges that may perpetuate crossing as an alternative view of globalization, and examining oppression grounded in the critical assessment of ethnicity, gender, and sexuality. One of Anzaldúa's most precious contributions is the possibility of re-signifying differences as the principle for constructing inclusive communities.

Anzaldúa's style proved to be essential for performing this deconstructive project—critiquing sanctioned knowledge by challenging its forms of articulation. The problem of identity to which my graduate professor referred becomes an endless restructuring of identity. This identity question must stay open until the machinery of oppression stops co-opting the emergence of subjectivities. This is one of the main principles that I consider invaluable as a legacy of Anzaldúa.

CHAPTER 11

Breaking Our Chains:
Achieving Nos/otras Consciousness

LEI ZHANG

For positive social change to occur we must imagine a reality that differs from what already exists. . . . Empowerment comes from ideas—our revolution is fought with concepts, not with guns, and it is fueled by vision.
GLORIA ANZALDÚA, "(UN)NATURAL BRIDGES"

I first encountered Gloria Anzaldúa's work as a graduate student in a literary theory class. After spending most of the semester deciphering writings by such luminaries as Jacques Derrida, Michel Foucault, and Homi Bhabha, it was refreshing to finally encounter clear, vibrant prose. My eyes flew with the lines; my fingers could almost touch the thick, full-bodied emotions streaming out of the pages. I kept turning the pages, amazed. Could she write in such an intensely personal, metaphoric way and still be anthologized alongside obscure postmodern philosophers in *The Norton Anthology of Theory and Criticism*? I put *Borderlands/La Frontera* on my reading list. When AnaLouise Keating at Texas Woman's University offered a writing-intensive seminar titled "Gloria Anzaldúa: Theorizing and the Politics of Imagination," I signed up early. In that class we read all of Anzaldúa's published work and were introduced to her promising post-*Borderlands* theories. After Anzaldúa's death, I found myself often going back to her writings to seek comfort, inspiration, or the simple enjoyment of reading her words. I found myself dwelling upon her nos/otras concept and wondering how it could help people such as myself to overcome a social phenomenon I term the *postcolonial inferiority complex*,[1] the sense of inferiority suffered by many inhabitants of developing countries in the postcolonial era and brought on by western political, economic, and cultural domination. Suffering from this inferiority complex, people internalize white supremacist ideologies and accept a hierarchical value system based on violent dualisms that prize "whiteness" over color. Anzaldúa's nos/otras theory can transform and eventually eradicate dualisms such as these.

Anzaldúa took the pronoun "nosotras," Spanish for the feminine "we" or "us," and inserted a slash to signify "we/others." The slash represents a bridge that connects "us" to "others" ("now let us shift" 570). Thus, the term "nos/otras" reflects a connectionist vision of bridging cultural divides and represents a fundamental desire to transcend binaries that have pitted people against one another. By connecting "us" with "others," nos/otras enables us to search for "an unmapped common ground" ("now let us shift" 570) and offers an alternative to the dominant dualistic worldviews. Furthermore, the nos/otras concept teaches us to accept the other as an equal partner and focus on the spiritual connection among us, finding "the best instead of the worst in the other," thinking of "la otra in a compassionate way" ("now let us shift" 572). Thus the nos/otras concept represents a postmodern effort to transcend binary oppositions and imagines a future "when the bridge will no longer be needed—we'll have shifted to a seamless nosotras" ("now let us shift" 570).

These discussions have inspired me to use the nos/otras concept as a grand vision, a blueprint to work at transforming the postcolonial inferiority complex into a positive sense of self. For many years I have observed a disturbing trend by which many Chinese, both in China and the United States, have embraced western concepts of beauty. Hollywood movies and American soap operas have brought images of blond, blue-eyed stars into almost every Chinese household.[2] A recent trip to China vividly reminded me how much my home country has changed. Upon my arrival, my thoughtful sister included, among my bathroom supplies, a bottle of L'Oreal White Perfect Whitening Facial Foam and Doctor Li Whitening Water Masks.[3] My fashion-conscious college friend showed up with a head of yellow/blond hair and told me it was the current fashion. When we visited a Japanese department store in Chengdu, the provincial capital in Sichuan province, my husband walked through the clothing sections taking note of photos of Western models and Western-looking mannequins yet could not find one that looked Chinese or Japanese. Chinese newspapers advertise plastic surgeries to add an extra fold, creating the more esthetically pleasing, occidental "double eyelid." On the billboards that decorate the city streets, we see digitally doctored, westernized "beauties" with sparkly white skin, big eyes, and "double eyelids."

While practices such as whitening one's skin, highlighting one's hair, and cutting folds in one's eyelids do not necessarily damage the body, they do suggest an unhealthy psychological makeup, which may in turn contribute to antagonistic behaviors. These behaviors are symptoms of the postcolonial inferiority complex. Suffering from this complex, we equate whiteness with beauty and superiority,[4] a habit that inevitably leads to horizontal racism—racism against other people of color who might be poorer or darker-skinned than ourselves. Assuming a "white" identity, we project our internalized white-supremacist judgments onto other people of color. As an immigrant, I have often heard my Chinese friends make racist remarks about Latinos/as and African Americans. These remarks typically echo mainstream white racism. Horizontal racism thus takes many expressions: *they* are lazy, *they* are law-breakers, *they* are statistically proven to be more dangerous, and so on. It manifests in small incidents. For example, a Chinese friend in Houston opted to pay more to buy a house in a predominantly white neighborhood. An extra fifty thousand dollars helped him to avoid middle-class black neighbors. Another male Chinese friend vowed to protect me from an approaching group of Latinos/as at a gas station in Dallas.

Some of us have digested racist ideologies so well that we move like programmed robots. We don't think, we don't act, we merely move, passively.[5] Horizontal racism represents the postcolonial inferiority complex at its ugliest.

The postcolonial inferiority complex has roots in the nos-otras divide and results from what Anzaldúa calls "a new colonization of people's psyches, minds, and emotions" (*Interviews/Entrevistas* 216). The postcolonial inferiority complex, along with its predecessor, the colonial inferiority complex, arose from a masculinist, eurocentric epistemology, internalized by the colonized, that sharply divided people into opposing camps: superior versus inferior, "white" versus "colored," civilized versus savage. In *Black Skin, White Masks,* Franz Fanon advocated emancipation from the colonial inferiority complex through the abolition of colonialism. Yet the devastating psychological effects of colonialism, so accurately captured in Fanon's book, have spread beyond the colonial era. According to Edward Said, "The meaning of the imperial past . . . has entered the reality of hundreds of millions of people, where its existence as shared memory and as a highly conflictual texture of culture, ideology, and policy still exercises tremendous force" (12). The colonial legacy, coupled with the contemporary western dominance of economic, media, and popular-culture resources, exacerbates the sense of inferiority experienced by many people living in "developing" countries.[6]

Surprisingly, despite the overwhelming evidence of the new colonization of the Chinese psyche,[7] this phenomenon has received little scholarly attention. Although publicly airing one's dirty laundry can be humiliating—there is a danger of "losing face"—silence cannot erase an urgent social problem. Like many of us, I have remained silent for too long. I hope this essay will contribute to the dialogue and increase awareness of this issue.

A deeper awareness requires that we recognize the causal link among those social ills: dualism, as an epistemology, breeds racism and the postcolonial inferiority complex. Thus, to transform the postcolonial inferiority complex into a positive consciousness, we must uproot the dualistic mentality.

Functioning as an overarching vision for social reform, Anzaldúa's theory of nos/otras requires that we look into the causes of the "othering" process that creates dualisms and offer alternatives. Admittedly, "othering" manifests on many fronts—class, religion, ideology, region, sex, age, race, and so on—but I want to focus on the gaze as a way of knowing that separates people into "nos" and "otras."

The gaze has risen to dominance in our image-saturated world. The cornucopia of images channels both subtle and blunt messages to us, telling us how we should dress, look, and judge other people. Through the gaze we say: she is black, she is Asian, and she is Mexican; he looks middle class, he looks handsome, and he looks fat. Through the gaze we objectify people and tell ourselves that we know something essential about them. In fact, obsessed and beguiled by the gaze, we forget what truly matters: our common humanity.

The postcolonial inferiority complex is triggered by the gaze. Measuring ourselves against glamorous models, we experience a lack. Movie stars and fashion models play a double role in this othering process. They are both sexualized and objectified through the gaze and represent and reinforce eurocentric beauty standards.

An alternative epistemology would replace looking with listening and would break free from all notions of beauty rooted in the masculinist, objectifying gaze. Listening encourages us to focus on the spiritual, emotional dimensions of our existence and reach deeper, more meaningful self-definitions as generated by nos/otras. Through listening, we recognize the deep, intricate connections among people, thus rendering the exterior appearance irrelevant, superficial.

We can begin by listening to our own voices. Prompted by the longing to understand ourselves, we listen to the intuitive voices in our minds and the desires in our hearts and bodies. Our voices whisper to us our spiritual and emotional needs and prod us to live to our full potential. Listening frees us from the gaze, which has trapped us in an endless oscillation between insecurity and inferiority. Listening frees us from the tyranny of the mirror, giving us energy and time to explore the meaning and purpose of life.

We can listen to other people's voices. Listening bridges the distance between "nos" and "otras" and encourages our connectionist vision of the world. Listening to other people increases our knowledge and expands our awareness; knowledge of others brings empathy and acceptance. Racism springs from a lack of knowledge—a fear of getting to know people and a desire to objectify people. Listening alleviates the fear of others, melting the emotional walls we have built around us. People who suffer the most are often the most silenced. We have to seek out those muted voices from diverse communities and focus on the social issues that have drowned their voices.

Listening to other people's voices increases our awareness of cultural diversity and prompts us to question the white-supremacist worldview. Through our effort to understand other people, we form a holistic worldview that transcends antagonistic divides; we compose a new multicultural, collaborative narrative of hope that "recognizes nurturance and reciprocity and encourages alliances among groups working to transform communities" ("now let us shift" 568).

We can listen to voices of resistance. Oppression often brings out the resistant spirit of people. Voices from history tell us that buried under the colonial falsehoods is the brutal exploitation that has pushed the colonized to the brink of annihilation. Voices from the present warn us against the hegemonic power of the western entertainment and commercial industries. An understanding of the past increases the awareness of the present: the colonized have not stopped resisting.

We must listen to the voices with which we disagree. It is fairly easy to listen to people with whom we wholeheartedly agree, but we may resist listening to differing views, especially when those views challenge our deep-seated beliefs. It takes extra effort to open our minds and listen to those voices. Those voices might force us to reconsider our identities, convert our belief systems, and make crossings. A difficult crossing may mark the beginning of a fresh, fulfilling life.

Sometimes those differing views may be sexist, racist, or religiously extremist. However, listening to them marks the first step toward engaging in an effective argument. After all, how can we expect those people to listen to us if we refuse to listen to them? We must listen carefully and be able to fairly represent their views. We have to be able to state the other person's views to the point that he or she will say, "Yes, that's what I mean." Wayne Booth calls this process "listening rhetoric" (101–02).

We can listen to our reflections on our lived experiences. We listen alone; we listen together. We can tell our families and friends that what matters is not how they look but how they listen to their own voices and other people's voices. Listening holds the promise of transcending the nos-versus-otras mentality that lies behind the postcolonial inferiority complex.

The nos/otras concept inspires us to envision a nondualistic future when we will have shifted to "a seamless nosotras" that recognizes "the deep common ground and interwoven kinship among all things and people" and an absolute reciprocity and connection in the universe ("now let us shift" 567–68). Through what Keating calls "re(con)ceiving the other," we recognize the "other" within ourselves (*Women Reading Women Writing* 75). If we realize the absurdity of the concept that "white equals beauty," people of color will stop feeling inferior because of our skin color or exterior looks. In this postcolonial era, we have to form a critical consciousness to recognize how we have been enslaved again by a hegemonic western ideology and then actively resist its insidious influence.

Genuine personal and social changes can only happen through the acquisition of critical awareness. We need to realize that horizontal racism originates from a postcolonial inferiority complex, the result of a new type of colonialism that thrives on a violent nos-otra divide. Many "nonwhite" colonized people, trapped by the concept of "whiteness," want to assume a "white" identity and at the same time otherize fellow people of color. Once we recognize how hegemonic cultural values have warped our own consciousness, we can actively resist these damaging influences by adopting an alternative epistemology. Through listening we connect with ourselves and others and create more meaningful self-definitions envisioned in the nos/otras concept. To achieve a healthy society, humanity must renounce the us/them, superiority/inferiority oppositions and make "a simple attempt to touch the other, the feel the other, to explain the other to myself" (Fanon 231).

CHAPTER 12

Conocimiento and Healing:
Academic Wounds, Survival, and Tenure

GLORIA GONZÁLEZ-LÓPEZ

"Congratulations on your promotion to associate professor with ten-ure!!!! I'll look forward to having you as a colleague for many years to come." I received this note from my department chair in an e-mail dated December 18, 2007. For about a week or two, I had been waiting to hear the official announcement. I felt blissfully happy and profoundly grateful when I received the news of my tenure. I experienced a deep sense of relief that I did not have words for, and I wanted to have a good cry, but I just couldn't. Gradually I took in the joyful relief, and eventually I cried and felt deep peace. Days later, I learned that another colleague and friend at my university had received sad news with regard to his tenure, which had been denied. We had shared the experience of "coming up" for tenure at the same time, and I felt deeply sad for him. The contrasting feelings of joyful relief for myself and sorrow for my col-league took me back to my academic journeys of intense indecision and struggle as I deciphered the best way to survive graduate school, obtain an assistant professorship, and eventually caress the dream of receiving tenure and promotion, all while trying to keep my sanity intact. Since entering graduate school to pursue a Ph.D. in 1993, persistent ques-tions have haunted me: "Do I really want an academic career? Is aca-demia really for me? I really love teaching, doing research, and writing . . . hmmm, but then the tenure process? It is so much pressure! Maybe this is for me, maybe not."

During one of the endless conversations AnaLouise and I engaged in while working on this anthology, I suggested that I wanted to write an essay that could potentially benefit other compañeras y compañeros in their struggle as they explore ways to have a satisfying academic jour-ney, especially on the path to tenure, while also trying to have a healthy, happy personal life. I began thinking about writing this essay during the fall of 2007, but I just couldn't bring myself to do it. "How can I write about surviving academic life and getting tenure if I don't even have tenure yet?!" I asked myself. Although I knew that this anthology would be published regardless of my tenure outcome, I had dreams of having this experience included in the publication. In reality, however, my professional future was on hold or at least not entirely within my control. The feeling reminded me of nepantla: I was in the process of transforming myself through an ambiguous and unknown state of consciousness.

Again and again I realized that nepantla had been my state of mind since that first day when I entered graduate school in the early 1990s. Until December 18, 2007, I had lived in a process of continuously challenging transformations, personal and professional, always unpredictable, always in a state of alertness to the unexpected. Now as I look back in time, I find myself revisiting the many complex and varying experiences of my academic journey. This journey has included many meaningful experiences of intellectual, personal, and spiritual growth, but often when I least expected it, it has involved various forms of institutional trauma. As I revisit the past fifteen years of my life, I open up to multidimensional forms of growth; *from within* the wound, I revisit other types of pain that I did not know existed until I decided to pursue graduate school and then to become a professor. Thus, as I close this deeply rewarding yet challenging chapter of my life, I immerse myself in the gold mine of Anzaldúan thought to explore ways in which her theorizing on the different forms of intellectual inquiry helps to explain my own academic journeys.

Conocimiento before, during, and after getting tenure has become a way of knowing, feeling, and healing. Conocimiento becomes a way of sensing and learning, a way of taking in and reaching out to others on a similar path. According to Anzaldúa, conocimiento is "skeptical of reason and rationality, conocimiento questions conventional knowledge's current categories, classifications, and contents" ("now let us shift" 541). Conocimiento transcends all binaries, the subject vis-à-vis object division, the emotional from the intellectual, the spirit from the body; conocimiento humanizes me while explaining to me the process of stretching out, hurting, and healing that I have been through during the past fifteen years. My own experience has enabled me to realize more fully how crucial Anzaldúan theorizing is for looking closely at scars and healed wounds and especially for exploring potential ways to share these experiences with others. In the process of writing this essay,

I felt validated and inspired by Jessica Heredia, who (in this anthology) uses the Anzaldúan theory on conocimiento similarly to share with us her own experiences as a graduate student.

This essay is my humble attempt to open myself to others while reflecting on my personal academic journeys through conocimiento and its seven stages. Reaching out to others after receiving tenure is a way to continue healing and, I hope, to help others avoid unnecessary pain. Sharing this journey is also a practice of spiritual activism. Conocimiento and its seven stages offer an alternative way of embracing and understanding academic life and growth. Anzaldúan conocimiento me acompaña as I remember, as I share with others and heal.

1. El arrebato . . . rupture, fragmentation . . . an ending, a beginning

cada arrebatamiento is an awakening that causes you to question who you are, what the world is about.

1992. I am crying tears of happiness while reading the letter of acceptance to a Ph.D. program in Los Angeles. As a Mexican immigrant woman, I felt so honored to be accepted, even if it meant that I would have to accumulate a huge financial debt to pay for the education. The concept of "graduate student funding" was foreign to me—I did not request it and it was not offered. The prospect of being inside the university system made me blissfully happy, and I figured I would sort out the financial details as I went along. Accordingly, I postponed official enrollment for a year in order to secure a government loan and pull together my modest savings. Despite these efforts, when I entered graduate school, I realized that I didn't have adequate funds to support myself, and the first week of classes found me driving all over East L.A. in hopes of finding some kind of bilingual job that would supplement my income and allow me to survive while attending graduate school. Then a miracle happened: a lectureship in the Spanish and Portuguese department was offered to me. Along with a modest stipend and the hope of this lectureship being renewed every year, I would be able to survive.

Despite what felt at the time like financial assurance, many other experiences left me feeling miserable, sad, and confused. Witnessing the early departure of the only other Latina student in my cohort made me anxious, and I found myself wondering if I would repeat the same story. This fear of failure was exacerbated as I realized more and more that I did not have the courage to participate in class discussions. I got lost in my own screaming silence as I witnessed the apparent confidence and knowledge of students whose English as a first language offered them the trust that I did not feel in my insecure heart. Typing up an intelligent comment prior to coming to class gave my sweating palms something to hold onto as I prayed that another student would not steal my idea before I found the courage to raise my hand and read my pre-typed comment out loud. Working on my papers required proofreading of my slightly imperfect writing by a native speaker. Because of this, I felt both flattered and confused when at least one of my professors commented that "for someone like you, your papers are really good." In the midst of this linguistic emotional labor, I learned to suppress what I thought and felt in Spanish as I struggled to organize my ideas and make sense to myself and to others in English. The ceaseless work of trying to make sense in academic lexicon and in a foreign language was a source of insecurity and shame—the quintessential vergüenza became part of academic life.

Paradoxically, I learned to live on the verge of an emotional cliff through the recognition that even my fellow students who were linguistically and academically privileged were also struggling and in pain. This awareness actually validated and soothed my own pain. As I looked around in my misery, the awareness of a life of professional transition became exhausting; my past experiences of emotional safety were gone, and the future seemed so uncertain and ambiguous. I was barely beginning to embrace a professional dream, and at the same time I felt increasingly uncertain about continuing an intellectual journey that hurt, especially as part of a life experience that I wasn't confident was for me.

2. Nepantla . . . torn between ways

Nepantla is the zone between changes where you struggle to find equilibrium between the outer expression of change and your inner relationship to it.

"I am becoming a translated woman. I am becoming a shadow to myself, a misspelled and mispronounced translation of who I am." This is the phrase I began repeating to myself. I felt confused, always having to translate myself to myself and to others. "When is this painfully confusing split going to end?" I asked endlessly. I still wasn't certain this intellectual journey was for me, and I was feeling worn to shreds. Finally, in desperate need of grounding, I sought alliance with another graduate student who also felt out of place and stigmatized, in her case for reasons of age and marital status (she was "older" and had been married more than once). She became a confidante and a close friend with whom I was able to share my deep vulnerabilities. Another woman, a Chicana student, also became my sister in despair as we gravitated toward one another. A split awareness—un doble saber—became a soothing part of my survival as I nodded with empathetic recognition when I listened to her experiences of struggle, survival, and pain. My friendship with both women was invaluable in helping me establish a sense of connection or equilibrium in my graduate school experience. At the same time, these alliances forged through mutual marginalization only served to reinforce my own sense of disjuncture or disconnection, taking me deeper into nepantla.

3. The Coatlicue state . . . desconocimiento and the cost of knowing

Though you thank the universe for your illness, emotional trauma, and habits that interfere with living fully, you still can't accept these, may never be fully present with the pain, never fully embrace the parts of self you ousted from consciousness, may never forgive the unconscious for turning hostile.

Spring 1996. Being Mexican hurt me in a way for which I had no words as I repeatedly watched the TV images showing two Mexicans being beaten up by members of the sheriff's department in Riverside, just a few miles away from where I was living. I continued to feel exhausted in my struggle to survive graduate school. Yes, the institution was not designed for people like me, but as I witnessed the brutal attacks on my fellow Mexicans I realized that no matter how much it hurt, I couldn't afford to leave. My pain was nothing compared to the humiliation and pain these human beings had to endure. They could have been me, or my brother, or my cousin. What if I did not have a green card or some of the years of college education that I had accumulated so far?[1]

Ironically, my graduate school experience was providing me with the language to more fully comprehend the oppression and indignities being suffered by marginalized groups. At the same time, this education was conferring on me a position of privilege, which also served to distance me from the same people. This small example was one of the many ways in which I was learning the costs of knowing through being confronted by my own desconocimiento.

The more I witnessed the comparative experiences of other Mexicans and marginalized people, the more I became aware of my privilege within the margins. I was learning to survive in my fragmented position while enjoying the privilege of graduate school, the possibility of a better life for my family and myself, and the dream of making a modest contribution to transforming our wounded world. My own pain and that of others like me became a form of knowing and awareness. No, I couldn't afford to give up; leaving graduate school was no longer a choice. There was no escape. I had to see this through to the next level.

4. The call . . . el compromiso . . . the crossing and conversion

You begin to define yourself in terms of who you are becoming, not who you have been.

Fall 1996. I am becoming more confident and comfortable with my writing and find myself participating more in my sociology classes; this experience becomes more and more healing as I prepare for my qualifying exams. I had a good cry after such an intense evaluation, which was followed two weeks later by more tears of celebration as I read the official letter confirming that I had passed my exams. What a relief! I passed! Gradually, across the distance of my experience, I began to get a glimpse of the horizon of my unfolding professional destiny. Within this glimpse I finally allowed myself a feeling of passion for this destiny. This unexpressed passion had nurtured my motivation to stay in school, and now I was finally able to fully embrace this dream with no fear.

As an academic focus I had chosen to become a sexuality researcher. I was fascinated with Latina women's sex lives, and I was excited about what this professional path could mean for me as a Mexican and a woman. I was becoming someone I had never imagined I could become. Being a researcher of sex and society would help me as a woman who grew up feeling deeply shy and intimidated with regard to matters of the erotic and romantic relationships. I was transforming, growing, expanding, but my personal and professional evolution would hurt in unexpected ways as I stretched out to grieve and let go of who I used to be. This self-transformation occurred as I recognized the contributions that I could bring to my academic work based on my experiences as a Mexican immigrant woman working with Mexican immigrant populations. This initial insight has become a constant reminder in the unfolding of my career: my own experiences of marginality reflect gaps in academic knowledge, and I contribute by translating these experiences into useful knowledge to share with others.

5. Putting Coyolxauhqui together . . .
new personal and collective "stories"

Coyolxauhqui personifies the wish to repair and heal, as well as rewrite the stories of loss and recovery, exile and homecoming . . . stories that lead out of passivity and into agency, out of a devalued into valued lives.

Graduate school had opened up many emotional wounds and scars, but being aware and despierta became a handy tool for survival. During this time I encountered an assertive Chicana psychotherapist who became a blessing while helping me in this transformative process. I still felt exhausted but at the same time more awake than ever. Feeling so alive through my confusion and pain, I learned that the awareness also enabled me to be present in the moment and to be absorbed in completing tasks and deadlines one day and one week at a time. I learned to have moments of joy and fun and reward myself for achieving my goals for that week as part of my struggle. The dream of completing the Ph.D. was coming true. These achievements were exhilarating, but again, the joy was shadowed by sustained feelings of intimidation and the ongoing deep self-doubt of whether academia was the life for me. By acknowledging this complexity and splitting I was able to remain centered, and in this centering I learned that taking good care of myself was the basis of a new level of transformation.

6. The blow-up . . . a clash of realities

You think you've made progress, gained a new awareness, found a new version of reality, created a workable story. . . . But when you cast to the world what you have created and put your ideals into action, the contradictions explode in your face.

2000–2001. The path of the academic job market is pitted with challenges and disappointments. My own experience bore witness to this dehumanizing process as I endured the initial excitement of being on the "final list" of candidates for four different academic jobs only to be rejected for reasons that were never entirely clear. Nonetheless, because of the pain and disillusion that I experienced in the job market, I felt both humble and grateful when I realized that these experiences had paved the way toward my dream job in Texas. Being close to my aging parents and returning to a region of the United States that made feel at home was more than I could have hoped for.

My first year as an assistant professor revived some of the old wounds as I transitioned into a professional identity that evolved as I deciphered institutional politics and survival. More than one generous mentor on campus confirmed that saying "No" to many demands that would not count toward tenure would be my salvation, a sacred act. I struggled and felt sad and fearful, while declining attractive but time-consuming invitations knowing that I would feel joyful in retrospect—I wanted to get tenure and stay. I did my best while extending a hand to students in struggle and attempting to remain centered and to maintain my writing and publishing as a priority.

Unexpectedly, the evolution of my academic projects revealed contradictions that eventually led to shifts in my feminist ideologies and theorizing. My research on the sex lives of Mexican immigrant women had now expanded to include the sexual stories of Mexican immigrant men who had endured different forms of sexual control. In the process of this research I was prompted to reconsider and transform the rigid views of gender inequality that I had embraced so passionately as a feminist. Expanding this paradigm helped me grow intellectually as I became motivated to teach not only on Latina women and sexuality but also on men's lives, feminism, and society. My teaching created new bridges as I learned an important lesson from my students, readings, class discussion, and women and men participating in my research: where I used to see contradiction and tension I began to discover and explore manifold opportunities to find creative ways to agree and reconcile seeming ideological and theoretical disparities. The beauty of poet Antonio Machado's words kept coming to mind: "caminante no hay camino / se hace camino al andar." My lived experiences in academia began to help me build a bridge as I learned to walk.

7. Shifting realities . . . acting out the vision or spiritual activism

[La nepantlera] realizes that to make changes in society and transform the system, she must make time for her needs—the activist must survive burn-out.

July 2005. I am in Machu Picchu at the break of dawn meditating and praying. Being here is not only another dream coming true, it is also a sacred place to give thanks during this week that my first book is going to be released. After completing my third-year review as part of the process toward tenure, these two weeks of meditation in solitude and silence while hiking in the Andes are a welcome blessing. Here in this quiet place far removed from institutional walls I take time to affirm my journey in academia up to this point and reflect on the direction of my next research project. As I realized that I was indeed going to become a tenured professor, I increasingly found myself wondering how to develop a professional career that would also nurture my spirituality. This question of spiritual engagement had not been in the foreground of my experience as I worked on my first project. But my personal and professional evolution had led me to think increasingly about how to create intimate bridges between my spiritual journeys and personal growth on one side and my academic life on the other. Anzaldúa's theorizing on "spiritual activism" has helped me expand on this vision and has motivated me to stay in deep interconnection with the people participating in my research, the activists with whom I share a common path, and with colleagues, students, and others interested in promoting social change while also surviving academia. The paradigm of "public sociology" (Naples, *Feminism and Method;* Burawoy, "For Public Sociology") has been similarly useful in examining issues that have relevant implications for the benefit of entire communities and societies. And finally (and most importantly), the concept of bodhicitta from Mahayana Buddhist philosophies inspires me deeply to explore ways to nurture the intimate interconnections between my personal life and professional life and between myself and others.[2]

My second project was inspired by the many questions that came to mind as I considered the ideas of spiritual activism and public sociology: how can I use my academic and institutional privilege and location for the benefit of the communities participating in my future research projects? How can I work on projects that will provide me with the intellectual legitimacy I need for tenure and at same time help me become sensitive and receptive to community needs and concerns? How do I protect myself from the "maquiladora syndrome"—that is, going south to get my data, assembling it, and then going north to profit from it? How do I identify urgently needed work? In short, how can I be of help as a researcher?

In my previous project, I was moved by the narratives of coercive sex within immediate and extended families. This led me to consider research on sexual violence with immigrant families and communities as a possibility for my next project. I conducted preliminary research and noticed immediately the invisibility of sociological research on these topics on the Mexican side of the border. Inspired by feminist models of activist scholarship and spiritual activism, I went back to Mexico, where I approached activist friends to ask what is an urgently needed area of research in the field of gender and sexuality. These community activists repeatedly confirmed my own impressions regarding the urgency of studying incest in Mexican society. Thus it has become the focus of my second major research project.

Immersing myself in the lives of sixty women and men through in-depth individual interviews on their histories of incestuous relationships has made me vulnerable as a human being and a researcher. While incorporating my spiritual, emotional, and intellectual dimensions as part of the research project, I have identified my informants' sexualized wounds as a vulnerable place for me and for my informants. The wound has become a place where I have immersed myself in order to explore how sociological knowledge is generated. At the same time, I have become unexpectedly liberated and humanized in the process of exploring new ways to connect my own inner transformation with larger processes of the production of knowledge and social change.[3]

In 2006, after eighteen months of ethnographic work, I completed my data collection with a sense of deep gratitude. Shortly thereafter, while preparing my tenure dossier and also grieving the unexpected death of my father, I was reminded of the ways in which conocimiento is a multidimensional cycle rather than a linear process. I have also realized how some dimensions of each one of the seven stages of conocimiento has been present in subtle and exquisite expressions in all levels of my professional development since my first year in graduate school. My awareness has led me to recognize that all stages are multidimensional, yet each stage of personal evolution emphasizes one specific form of consciousness, which can only be recognized retrospectively. Now I know.

As my personal transformation and my engagement with the struggle for social justice become more and more intimately interconnected, the last stage of conocimiento is becoming a more stable and persistently motivating state of existence for me. The Coyolxauhqui in me is also begging to heal. Each one of her tender scars becomes an Anzaldúan promise to myself and others: "May I always do work that matters."

III

BORDER CROSSINGS:
INNER STRUGGLES, OUTER CHANGE

CHAPTER 13

Letters from Nepantla: Writing through the Responsibilities and Implications of the Anzaldúan Legacy

MICHELLE KLEISATH

Bridges span liminal (threshold) spaces between worlds, spaces I call nepantla, a Náhuatl word meaning tierra entre medio. Transformations occur in this in-between space, an unstable, unpredictable, precarious, always in-transition space lacking clear boundaries. Nepantla es tierra desconocida, and living in this liminal zone means being in a constant state of displacement—an uncomfortable, even alarming, feeling.
GLORIA ANZALDÚA, "(UN)NATURAL BRIDGES"

Dear Gloria y AnaLouise,

Having received your e-mail informing me that the book manuscript would be going into production soon, I decided to re-read over the original piece I wrote for your collection back in 2006, when I was teaching in Tibet. I was not surprised to discover that I am now deeply critical of the many assertions I made then. I am now a graduate student in anthropology at the University of Washington, and my dissertation project focuses on white privilege and the production of expert knowledge on Asia. In my current work, I explore how, as a white English teacher and development worker in Tibet, I was highly complicit in the normalization and over-valuing of white ways of thinking and being. A disturbing lack of self-reflection in my original essay reveals this complicity. Reading over the essay now, I cringe at what I could not then see, and at what I reproduce in my ignorance as I write. That piece neither honors Gloria Anzaldúa's legacy nor reflects my intellectual awareness and growing maturity as an anthropologist in training. But what to do? I am writing to ask for your thoughts. I would be happy to revise the piece, or pull it from the collection altogether, if that is better. I am hoping that one of these options is a possibility, as I am convinced that the piece as it is may very well undermine the original intentions of the collection.

Looking forward to hearing your thoughts,

Michelle

I did not expect to write such a letter in my effort to honor the life and work of Gloria Anzaldúa and explore the specific ways we can expand and build on her intellectual legacy. I wrote this letter to *Bridging*'s generous editors in response to their request for final permission to publish the piece I submitted three years earlier. In the original essay, I had attempted to describe the resounding effects that Anzaldúa's work had on me as a college freshman and compare my own growth as a feminist to the dramatic changes I witnessed among a group of Tibetan women students with whom I shared Anzaldúa's work while teaching in a Tibetan area of China. As the publication date quickly approached, I reread my former essay with both curiosity and trepidation. I guessed that it would reveal some of my own ignorance, ignorance I am continually confronting and working through as a white scholar of critical race theory. As I read, often with a grimace, I wrote notes in the margins, outlining a dialogue between present and former versions of (my)self.

As I madly scratched out this awkward and confusing conversation, Anzaldúa's voice validated my consciousness in transformation: "In this liminal transitional space, suspended between shifts, you're two people, split between before and after" ("now let us shift" 544). Here, I engage the voices of these two versions of self in a dialogue about Anzaldúa's invaluable contribution and her power to incite and sustain the constant transformation of self, necessary for ultimate consciousness and true freedom. I offer some reflections about the ways in which Anzaldúan thought has the potential to build on anthropology, my discipline.

Xining, Qinghai, China, 2006

I took my first class in gender studies in 1999, during my freshman year at the University of California, Davis. When my eyes scanned the readings, a chorus of women's voices rang in my ears: angry, proud, critical, ecstatic, decided, undecided. Women of every race, sexuality, religion, creed, and ethnicity, from every corner of the world, living in the state lines and the borderlands, roaring one resounding message: We will have our voices. Outraged, demanding, their words burned into my brain, and as quickly as a fire consumes a dilapidated house, feminist thought consumed my old self. No voice was more jarring than that of Gloria Anzaldúa. Reading Anzaldúa's work, I felt as if I could suddenly penetrate the constructs and artifice that had ensnared me. She didn't hold my hand and walk me through her ideas. She was there on the page, without apology, without explanation, confronting her readers: Here I am. Deal with me.

After I graduated, in 2003, I abandoned my comfortable home, culture, and landscape and moved to a Tibetan region of China to teach English. I hoped that in this new location, in a new incarnation of my self, I could broaden my feminist revelation. I couldn't have made a better decision. Shortly after arriving, I began teaching an extracurricular gender studies course for female students in my home. They hailed from across the Tibetan Plateau and knew well what it is to grow up as marginalized others. They were "born low" as women in their own communities and invisible as Tibetans in a sea of ethnic Chinese.

We began our course with admonitions from the Buddha Siddhartha Gautama:

Do not believe in anything (simply) because you have heard it. Do not believe in traditions because they have been handed down for many generations. Do not believe in anything because it is spoken and rumored by many. Do not believe in anything (simply) because it is found written in your religious books. Do not believe in anything merely on the authority of your teachers and elders. But, after observation and analysis, when you find that anything agrees with reason and is conducive to the good and benefit of one and all, then accept it and live up to it.[1]

This advice from the Buddha Sakyamuni, a central figure for Tibetans, set up the context for our gender studies course, in which students thought critically about their lives as women and Tibetans. This counsel also encouraged students to think critically about me, their western teacher, and the ideas I shared. Because some western feminist logic is incongruous with the social and political contexts of modern Tibet, I encouraged students to try on the ideas I shared like they would pieces of clothing: if they didn't fit, put them aside. In this course, this bridging across cultures, no voice struck more incisively than that of Gloria Anzaldúa. Five years after my first encounter with Anzaldúa's work, I found myself engaging it again in an entirely new context. Here, in our makeshift classroom, thousands of miles and an ocean away from where they were originally voiced, the words of Gloria Anzaldúa took shape and transformed the lives of a very different group of young feminists. As we read "How to Tame a Wild Tongue," a di-alogue emerged between Anzaldúa and the women attending my classes:[2] *"En boca cerrada no entran moscas. 'Flies don't enter a closed mouth' is a saying I kept hearing when I was a child" (Borderlands/La Frontera 76), opens Anzaldúa, pressing the women to reflect on their own experiences. In a chorus of voices, some of my Tibetan students add: "When I was young, whenever I talked to guests, my parents would say, 'You should be quiet!'" remembers Sonamdrolma. "This idea was rooted in my mind."*

"My mother always told me, 'If you are born a girl, you must behave properly, or others will destroy you with their tongues,'" echoes Gesanglhamo. "At that time, I was automatically on my mother's side."

"I was stressed by the words 'Girls should be gentle and quiet,'" finishes Gawangjyid, a somber look on her face.

"What can we do about this?" the women question, and Anzaldúa responds:

"I will no longer be made to feel ashamed of existing. I will have my voice: Indian, Spanish, white. I will have my serpent's tongue—my woman's voice, my sexual voice, my poet's voice. I will overcome the tradition of silence" (81).

It is December 2006, and in a few months, I will return to the United States. My students will also move on, to become teachers, mothers, trans-lators, and nongovernmental organization workers. But as we progress to our different futures, we will be forever changed by the work of Gloria Anzaldúa. Her writing is at once universal and individual, speaking to the experience of both third- and first-world women. Just as her words ig-nited a passion in me as a college freshman, they sparked a fire inside these young Tibetan women.

Seattle, September 2009

Dear Michelle of 2006,
It is now 2009, and I am writing to you, my former self, to explore some of the problematic logics in your essay. I hope that revealing these can push our present and future selves to understand the implications of your work and words and take responsibility for our contribution to the Anzaldúan legacy.

When Gloria Anzaldúa puts herself on the page, demanding of her readers that they hear her words, what is she demanding of you? You revel in all of the ways that you can identify with her voice, how she names and challenges so many of the same overwhelming forces that have silenced and immobilized you as a woman. She speaks to you when she says, "I will no longer be made to feel ashamed of existing," and her words give you strength. But there is another part of her challenge that you are not yet ready to face as you write in 2006: your difference from her, your privilege. You are the woman who will "have her voice," but you are also La Anglo, who, "con cara de inocente nos arrancó la lengua." Not knowing how to face this complicity, you distance yourself from your privilege. In college, all you know to do is identify, align yourself with the chorus of voices of women of color ringing in *This Bridge Called My Back,* not yet ready to hear how these voices are directed at you.

You distance yourself, in thought, words, and miles. You leave the United States, convinced that you are searching for discomfort and for a place where you can explore the unknown parts of yourself. But in so many ways, you are running away from your discomfort. You want to feel good about yourself. You want to help. You do not want to be La Anglo. With the best of intentions and a warm heart, you go to a place where you can help, where the voices and lives of a different group of subaltern women become catalysts for your own self-realizations. Unwittingly, you colonize these voices. You speak for and about Tibetan women. Unable to see or face your own social power, you over-essentialize your Tibetan colleagues with your words and reproduce colonial practices. You do the same with the voices of U.S. women of color as you share their insights and demands with Tibetan women. You shape and narrate a dialogue between Anzaldúa and your students and then convince yourself (and possibly others) that it "emerges" independent of your powerful presence. Not knowing what to do with your privilege, you try to hide it, mystify it. This slippery practice is comfortable, for in this new country, your white privilege works in unfamiliar and fantastic ways. You pick and choose the words you want to hear, when and how you want to hear them. Here, thousands of miles away from the heated voices that you know are also directed at you, with enough institutional power and cultural distance to ignore any challenges your Tibetan students may want to pose, you feel safe, protected. You feel good. You are afraid. This is delusion. Go back to Gloria Anzaldúa's work. Listen. Feel.

In 2009, in my inner dialogues, I have only just begun to understand what it means to confront my own privilege. On a daily basis I am frozen, incoherent, and terrified as I watch myself stumble through antiracist work, often failing miserably. Marilyn Frye captures this sentiment well:

> All of my ways of knowing seemed to have failed me—my perception, my common sense, my good will, my anger, honor and affection, my intelligence and insight. . . . Simple things like courtesy or giving money, attending a trial, working on a project initiated by women of color, or dissenting from racist views expressed in white company become fraught with possibilities of error and offense. If you want to do good, and you don't know good from bad, you can't move. (84)

I go back to Gloria Anzaldúa's work, searching for a way to understand my inner conversations. Her words have ripened for me, taken on new meaning to my present version of self: "Tu camino de conocimiento requires that you encounter your shadow side and confront what you've programmed yourself (and have been programmed by your cultures) to avoid (desconocer)" ("now let us shift" 540–41). I begin to confront: hear the heated words that are directed at me, see the oppressive consequences of my actions, feel the sting of recognition in my own complicity. In confronting my shadow side, I discover a paradox: the need to constantly acknowledge my racial identity and then decenter it. Understanding privilege without altering its embodied habits is a toxic practice. I strive to transform my ways of knowing and being: I listen and wait, see, notice, move my body, lower my voice, shift my gaze. When I find myself striving to do good, to be a good person, I am back where I started, frozen. Anzaldúa pushes me to move beyond the good/bad binary, for this will only freeze me and the world around me into place. Her words give me strength to stay as long as I can in an unstable, shifting space, a space of nepantla, where unsure, scared, I do not know what good is any more. I yearn to stay in nepantla because I know that this alarming space of constant change is one of magic, of infinite possibility.

Anzaldúa's remarkable legacy attests to the incredible power of disorientation. Her writing lays the groundwork for powerful transformation, both individual and institutional. As disciplines forged in the practice of colonization like anthropology open (or are wrenched open) to the incisive critiques that put them into a state of crisis, Anzaldúa's writing foregrounds the possibility of a profoundly powerful relationship to this crisis: "Seeing through human acts both individual and collective allows you to examine the ways you construct knowledge, identity, and reality, and explore how some of your/others' constructions violate other people's ways of knowing and living" ("now let us shift" 544).

In 2009, I go back to copies of the letters that I asked my Tibetan students to write to Gloria Anzaldúa in response to her "Speaking in Tongues: A Letter to 3rd-World Women Writers," the letters that were still in transit, floating on a barge in the middle of the Pacific Ocean, the day that Gloria left us in 2004. I try to salvage something that does not bear the mark of my influence. It is impossible. Despite this apparent impossibility, I have a lot to learn from my students' words. I must listen. Nepantla is also "the overlapping space between different perceptions and belief systems" ("now let us shift" 541). I don't try to describe, narrate, or relate the words they have put on paper. I wait and listen.

Dear Gloria,
Now I have your letter and suggestions in the gender class; I realize I can't have people talking in my ear. I must come out of my tiny mind, abandon myself, and warm up to being a woman. You encouraged me to face violence against women and write about my own experiences. I suddenly recognized the strongest impulse: Break Free, Free! Body and soul free! [It may seem] that women don't naturally shock, but it's the truth. Women's inequality compared to men is not just an individual problem, but [a problem of all] the world's women. I have a new understanding of women now.
—Lhamotso

What are the implications and responsibilities of being a white woman in nepantla? The most honest answer that I can give right now is that I do not know. I only know that this space of uncertainty is very different for Gloria Anzaldúa, Lhamotso, and me. And different still for the various versions of my self presented in this paper. As a freshman in college, Anzaldúa's incisive words, her anger, spiked me into a new consciousness; in Tibet, I saw how her work extended beyond the reaches of my cultural imagination, how she spoke across cultures, oceans, languages. In Seattle, she is helping me find the strength to face the fear I encounter beneath yet another layer of understanding. She cautions me to remain alert and awake, constantly checking myself.

How can we expand on the immense gift of Anzaldúa's work? It is a future beyond the current boundaries of my imagination. Instead of helping us build a solid foundation on which to stand and see ourselves, our identities, and others, Anzaldúa's work will forever push us to create ourselves from within and through our coalitions with our surrounding communities. Anzaldúa's intellectual legacy invites us to continue exploring these intimate connections in spiritual ways: the production of knowledge is like an intricate sand mandala—it might be created with care and stunning precision, but we transcend in many ways by embracing our fearless awareness that each grain is laid out in the design only to be swept away. This vulnerability to the production of knowledge, this deeply transforming Anzaldúan perspective, promises to be validated in the future as we continue incorporating and expanding her contributions, as we nourish our intellectual and professional agendas in anthropology and across disciplines.

CHAPTER 14

Challenging Oppressive Educational Practices: Gloria Anzaldúa on My Mind, in My Spirit

BETSY EUDEY

Words are blades of grass pushing past the obstacles, sprouting on the page; the spirit of the words moving in the body is as concrete as flesh and as palpable; the hunger to create is as substantial as fingers and hand.
GLORIA ANZALDÚA, *BORDERLANDS/LA FRONTERA*

I was grading papers one morning in May 2004, and Gloria Anzaldúa's voice was in my head (as it often, or perhaps always, is), recounting the experiences of Third World women writers. She tells me,

> Because white eyes do not want to know us, they do not bother to learn our language, the language which reflects us, our culture, our spirit. The schools we attended or didn't attend did not give us the skills for writing nor the confidence that we were correct in using our class and ethnic languages. ("Speaking in Tongues" 165)

She knew I needed to be reminded of this, that I had somehow forgotten about the true nature of white privilege, academic privilege, literary privilege as I constructed what I had intended to be an assignment dealing with these very issues. I had used a book in class that centered around the experiences of white, heterosexual, middle-class, educated women, and I had assigned my students to seek out works that addressed women excluded from the book, including women with limited schooling, women of color, women outside the United States, working-class and rural women, lesbian and queer women, and so on. I wanted my students to read these works alongside and against the course text, evaluating the benefit of seeking multiple perspectives and learning about the difficulties of finding information on women whose experiences are frequently ignored or marginalized. Thinking I was helping them develop research skills, I required them to utilize four scholarly journal articles and one nonscholarly source. As I graded the papers, I knew the assignment had gone awry. Gloria was reminding me why.

Gloria (we use first names, as friends always do) tells me that formal writing, whether fiction or nonfiction, limits the expression of ideas even as it provides rules that supposedly create or ensure a quality to the work. She reminds me that writers are encouraged to "bow down to the sacred bull, form. Put frames and metaframes around the writing. Achieve distance in order to win the coveted title 'literary writer' or 'professional writer.' Above all do not be simple, direct nor immediate" (167). I know that Gloria sees value in academic scholarship, but she doesn't privilege it over all other forms. I tried to justify the assignment's design, telling myself that to participate fully in U.S. higher education, students need to be able to understand the types of information produced by academics, which centrally involves scholarly journal articles. I told myself it's important to see that women's issues are not only represented in essays and newsletters but also are worthy of study by academics.

Gloria closed her eyes, shook her head, and sighed (I don't know if this was really a habit of hers, but I've quite often imagined her doing this to me). I didn't want to claim what was at the root of her disappointment. I had inadvertently created an assignment that silenced the very voices I wanted included. I bought into the privileging of the academic and sent this same message to my students. Including scholarly works is useful, but it needn't be the sole focus of such assignments since the marginalized are rarely represented in their fullness within academic discourse.

Gloria nodded slowly, encouraging me. I recalled her anthologies that created "space for some ethnic mestizas who have been silenced before uttering a word, or, having spoken, have not been heard. A few pieces give fresh, immediate voice to the issues facing women who, in university surroundings, are often thrown into confusion about their ethnic and/ or racial identity" ("Haciendo caras" xvii). The works she included were meaningful not only because of their subject but because of the manner in which they were written. Written (at least predominantly) by women of color, the works intended to teach others how to "read in nonwhite narrative traditions—traditions which, in the very act of writing, we try to recoup and to invent" (xvii). Through the class assignment I had allowed marginalized women's experiences to be given voice, but by requiring the experiences to be recounted through articles in scholarly journals, I had forced them to be shared in a language and location that was often not their own. It's clear that a powerful opportunity for learning and understanding was lost. Gloria smiled, sensing I'd been inspired enough for the moment, and let me get back to my grading.

Later that day, I learned that Gloria had died. It seemed impossible, for she was strong as ever when we were grading together. It was clear to me that Gloria Anzaldúa wasn't dead; her physical body was simply no longer here. Gloria is alive in those who have experienced her (as a friend, a teacher, an author, a mentor). Gloria is alive in the writings of those whose voices she helped bring to public notice and those who felt empowered to write because of her. Gloria is alive in people like me who learned (or more correctly are learning) to challenge unearned privileges and to question the ways in which we marginalize others. She'll write no more, but she can still teach us and live through (with) us.

Anzaldúa continues to live when white, heterosexual women in positions of influence in this country (women like me) remember that we have often achieved our status because routes to influence were more open to us (or were closed by us) than to U.S. women (and men) of color, women (and men) in nonwestern societies, and anyone claiming nonheterosexual orientations. Gloria reminds me "in the act of pinpointing and dissecting racial, sexual or class 'differences' of women-of-color, white women not only objectify these differences, but also change those differences with their own white, racialized, scrutinizing and alienating gaze" ("Haciendo caras" xxi). When I (we) strive to embrace and learn from a diversity of people and to value a range of expressive forms, Gloria continues to live.

Over the past decade, I've claimed Paulo Freire, John Dewey, and bell hooks as the most profound influences on my teaching. With their perspectives on the aims of education and the means through which education can be a liberatory experience, they each inform how and why I teach. Through them I come to better understand the value of education, the responsibilities and obligations attached to being a teacher, and some strategies for creating powerful learning environments. The four of us speak often in my mind, so it's no wonder I have called them my best teachers. Until recently, that is.

It's become abundantly clear to me that Anzaldúa influences the how and why of my teaching as well, even if she doesn't specifically address pedagogical strategies or educational outcomes. She offers a worldview that insists that all voices matter, all experiences matter, all people matter, and efforts to silence difference must be challenged whatever the

apparent cost. Indeed, failure to address and respect diversity (of people, of ideas, of modes of expression, of types of truths) not only limits
education but reinforces forms of oppression and limits human growth.
Gloria has shown me that struggling to understand and struggling to
share what we think we understand are two of the most rewarding endeavors we can undertake. Gloria reminds me that as a teacher I must
always seek to learn more, to share more, to inspire more, to expect
more, to give more.

I started to claim that Anzaldúa adds heart, soul, and spirit to my
teaching, but that's not really it. Instead, she helps me recall my own
heart, soul, and spirit as I engage in teaching. She reminds me that our
work can connect to our passions and that we need to share our voices,
our visions, with others in ways that are authentic for ourselves. Gloria
wrote; I teach (and will try to write more).

I teach because I know that education is transformative. I teach to
draw attention to voices I believe need to be heard, especially the voices
of women and the queer community, and let others decide what to make
of them. I do this because I know that doing so will improve lives. I
teach to share with others what I have learned and how this learning has
influenced my life. In many ways, I teach to provide the kind of education I wish I had experienced. But I also teach so that I may learn about
others and about myself. I teach so I may hear others' stories, interpretations, interests, and passions. I teach to make connections with others
in hopes of improving all of our lives. I teach to become a better me. I
teach because it's what I must do to be fully me.

Gloria Anzaldúa speaks to me as a teacher because she understands
the power of the written word and challenges me to seek out ways to
include a greater range of voices, ideas, and works. When I recall her
words I become more empowered to go beyond the readily available
sources, knowing that doing so enhances education and promotes the
humanity of the authors. She states, "I write to record what others erase
when I speak, to rewrite the stories others have miswritten about me,
about you. To become more intimate with myself and you. To discover
myself, to preserve myself, to make myself, to achieve self-autonomy"
("Speaking in Tongues" 169). What would have been lost had she not
written? I can't imagine teaching without her and without those inspired
by her. I wonder now what I'm losing by not writing more myself. It
seems this essay eases me along on a path I need to take. The question
now is where I'm heading.

The challenge (no, the *opportunity*) is to more intentionally, thoughtfully, gracefully incorporate diverse voices into the classroom. The inclusion cannot be offered as supplemental to the "core texts," but instead all works must be seen as parts of a whole or perhaps as pieces in a kaleidoscope where combinations of pieces and new perspectives can allow previously inaccessible patterns, connections, and discords to reveal themselves. Because of Anzaldúa's inspiration, in my classes I am including more collections of personal narratives, more art, more poetry and literature, more blogs and websites, more materials from activist organizations, more editorials, more newsletters, more of everything. This, of course, takes time to do, which is something I don't always feel that I have. But it's time well lived if it leads to transforming myself, transforming my classroom, transforming the world.

But inclusion isn't enough; what matters most is *how* these voices are included. I must become a stronger facilitator and assist my students in placing the author's ideas in conversation with each other, looking for areas of connection, exploring possible reasons for disjuncture, and describing how their own voices participate in the conversation. Indeed, a goal of all education must be the encouragement of student voice, each voice in conversation with others—whether in person or through texts. For this reason, the courses I teach are primarily discussion-based, with discussion occurring in small and large groups (and even sometimes via the Internet and satellite television) to allow perspectives to be shared in ways that are most comfortable for the students.

Anzaldúa reminds me that all voices matter, and care must be given to create environments in which both sharing and receiving of perspectives can occur. Students need to receive information but also must know how (and be inspired) to find additional perspectives and seek meaning from them. I question sometimes what is harder—creating a space for sharing ideas or creating an environment in which ideas are truly heard, considered, digested, internalized, analyzed, valued, appreciated, loved. I use case studies, interviews, analytical essays, service-learning projects, debates, and similar assignments to facilitate exposure to and consideration of multiple viewpoints and experiences, but I know that students will only internalize the lessons if they're ready to do so.

I've been considering how I can use my position as a professor, as a member of a women's and gender studies community, as an activist, and as a privileged (Anglo-American, middle-class, heterosexual, schooled, etc.) woman, to honor Gloria's influence on me. I've considered creating edited collections and developing websites drawing attention to people and perspectives I find powerful and introducing influential people I know to people whose works I find important. But none of these options destabilizes the structures that give me privilege and marginalize others (recognizing that I, too, am at times on the margins). While I may be able to serve as a bridge, we need a reconceptualization of valued territory and who gets to determine and establish connections. I must do more to challenge my own privileges as I work with and in support of those whose ideas inspire me. I also must continue challenging what counts as works worthy of "academic" consideration, including the kinds of works that allow people like me to maintain and further our status as academics.

One thing I'm still trying to learn from Gloria is to use my writing to express my voice, my passion, my fears, and my dreams. I seldom write, for myself or others. It's fear, of course. Fear of not being able to put onto paper what I want expressed. Fear that I'll say something I'll later regret. Fear that others may know me, or think they know me, because of my writing (what if someone put me in her head like I have done with Gloria, bell hooks, and so many others?). What if I offend? What if I don't? What if my writing (my soul) doesn't matter to anyone else? Gloria proclaimed, "I have never seen so much power in the ability to move and transform others as from that of the writing of women of color" ("Speaking in Tongues" 172). I may not be a woman of color, but I can still seek to move and transform others (and perhaps myself) through my own writing. Gloria had fear as well, but hers drove her to write. She asks, "Why am I compelled to write? Because the writing saves me from this complacency I fear. Because I have no choice. Because I must keep the spirit of my revolt and myself alive" (168–69). So Gloria pushes me, encourages me, shakes me out of my own complacency (and complicity). And indeed, I hope to inspire my students to be active in sharing their own voices—however they choose to do this.

On days when I set out to write, she reminds me that "the act of writing is the act of making soul, alchemy" ("Speaking in Tongues" 169). Gloria encourages me to write about what matters, not what I think others might want to hear. When I'm concerned about taking risks in my writing as a junior faculty member, my head rings with her words: "The danger in writing is not fusing our personal experience and world view with the social reality we live in, with our inner life, our history, our economics, and our vision" (170). It's clear that I have to write about (with) Gloria for a while because her voice, more than others, informs the kind of teacher (writer, person) I want to be.

I believe that Gloria Anzaldúa continues to teach me, to challenge me, to encourage me. I keep becoming a better me and a better teacher, hopefully a better writer, because of her. I'm seeking out new topics about which to write, new venues for publication, and new courses to teach. Through these endeavors I keep learning and expanding the range of works and perspectives I can share with others. How wonderful to recognize how much I keep changing. Gloria Anzaldúa whispers to me, "I am playing with my Self, I am playing with the world's soul, I am the dialogue between my Self and *el espíritu del mundo*. I change myself, I change the world" (*Borderlands* 92).

CHAPTER 15

Living Transculturation:
Confessions of a Santero Sociologist

GLENN JACOBS

"Omi tutu, ana tutu, ache tutu.
Tutu ile, tutu Laroye, tutu ariku babawa . . ."
[Fresh water; freshen the road, freshen my power; freshen my home.
Freshen Eleggua (Eshu Laroye).
Freshness that has no end; freshness so that
we do not see an early death]

These are the opening words, sprinkled with cool water, of the divi-
nation procedure—"throwing coco" (coconut)—used by santeros and
aleyos (non-initiates) when they address the orisha (the divinities of the
Yoruba pantheon) or the eggun (spirits of the dead).[1] Here, as is cus-
tomary, I propitiated Eleggua, the guardian of the crossroads, prior to
addressing my patron orisha, Changó, whose permission I asked to write
this piece because it entails saying things about the religion that might
be unflattering, and while none of these are insults to the orisha themselves, out of respect for them I consulted Changó. The answer was ejife
("eh-gee-fay"), the strongest affirmative.

Why write this essay on the bridges created—the roads opened—for
me by Gloria Anzaldúa, with a part of my identity (my spiritual "I") that
I have seldom written about and largely keep muted as a teacher and
writer? Here the propitiation of Eleggua, the orisha representing liminality, is strikingly appropriate, for it announces, as I explain below, the
opportunity Anzaldúa has given me to fashion a frame or a voice for my
own evolving identity and the resolution of dilemmas of in-betweenness
I have experienced in trying to integrate my several selves—intellectual/
scholar, religious layman, santero, Jew. The boundaries of our selves,
like the social boundaries they reflect, both include and exclude: they

shield us from the outside and outsiders but also numb our awareness and partition our consciousness.

I knew nothing about Gloria Anzaldúa before summer 2005, when the University of Massachusetts Annual Social Theory Forum committee decided to focus our annual forum on her work. Reading *Borderlands/ La Frontera* began a catalytic process on two levels: first, intellectual material that I have been musing over started coming together; and second, Anzaldúa's work gave me tools to forge a path out of a hazy, ambiguous identity to a more secure platform for a multicultural one. I have been striving to integrate and reconcile the Cuban anthropologist Fernando Ortiz's notion of transculturation (the creation of a new culture by hybridization and syncretization of discrepant and diverse cultures) with ideas suggested to me by subaltern-studies scholars concerning the authenticity of representation from various quarters, of the "wretched of the earth"—the marginalized and downtrodden minorities within our own society (Latinos, blacks, gays, Native Americans, and immigrants largely from the South) and the ex- and neo-colonized (by imperialism, globalism, and neoliberalism) peoples of Africa, Asia, and the Middle East—the subaltern.[2] Anzaldúa's thought and writing and, by example, her life embody an affirmative answer to Spivak's rhetorical question: Can the subaltern speak? While this is true of the subaltern themselves, what does it say regarding their representation by those who aren't?

Anzaldúa's integration of the spiritual elements of her own background—the mythology of indigenous Mexican (Aztec, Olmec, Toltec, etc.) religions and Catholicism—with her intellectual self and her gender and sexuality serves as a beacon for me, a heterosexual sociologist of Jewish heritage converted in middle age to Santería and to the possibility as a participant observer of writing about the religion. Having participated in and ruminated on Santería for more than a decade, this matter of representation has dogged me, for I have experienced doubt and conflict concerning my qualifications to write about a religion I joined as an adult, a culture very different from the ethnic Jewish secular agnosticism I grew up with. Anzaldúa's life and work have given me—a man in the middle—an awareness of the advantage of seeing both sides of the equation, as an insider and as an outsider. They have grounded my understanding of, as Clifford Geertz puts it, "how it is that other people's creations can be so utterly their own and so deeply part of us" (54).

I am the product of four experiential worlds (white, black-Cuban, academic, secularized Jewish), which evoked great doubts about my capacity and right to write about the Afro-Cuban one authoritatively. Inspired by Anzaldúa's writing and praxis, the matter of liminality, my own existential in-betweenness was dragged from the periphery to the center of my autobiographical reflection. Anzaldúa sped up the processes of intellectual fermentation, resulting in an epiphany wherein I could grasp, or at least find, tools to make the connections between my personal evolution and my intellectual life.

These are not matters academic folks are prone to write about. Religion, for example, is private, even if qualified as "spirituality"; moreover, it is not trendy to explore one's own spirituality, let alone admit that it has a bearing on one's professional practice.[3] Notice, however, how "religion" implies legitimacy and collective dominance and how "spirituality" reduces belief to the isolated individual. But confessing membership in a religion of Caribbean-African origin compounds the conundrum of faith versus intellect with that of race and class. Because of Santería's African (Yoruba) origins, its adherents are viewed as indulging in magic and superstition. (I recall a colleague incredulously asking me, "Do you believe in that stuff?") Moreover, crossing the public-private boundary implies the compromise of scientific objectivity or value neutrality and hence professional integrity.[4]

Consequently, Anzaldúa's method of autobiographical analysis, augmented by her synthesis of the folk elements of her own and others' cultural heritages, affirmed my quest to integrate my several selves and propelled me into a new intellectual direction. This has resulted in the overcoming of intellectual and existential barriers that have dogged me for years and were exacerbated when I became personally involved with Santería. In addition to the aforementioned conflict over spirituality and intellectual objectivity, I became at once more conscious, and in a way self-conscious, about my whiteness. To some degree this awareness occurred because Cubans and other Latinos in varying ways complimented me for my interest and participation in the religion and occasionally discounted me as an Anglo outsider. Thus, for objective and subjective reasons I hesitated to write about the religion and my research on Cuba. Moreover, the contradictions and personal failings I have seen and experienced in the religious community have occasionally been disillusioning and challenging, but in the face of these disconcerting elements (including my own experiences with unscrupulous practitioners) my relationship to the religion has been tested and grown stronger.

Reading and experiencing Anzaldúa catalyzed the integration of my apparently disparate worlds. As she puts it: "An individual is multiple and has multiple personalities and multiple little selves, along with the big self. I'm an individual but because I inhabit many worlds I can go from being at my mom's little pueblito to an academic classroom to a lesbian musical event to a writer's conference, and in each instance I can experience what the other people present are experiencing" (*Interviews/ Entrevistas* 20). Recalling my earlier reference to Geertz, Anzaldúa demonstrates how self-reflection about one's multiple selves, rather than resulting in confusion and doubt, can open a path to autotranslation of the worlds one inhabits, enabling one to use these disparities for intellectual and personal nourishment.

Beyond the *personal* implications of Anzaldúa's work is its historical and intellectual significance as a basis for what Antonio Gramsci identifies as a new hegemony: "From the moment in which a subaltern group becomes really autonomous and *hegemonic* . . . we experience the concrete birth of a need to construct a new intellectual and moral order, . . . a new type of society, and hence the need to develop more universal concepts and more refined and decisive ideological weapons" (388, my italics). This new hegemony is non-absolutist, dynamic, and non-elitist, undergoing constant revision and incorporating and synthesizing the new cultural elements added to it by the transculturative processes of folks liberating themselves in and through developing their own reflective awareness and consciousness. Gloria Anzaldúa's new paradigm of the border, of the liminal, of the multicultural, contributes to the new hegemony.

Anzaldúa's New Master Narrative

My intellectual epiphany concerning the real possibility of this new hegemony began when I read Anzaldúa's discussion of the syncretization of Coatlalopeuh and La Virgen de Guadalupe in *Borderlands/La Frontera*. Anzaldúa offers a genealogy of the creation, transformation, and development of contemporary Chicano culture and, moreover, of its constituent gender roles as that totality ultimately bears on the development of a "new consciousness." She carefully delineates the trajectory and transformations of the Mesoamerican indigenous female and serpentine pantheon into "a synthesis of the old world and the new, of the religion and culture of the two races in our psyche, the conquerors and the conquered," wherein "*La cultura chicana* identifies with the mother (Indian) rather than with the father (Spanish)" (52). This genealogy, tracing "The Loss of the Balanced Oppositions and the Change to Male

Dominance" (53) and the associated transformation of the image and mythology of the serpent and Cihuacóatl, the Serpent Woman represented or incarnated in the contemporary (modern) split consciousness of rationality and the spirit, *is truly a masterful sociology of culture*! As Anzaldúa suggests, other syncretized mythologies (for example, Vodun, Santería, shamanism) embody and suggest similar narratives (59). She tells us:

> Don't give me your lukewarm gods. What I want is an accounting with all three cultures—white, Mexican, Indian. I want the freedom to carve and chisel my own face, to staunch the bleeding with ashes, to fashion my own gods out of my entrails. And if going home is denied me then I will have to stand and claim my space, making a new culture—*una cultura mestiza*—with my own lumber, my own bricks and mortar and my own feminist architecture. (44)

Reading this account set me on fire. Here were gods like my own syncretized ones with human virtues and vices, coming out of a hybridized border-transgressed past, infused with sex, rebellion, and domination. The syncretizing of La Malinche (the traitor-whore), La Llorona (the tragic weeping mother), the serpentine Coatlicue/Coatlalopeuh/ Tonantzín with La Virgen de Guadalupe, resonated strongly with the Yoruba pantheon in Santería, for example, with respect to Ochún, the riverine goddess of fertility, sexuality, and reproduction—she is nicknamed La Puta (the whore). Ochún, syncretized with the Virgin as La Caridad del Cobre, the patron saint of Cuba, is sweet and is typified by the balm of honey: she weeps easily and is generous with her blessings. But woe betide one who crosses her. She will stick and stab with piercing laughter and is verily impossible to placate. And there also are the warriors Oya, who gave Changó lightning, and the machete-wielding Yemayá Okuti.

Lost Illusions and the Liminal Life

The multiplex or multivalent self captures the essence of Anzaldúa's new tribalism or mestiza consciousness. This consciousness serves as a platform for, or base of, constructive social change, so that "living on borders or margins, keeping intact one's shifting and multiple identity and integrity, is like trying to swim in a new element, an 'alien' element."

This evinces "an exhilaration in being a participant in the further evolution of humankind, in being 'worked' on" (19).

Standing on the border, at the margins or where "phenomena tend to collide," represents what Anzaldúa calls a "tolerance for contradictions," which is a keystone of the mestiza consciousness. La mestiza "learns to juggle cultures. She has a plural personality" (101). This new consciousness will depend on the "breaking down of the unitary aspect of each new paradigm" and the creation of "a new mythos" out of the plurality that stands before us (101–02). I have already discussed the new mythos—the master narrative—she speaks of, and I also have discussed the contradictions of my *identity*—my several selves, and the conflicts and blockages connected with them as they bore on my intellectual production. This liminality also enables one, beyond the issue of toleration, to *understand* the contradictions of the world around us. This is especially true in my case within the world of Santería with respect to matters of sexuality and race. I have learned not to romanticize the religion and now am able to simultaneously appreciate its creative and fulfilling aspects, its Bakhtinian carnivalesqueness, and its practitioners' occasional folly when (as with all religions) they fall victim to the ravages (the soporific dangers) of blind faith.

The simultaneous awareness of the inner life's and outer world's contradictions is valuable, obliterating negative value judgments and cultivating appreciation of the richness afforded by crossing the borders and boundaries marking differences. No longer barriers, borders offer opportunities for personal growth, creativity, and social change. Awareness of boundary-crossing potential for growth can be part of conocimiento, a theory Anzaldúa developed to describe the consciousness work that "connects the inner life of the mind and spirit to the outer worlds of action" (*Interviews/Entrevistas* 178). As Anzaldúa says, "Living in a multicultural society, we cross into each others' worlds all the time. We live in each other's pockets, occupy each other's territories, live in close proximity and intimacy with each other at home, in school, at work." Although many are unable or unwilling to recognize it, we become "simultaneously insider/outsider," hyphenating nos (us) and otras (others—them). Despite this nos/otras status, society has yet to evolve: "This country does not want to acknowledge its walls or limits, the places some people are stopped or stop themselves, the lines they aren't allowed to cross" (*Interviews/Entrevistas* 254).

Applying this insight to my own experiences has enhanced my abilities as a participant observer and tamed the outsider's impulse to be-

come a zealot once s/he feels comfortable in the world s/he has recently joined. I confess that for a long time I was a zealot. After a decade
in the religion and several trips to Cuba, I became disappointed with the
religion. Reading Anzaldúa's frank discussion of her own cultural and
personal background at a critical time in my life made me a "realist,"
understanding that *my* wish-fulfilling enchantment, and consequent dis-
enchantment, were not prompted by deceptions and betrayals enacted
by "them."

Assisting my search for the connection between my need to integrate
my several selves without burning bridges to my various communities, Anzaldúa's nepantilism helped me avoid bitterness and the endless
search for identity nostrums—new subcultural interests to assuage my
bitterness over my failed ideals. Thus Anzaldúa's insights have assisted
me as a sociologist in interpreting, although not necessarily excusing,
some of the opportunism and greed I have occasionally encountered
among some money-hungry santeros as byproducts of immigration of
Cubans from a society undergoing severe economic deprivation. I see
internalized racism and homophobia in divinations pronouncing the necessity of a client not associating or working closely with those darker
than they and in remonstrations to gay clients that they renounce their
homosexuality and seek heterosexual mates. Then there is the "institutional sexism" of permitting only men to be babalawos (master diviner
high priests) and the stereotypical practice of frequently assigning female
patron orishas (Ochún and Yemayá) to gay male would-be santeros.

Emphasizing the significance of racism, sexism, and homophobia, Anzaldúa notes that both subjects and victims of these plagues can "mine
some kind of meaning" from them. "That's how we make our soul,
how we evolve as humans" (*Interviews/Entrevistas* 74). While Anzaldúa
underscores the "need to switch between looking at differences and
looking at commonalities," as she implies, the switch goes both ways;
consciousness of both our commonalities and differences are required at
different times to gain perspective on our various contexts.

Trusting Our Devils More Than Our Angels

It is pleasant to think—to fantasize—about the new world that mestiza
consciousness will fashion, but just as we need visions of the finished
utopia, we also require tools for the struggle to achieve it. My prescrip-
tion is tautological: we need inner struggle in order to struggle for jus-

tice! Struggle comes in many forms and appears in different guises. It can, and most certainly will, take the form of movements and rallies. It will have its heroic and dark moments. But for me, Anzaldúa's most poignant and urgent struggles are those she grappled with inwardly about her illnesses and disabilities, her sexuality, her multiple selves, and the agonies she experienced in her family, school, and other communities as these played out in the battlefield of her mind and soul. As Anzaldúa suggests, this struggle results in conocimiento, "the awareness of facultad that sees through all human acts whether of the individual mind and spirit or of the collective, social body" (*Interviews/Entrevistas* 178).

Anzaldúa's distrust of Manicheanism—the division of the cosmos and the social world into absolutely opposed, mutually exclusive good and evil sides—thus aligns itself with sophisticated esoteric spiritual traditions such as Sufism and the "fourth way" schools of Gurdjieff and Ouspensky, which counseled looking at and embracing fully and impartially all sides of oneself under the condition of daily life. As she says, "The idea central to my autobiography is the return of the spirit, the idea that God and the devil are the same person, that evil and good are the same" (*Interviews/Entrevistas* 99). Thus, she embodied her gods as much with evil as with good, darkness as with light, menace as with promise, cruelty as with mercy. Through this nondual embodiment, she transforms the meaning of "evil" and "good," for they are mirrors we hesitate to gaze into, and their stories offer parables warning us about what we are and can be and what horrors we might visit upon ourselves.

Lying at the heart of the "Coatlicue state," that is, at the heart of our contradictions and the dark forces that move us, Anzaldúa saw arriving at self-knowledge as her deepest challenge. She likens it to a descent into the self's underworld and the unconscious associated with the place of the dead: "When I reach bottom, something forces me to push up, walk toward the mirror, confront the face in the mirror." But she resists: "I don't want to see what's behind Coatlicue's eyes, her hollow sockets," for "behind the ice mask I see my own eyes" that will not look at her (*Borderlands/La Frontera* 70). Seeing our many selves provides the key to personal *and* social liberation, for it entails a keen perception of the ubiquitous boundaries so thematic of Anzaldúa's life and work. For the privileged, it entails awareness of how the boundaries of our selves remain insulated and unexamined, thereby buffering how we exclude others.

For those coming from the precincts of racial, gender, sexual, and class oppression, the challenge lies in understanding the extent to which we in our personal perceptions and attitudes identify with the oppressor and find ourselves re-erecting boundaries with tribalistic exclusion and even oppression. Thus border crossing results in seeing double, and as Anzaldúa says, "You glimpse the sea in which you have been immersed but to which you were oblivious, no longer seeing the world the way you were enculturated to see it." In her words, "You see through the fiction of the monoculture" (*Interviews/Entrevistas* 129).

It is my feeling that we are already witnessing widespread discontent of much of the population with imperialism and war as diversionary solutions to our social problems: inadequate decent jobs with health care, child care, and retirement benefits; scarce affordable housing; despoilation of the environment; restricted and overpoliced public and recreational space. These problems are the manifestations of a hypertrophied and mythologized monoculture. I also see a readiness to embrace difference but in the near future one teetering on the edge of an abyss containing the possibility of the opposite—a plunge into a turmoil of racial and ethnic civil strife manipulated in the interests of privilege and profit. We intellectuals need to continue our struggles but also to write with more moral courage that "connects the inner life of the mind and spirit to the outer worlds of action" (*Interviews/Entrevistas* 178). We can thereby rest easily with the antinomy Geertz posits regarding sociocultural differences: "The differences *do* go far deeper than an easy men-are-men [*sic*] humanism permits itself to see, and the similarities *are* far too substantial for an easy other-beasts, other-mores relativism to dissolve" (41). By themselves neither of these extremes inspires or fuels the kind of fire-in-the-belly writing Anzaldúa proposes, but as she says, conocimiento, in producing self-reflectivity, encourages empathy with others and recognition of commonalities (*Interviews/Entrevistas* 178).

CHAPTER 16

Acercándose a Gloria Anzaldúa
to Attempt Community

PAOLA ZACCARIA

Encantada to Meet GEA

I came to know Gloria E. Anzaldúa toward the end of the 1980s through quotations that sounded very new and interesting, mostly from *This Bridge Called My Back: Writings by Radical Women of Color* but also in essays on cultural studies or feminist studies. In 1996, during one of my periodic study trips to the States, I bought a copy of Anzaldúa's *Border-lands/La Frontera: The New Mestiza* and retrieved her other works in Harvard University's Wiedner Library. I was struck by Anzaldúa's skill in naming new formations and figurations. She elaborated a theory on commonality and fragmentation that helped me name and think about the 1990s Balkan conflict, which, following the death of charismatic President Tito and the fall of the Berlin Wall, exposed the political and cultural divide inside a people that Europe had viewed as undifferentiated "Yugoslavs"—Serbs, Croats, Bosnians, and Albanians. This awful intestine war inflamed old and new Euro-American interests in an area that those of us in southeastern Italy had perceived simply as the other side (el otro lado) of the Adriatic Sea, the osmotic element seen on both shores not as a barrier but as an incessantly fluid, crossable threshold.

In 1993 we (the women affiliated with the Centre for Women's Doc-umentation and Culture, the CDCD, a feminist association in my city, Bari) worked passionately to develop a critique of conflict and gender, following the despair that had seized pacifists, left-wing activists, and feminists at the conflagration of ethnic hatred on the eastern side of the Adriatic Sea. There was not much relevant theory available, so we (the women of the Italian movement and the activists in women's associations in Belgrade, Zagreb, and Mostar) started from women's practice of re-latedness and developed a women's network, trying to stop the hatred.

Meanwhile, people from Albania, Yugoslavia, and Kosovo arrived on despair boats in Bari and other harbors along eastern Italy's southern coast. We helped establish refugee camps, but soon these camps were insufficient. We worked through the network created by Women in Black, but it was difficult to mediate the encounters among Serb, Bosnian, and Croatian (often feminist) women. It ached; it split us. This conflict demonstrated that shared gender did not guarantee disloyalty to war issues and agendas. Sorrow and despair almost silenced those in the pacifist movement, although we realized that we must deconstruct terrorism's shifting faces and reconsider categories and formations such as conflict, ethnic group, nationalism, frontier, belonging. We must question the neutral universal logocentrism and unveil the subterranean strategies that worked in the male/neutral discourse rooted in the deep drive to change multiplicity to unity, differences to sameness, diversity to homogeneity.

Feminist practice and theory helped those of us (Italian and Yugoslavian feminist activists alike) who had already worked for the recognition of gender difference; we recognized that in order to articulate and enact new visions and formations, we must begin by reconsidering the primary duality—*you* and *I*. To do so required moving beyond sheer binarism and oppositionality, out of a subjectivity formation in which this encounter is framed as familiar/stranger-enemy. Some nuclei of the conflict discourse, such as rootedness and unrelatedness, had been emptied by feminist theory and practice from the burden of binarism since for us "locating oneself in one's place" was not fixing one's roots forever but rather developing the necessary awareness and strength outward and creating gender and social relationships. We also knew that the feeling of dislocation, although a space of woundedness, can trigger metamorphosis.

The Balkan War compelled us to reconsider the meanings of "limen" and "cum-finis," the Latin words for the borderlands.[1] At that time, not knowing Anzaldúa's thinking, we tried to understand the source of ethnic prejudices, questioned the relationship between borders and identities, and explored the stakes involved when male warfare marked the frontier as dominium, potestas, property, fatherland.

In the 1990s we, on this side of the world,[2] were raising questions that Anzaldúa had explored in the previous decade. Her works exposed the sexual, cultural, linguistic, political contradictions inherent in both the Anglo way of life and Mexican traditional culture; she argued for the necessity of subtracting oneself from the despotism of "home" and the requirements of "belonging" that imply rooting oneself in one language, one soil, one blood. To live in the borderlands, she demonstrated, means to live on the world's threshold.[3] But during the 1990s almost no one in Europe knew her work; the great divide between Mexico and the United States was not discussed in Italy.

When I first read Anzaldúa, in the mid-1990s, I was extremely interested in her theories and strategies to heal dualisms and conflicts—her challenge that we not be afraid of contradiction, ambivalence, lo contradictorio. In her body-text she showed how to cross differences, how to "conectar across colors and other differences to allies also trying to negotiate racial contradictions" ("now let us shift" 571), how to move toward conocimiento and relatedness through a(nti)systemic or cross-systemic strategies.

When *Borderlands/La Frontera* entered my personal library, I wrote widely about it in my *Maps without Frontiers: Literary Cartographies from Modernism to Transnationalism*, where, in the appendix, I translated the book's preface and one poem, "To live in the borderlands means." I was left with the urge to translate her whole book,[4] which I viewed as poetically and politically central to the ongoing process of global multiculturalism, hybridization, and crossings. Because both Gloria Anzaldúa and I had a feminist formation, I wanted to translate her book from a gendered perspective, "as a woman" (Godayol 99). Because Anzaldúa is, simultaneously, a poet and a self/intra-translator who tries to establish a dialogue and confrontation among multiple languages, it was my duty as a translator not to put myself in a monolinguistic space; on the contrary I stressed the co-presence of at least three languages and "five races." *Borderlands/La Frontera* was a text absolutely necessary for Italy. Through the incoming flux of extra-European migration, Italians needed to rethink internal migration and the babel of tongues and cultures that had been removed in the name of a still young national unity.

If Anzaldúa had established a dialogue among the mestiza subjects' diverse languages, as a translator I had to locate my voice *across* and *beside* her different languages; I had to expose contamination, betrayal, rajadura, difference . . . driven by the urge to come as close as I could to difference(s). Disclosing this Chicana/o difference enabled me to disclose unspoken Italian differences, historical colonization, and mestizaje. Translation became trans-action, transfer, transformation, transfiguration, and difference.

To translate, I realized, is to acercarse to the other, cortar, open the other's tongue. Translating borders allows us to call "home" the bridge,[5] to receive the other of the other side at least on the threshold.

Translating is a positionality akin to that of living on the borderlands: the translator inhabits the borderlands, s/he is inhabited by border-languages, bordervoices. To translate means to live in a two-way tunnel, to make two languages incessantly interact, to "have (inter)course" with the other, feel attraction toward the other (tongue). Translating means bridging, "loosening our borders. . . . to attempt community" ("(Un)natural bridges" 3); it obliges us to see ties, links, differences. Translating borders allows us to "reimagine our lives, rewrite the self, and create guiding myths for our times"—myths that are "multicolored theories" (5).

While I was teaching Anzaldúa's poetics and theories in my classes and discussing her work at national and European seminars and conferences, I encountered the Bosnian writer Ivo Andric's *The Bridge on the Drina* (1945). At this time, the second act of the Balkan War, the Kosovo conflict, was occurring. Invited in 1999 to speak at the Conference of the Italian Association of Semiotic Studies on "Encounters of Cultures: Languages, Frontiers, Translations," I tried to conjugate the United States and Europe with the help of Anzaldúa's *Borderlands/La Frontera* and Andric's *Tales from Bosnia* and *The Bridge on the Drina*.

Andric's painful insights into living in the borderlands, his narration of Bosnian Muslims torn between their love for their land and feelings of disloyalty toward cultural ascendancy in Turkey, reminded me of Anzaldúa's concept of rajadura. Although different in sex, culture, geography, race, and history, in my eyes and sentido, Andric and Anzaldúa shared the experience of being impaled on la frontera, crossed by two homelands (says Andric), rajada y atravesada by five races (says Anzaldúa): their writings sweat, swing, and swell with the unending sensation of being alien, an illegal everywhere, never at home.

Now it seems ominous that I started to "Europeanize" Anzaldúa's thinking and vision by foregrounding it not so much against the conventional western cultural heritage I belonged to, but by comparing it with the "other Europe," the Balkan area so close to my own land and yet so unknown because of the Cold War, which set the countries within the Atlantic alliance against (or, rather, speechless, mute to) the Soviet bloc countries.

Starting from the semiosis of the borderlands, illuminated by two texts belonging to two border countries apparently very unlike mine, I had the urgent need to question the semiotic and political implications of the threshold (both as terminus and as solum): frontier, limen, door, bridge, crossing, and (en)closure. I could see how the transitional subject tries to cross and recross the frontiers by stitching together the edges.

On the level of art figura(c)tions, the transitional subject not only maps hyphenated psychospatial forms but gives life to hybrid aesthetics and styles that display the will to conjugate the real and imaginary lands touched by the migrant mestizo criollo. This illegal desaparecido fugitive subject creates the new without completely amputating her/himself from the original space-perception. These cartographies are the exact reverse, el otro lado, of the cartographies of colonizers, whose graphomania was a sign of the will for potestas and dominium—the hegemonic drive.

Mirroring Auto(bio)graphies

Born in the 1950s in the beautiful olive-tree landscape verging on the Mediterranean seaside of southeastern Italy, the youngest of four daughters of poor farmers, I spent my first six years in wild bliss, nourishing my physicality with runs at sunset accompanied by our small dog, Nerino, negrito. Sometimes, on the brink of twilight, together with my sisters, I sang (or rather I howled and screamed), calling the distant invisible otherness so far, so mysterious, so fathomless. I did not speak a word of Italian. Father, mother, sisters, and laborers spoke dialect, a vernacular language completely different from the national tongue, with words and sounds bearing traces of the Greek, Latin, Arabic, French, and Spanish domination/colonizing of southern Italy. My physical wilderness went side by side with linguistic wilderness.

At six I first entered a school door, or should I say the thresholds of conocimiento? Ten children of different grades in the same classroom, with the same young dark-looking clever sweet maestra. The teacher spoke Italian and taught us to write and read. Delight in discovering funny signs with meanings that, if read one after the other, could tell stories. Elation in discovering that through the necklace of words I could connect to numberless invisible voices and tales. I do not remember as difficult the passage from my childhood vernacular tongue, though very unlike Italian, to the national tongue. The discovery of the numberless worlds I could enter just by learning to read enhanced my willingness to shift to another tongue. My father bought a transistor radio through which the standard national language entered our house. Repeating the song lyrics made us feel almost like the city girls we met from the third grade on, when I went to school in the nearest town, traveling alone by train. And through the trains, newspapers and magazines entered our home because the station master gave us the materials he read in the long, boring hours in the little railroad station of Egnazia, the country place where we lived.

Today I realize how lucky I was to receive magazines as gifts at the age when other girls played with dolls and went to dance lessons; how unusual it was to live on the borders of poverty and analphabetism and be able to go to school, read good press, and sing rhythm and blues after Otis Redding or soul music with Aretha Franklin, jamming it with melodic Italian lyrics.

I recount my childhood languages and schooling—the fight with my father to have the opportunity to attend high school and then college while still helping my parents work in the field—only to hint at the many vernacular languages scattered throughout the world, to remind us that you can enter school and discover you speak a foreign language although you live in your homeland and see in the eyes of your high school classmates that though you are smart and one of the top five in the class, you are always a bit "strange" because you live in the country-side and wear your sister's outgrown coat, and your hands are not student's hands but rough fieldworker's hands, and at home your parents speak dialect and you shift to dialect when you are with them or with the fieldworkers, who start looking at you as a bit "strange" because although you still go barefoot in the summer when irrigating the orchard with them or still shout and laugh in vernacular wild sounds with them, they know you go to high school and can see how when classmates contact you at home you shift to Italian.

Did it begin then, my fondness for difference? Was my later dedication to "minority" causes—the women's movement, peace activism, emigration, etc.—an attempt to caress the difference in myself, the difference so often stigmatized in others' eyes? Was it an attempt to make amends for my mother's hard life and respond to her silent stares asking for me, from me, a different life? Twenty years after her death, still processing the loss of my mother and reflecting "on the many implications" of Anzaldúa's death, I feel the urgency to face this drive toward the marginalized, the different, the clandestine, the oppressed, the queer, the subdued, the dispossessed. Confronted with the question of why I responded so passionately to the call of Gloria Anzaldúa's thinking and utopian vision, I feel again the need to look back to my mother, to my motherland, to my mother tongue . . . and suddenly I realize that one reason behind my dedication to Anzaldúa's work is *her* dedication to "the prohibited and forbidden. . . . *Los atravesados* . . . the squint-eyed, the perverse, the queer, the troublesome, the mongrel, the mulato, the half-breed, the half dead" (*Borderlands/La Frontera* 25). We both have devoted intellectual and emotional energies toward repairing the rajadura inflicted on our sexual and cultural matrices.

Why do we take sides with the forgotten, the racialized, the untouchable, the medio y medio? The reasons might go back to our psycho-bio-cultural geography, to our preformative and formative years. Basically, I feel, both Gloria Anzaldúa and I realized that notwithstanding economic deprivation, we were lucky to escape utter deprivation and to know both sides of la frontera between power-oppression and liberation-through-resistance-to-oppression in order to live a free existence and celebrate art and earth as our common homeland. This struggle helps to develop la facultad and agency, which in turn bring about conocimiento and the realization that once you have known the frontier, the wall, the closure, you will forever stay aware of the borderland and try to make of it your place. Shaping the frontier as bridge, Anzaldúa taught me to name it "home."

Furthermore, Anzaldúa showed me/us how to "put in figure"—how to name and shape—what border people, endowed with la facultad, feel when they *sense* something new on the verge of being born. As a poet, she believed that it was her task to bring new formations and conocimientos into the world, so that the auroral figure-feeling can become public, communal knowledge and, by engendering transformation, metamorphosis (Braidotti), metramorphosis (Lichtenberg Ettinger), and transfigurations (Anzaldúa, "now let us shift"; Zaccaria, *La lingua che ospita* and *Transcodificazioni*), the figure becomes a figuration, a kind of tension-knot where many lines-paths-meanings converge, where what is usually considered the domain of the aesthetic touches the arena of the political.

The Nepantlera's Nurturance

What, then, does Anzaldúa's work contribute to Italian methodology of research? How might we nurture her poetics and politics? Anzaldúa has taught me to think of artwork as "public property," not as a museum piece. As I attempt to forge a kind of "dialogue of errancy" with/across

different transnational-thinking travelers, crossers of cultures, expatri-
ates, mestizas, builders of new poetical and political formations, Gloria
Anzaldúa is the guide who invites me to enter a supranational sphere
resonating with interwoven voices containing dialogues between poetics and politics of women and men from all over the world who, having accepted that in our times being a writer means to be doomed to
expatriation (Djebar 200), go on the traces of diasporas, utopianisms of
commonalities, constellations of "living democracies" (Shiva 84).

Because writers involved in the dialogue of errancy, in the fronterizo
positionality and mestizaje condition, believe in the great role of translation and so that the dialogue does not become babelogue, I suggest
that Anzaldúa's works be translated into as many European languages as
possible. We have much to learn from her testimonial work on turning
marginalization, multiculturalism, and hybridity into transformational
strategies. Through her experiences and bold visions, Europe can re-
examine the backlashes of its past and still-enduring colonialisms. European readers will finally see that the "ex"-conquerors are translated
people, because Anzaldúa gives names to old and new colonizations; she
unveils internal colonizations and interiorizations of colonial acts and
stereotypes. Europe in general, and Spain in particular, will realize how
the Spanish language has been creolized in the incessant workings of
translation. In realizing that all our national languages are made by the
multiple voices coming from the past but also formed through knead-
ings and borrowings (like my childhood dialect), Europe, if it will take
care of the richness offered by transits, will hopefully open the frontiers
to the earth wanderers: language—both as literature and as spoken word
resonating with creolization—will be a means of/to transformation.

Anzaldúa's discussions of how to move beyond nation boundaries
teach us to disidentify with the nation, create a new nondualistic epistemology, and demonstrate the necessity of negotiating and working
through conflicts. Europe (and not only Europe) needs to learn the path
leading to interconnectivity, relatedness, and conocimiento, which originates in nonlinear thinking and teaches el compromiso, crossing, conversion ("now let us shift").

Con-version hints both at a camino undertaken together with others and the works of translation: *con*-version, a (linguistic) version given
together with the/an other. Again we are within the semantics of the
cum and *across* and *toward* (Latin: *ad*), which builds a world on dialogue. We discover that in frontera writings such as Gloria Anzaldúa's
breathes a poetics that engenders a yearning for conocimiento. I am sure

Anzaldúa's views in "now let us shift" are right: a large part of America, of Europe, a large population all over the world is already building a relational model of culture, an interactive, dynamic, intersubjective, spiraling, polyphonic, multicoded, multimedial, asystemic, comparative, and polydiscursive method of researching, existing, and envisioning. Activating this complexity, we bring into the world the intellectual mestizaje and theory of conocimiento inherited from Gloria Evangelina Anzaldúa. We are ready to change, so let us shift, let us act out community-centered transformations and transfigurations.

CHAPTER 17

Learning to Live Together:
Bridging Communities, Bridging Worlds

SHELLEY FISHER FISHKIN

I found *Borderlands/La Frontera* a few months after it came out on the shelf in Old Wives' Tales, a feminist bookstore in San Francisco. Or it somehow found me. I could never be sure. In either case, I was convinced that fate had a hand in the matter. I was a visiting scholar at Stanford's Institute for Research on Women and Gender in 1987–88, giving myself a total-immersion course in feminist cultural studies and working on a soon-to-be-aborted novel, when *Borderlands/La Frontera* entered my ken. I found it riveting, challenging, and brilliant. From the start I was proselytic: I talked about it constantly, bought multiple copies to give to students, friends, and colleagues, and decided that any graduate student who hadn't read it didn't deserve to pass her Ph.D. orals in American Studies at the University of Texas, where I taught.

I've taken special pleasure over the years in bringing *Borderlands/La Frontera* into the cultural conversation in places where people had not encountered it—such as an American Studies conference in Izmir, Turkey, where scholars decided that "To Live in the Borderlands" was really a poem about *their* country. Or a symposium in Seoul, South Korea, where Anzaldúa's attentiveness to the artificiality of borders and the pain they inflict struck a particularly responsive chord. In 1988, when I was invited to contribute to a volume on twentieth-century literary journalism that a prominent press was publishing, the editor looked at me quizzically when I said that one of the authors I planned to write about was Anzaldúa. Hadn't heard of her. He had to read her, I insisted: he'd be glad that he did. He was. He even ended up beginning the volume with an epigraph from her book.

My contribution was titled "The Borderlands of Culture: Creative Experimentation in American Nonfiction Narrative." It put Anzaldúa in good (if somewhat unexpected) company. "While conflicts over physical territory are usually resolved by force or by negotiated treaty," I wrote,

few comparable mechanisms have been devised for resolving conflicts over cultural territory—of choosing whose realities become reified and whose get "redlined." He who wields political and economic power usually manages to control the power to name and narrate as well. A vast substrata of social, cultural, economic, and historical conditions make it seem "natural" that the dominant paradigms in the culture should dominate.

W. E. B. DuBois, James Agee, Tillie Olsen, and Gloria Anzaldúa were all concerned with stories that did not fit the dominant paradigms. They were stories of people who were dismissed and devalued because they had the "wrong" race, class, gender, ethnicity, or sexual preference. They were stories of the powerless, their pain invisible, their cries inaudible, their membership in the human community implicitly denied. Speaking for them, from them, to them, and through them, DuBois, Agee, Olsen, and Anzaldúa brought to a broad, general audience dimensions of experience previously absent from American newspapers, magazines, and books. The formal experiments they embraced were the sort of thing modernist poets tended to fool with: these four writers pressed them into the service of nonfiction. The truths they had to tell concerned subjects routinely dismissed as too boring or dull by the nation's journalists: these writers told those truths with poetry and passion usually reserved for fiction. Their agenda was clear: make the reader feel what you have felt, even if you have to break rules, customs, and conventions to do so. The passionate cultural reports they produced transcended existing paradigms and stretched the boundaries of our culture in enormously rich and fruitful ways. They also helped map new directions and set new standards for literary nonfiction in the twentieth century.

American literary history is punctuated by the appearance, from time to time, of literary experiments that transform the discourse of which they are a part. W. E. B. DuBois's *The Souls of Black Folk,* James Agee's *Let Us Now Praise Famous Men,* Tillie Olsen's *Silences,* and Gloria Anzaldúa's *Borderlands/La Frontera* are four such transformative works. (133–34)

I argued that all four writers found that generic conventions and available narrative forms could not do justice to their experiences and their thoughts. As a result, they broke through those conventions in particularly innovative ways in boldly original experiments: DuBois pasted bars of musical notation across the page; Agee inserted a line of pure punctuation into his text; Olsen left several pages nearly blank; Anzaldúa often moved back and forth among multiple languages within a sentence. The four of them, I believe, shared a common goal: they wanted to disrupt patterns of perception familiar to the reader. They wanted to explode conventional expectations, break down the reader's sense of equilibrium, surprise, challenge, and throw the reader off guard. In short, they wanted their readers to respond to the texts in ways that had not been required of them before and to be changed, profoundly, in the process. The discussion of *Borderlands/La Frontera* that followed showed Anzaldúa laying out her facts with the clarity of a good journalist or historian while infusing them with the power and beauty that only a multilingual poet able to move with ease from English to Spanish to Náhuatl could impart. The essay went on to examine the interplay not only of multiple linguistic codes in the book but of multiple genres as well.

I was thrilled by the ambition of her book—by the fact that Anzaldúa seemed to want to do more than simply validate her language or her vision: she wanted to wrench from her own experience as an outsider the guideposts of a new way of being in the world. I was exhilarated by the strong case she made for the idea that the sense of disruption, discontinuity, dislocation, ambiguity, uncertainty, and fear that living on cultural, social, linguistic, and sexual borders entails can be a positive force for the artist. And I was inspired by the ways she wanted to help her readers break through their "everyday mode of perception," taking them beyond their "habitual grounding," whether the reader was a Chicana ashamed of her language, a lesbian afraid to express her love of women, an Anglo who suspected that the words "Chicano culture" were an oxymoron, a poet who thought history should be left to the historians, or a man who took women's silence as tacit assent. I was awed by *Borderlands/La Frontera*'s ability to convey facts shot through with the poetry and passion of fiction, cultural reports bursting with the energy of felt life and with the power to convey important truths about that life.

I then did something I had never done before: I sent the subject of my essay a copy of what I'd written. To my delight, Gloria loved it. She was also pleased by my interest in organizing a session about her work—with her as a respondent—at the next American Studies Association annual meeting, which would be held in New Orleans the following fall. She suggested that we get together when she was next in Austin.

That winter we had a long, leisurely, wonderful lunch at a Mexican restaurant on South Congress Avenue called Seis Salsas. She wrote on the inside cover of my copy of *Borderlands/La Frontera*, "Para Shelley, me dio tanto gusto comadrear un poco contigo en el 'Seis Salsas.' Espero que todos tus proyectos lleguen a dar fruto. Contigo, Gloria 12/6/89. Nos vemos en Nueva Orleans."

It was a special pleasure to introduce Gloria Anzaldúa and *Borderlands/La Frontera* to the ASA that fall, to a community that, I felt, needed to know her and that could help extend the reach of her ideas. Although this was the first time the book was featured at the ASA, it was far from the last. In 2001 the ASA would give Gloria Anzaldúa—along with Cherríe Moraga—the Bode-Pearson Lifetime Achievement Award. And after her death the ASA took steps to create an award in her name to be given to an independent scholar who has made transformative feminist contributions to issues of gender, race, and sexuality in the field of American Studies.

Knowing that Gloria had never visited Mexico City and that Mexican readers were largely unaware of her work, I jumped at the opportunity, the following year, to invite her and other colleagues to develop and teach a minicourse with me there in June 1992 at the Universidad Nacional Autónoma de México. In the winter of 1991 and spring of 1992, Gloria and I, along with Carla Peterson, Lillian Robinson, Jeffrey Rubin-Dorsky, and Richard Yarborough, pulled together a large packet of readings that were photocopied for our students as the core of an intensive two-week course sponsored by UNAM's Centro de Investigaciones sobre América del Norte (CISAN) on "Identity in America from a Multicultural Perspective." Gloria was delighted to be able to visit Mexico City, and—no surprise—the students loved her.

I had little sense, when I first read it, that *Borderlands/La Frontera* would help shape my research agenda for the next two decades. But I recognize in retrospect how much it helped me understand structures of knowledge that reified certain paradigms and voices while ignoring others—and how much it helped give me the courage to ask questions that had not been asked before, to challenge categories that were widely accepted, and to pursue transgressive lines of inquiry.

I suspect that reading Gloria Anzaldúa's work and talking with her about mestizaje and mestiza consciousness, particularly in the spring of 1992 as we planned the course for UNAM, probably influenced some of the ways I thought about the blending of black and white voices in American literary traditions as I researched my book, *Was Huck Black? Mark Twain and African American Voices*, which came out the follow-

ing year. Gloria Anzaldúa's theories about mestizaje and mestiza consciousness were rooted in the specific cultural borderland that was the
Texas-Mexico border; but she encouraged others to apply and extend
her ideas to varied cultural borderlands as well. My research on Mark
Twain had shown me that African American voices, speakers, and rhetorical traditions had played a key role in the genesis of the book with
which he transformed American literature; meanwhile, conversations I'd
had with Toni Morrison, Ralph Ellison, David Bradley, and other black
novelists made it clear that *Huckleberry Finn* had been a central and em-
powering literary model for black writers in the twentieth century (*Was
Huck Black?*). Gloria Anzaldúa's work helped embolden me to investigate other instances of cultural cross-fertilization. It encouraged me to
recognize the mestizaje at the heart of many artifacts that had previously
inhabited largely segregated cultural histories. One result of this line of
investigation was my review essay of more than a hundred books and
articles in literature, history, folklore, art history, popular culture, music, and anthropology, "Interrogating 'Whiteness,' Complicating 'Blackness': Remapping American Culture," which appeared in *American
Quarterly* in 1995.

Gloria Anzaldúa's candid and lucid explorations of both racism and
sexism also had a big impact on my writing over the next few years, and
her brilliant blending of the analytical and the autobiographical served
as a beacon as I struggled to find narrative strategies for exploring these
issues. In addition, her work—and her friendship—encouraged me to
embrace parts of myself that mainstream American culture devalued and
that I had never foregrounded in my work, such as the Yiddishkeit that
surrounded me in my grandmother's kitchen during my childhood. I
learned lessons from reading and talking with Anzaldúa that helped inspire me to edit *Listening to Silences: New Essays in Feminist Criticism*
(co-edited with Elaine Hedges) and *People of the Book: Thirty Scholars
Reflect on Their Jewish Identity* (co-edited with Jeffrey Rubin-Dorsky),
both of which came out in 1994; and the *Encyclopedia of Civil Rights in
America* (co-edited with David Bradley) and *Lighting Out for the Territory: Reflections on Mark Twain and American Culture*, both of which
came out in 1997.

If Anzaldúa's exploration of the dynamics of racism and sexism and
her experiments with blending the autobiographical and the analytical
shaped my work in the 1990s, the attention she drew to the arbitrariness
of borders shaped my work more recently. In searing prose and wrench-
ing poetry, *Borderlands/La Frontera* required me to think in fresh ways
about the "constructed" and artificial nature of political borders like the

one dividing the United States and Mexico. It was Gloria Anzaldúa who first enabled me to understand (as I put it in my presidential address in 2004 to the American Studies Association) that we needed border-crossing scholarship to examine cultures and histories that have never been confined within political or geographic borders. Sadly, Anzaldúa passed away six months before I delivered "Crossroads of Cultures: The Transnational Turn in American Studies." I dedicated the address to her memory.

Gloria Anzaldúa continues to have a major impact on the field of American Studies. If *This Bridge Called My Back* helped bring the voices of women of color into U.S. college classrooms in the 1980s at a time when such voices were almost completely absent, *Borderlands/La Frontera* paved the way for the paradigm shift of the early twenty-first century—a time when ideas of personal and national identity are being dramatically reconceived; when transnational questions are increasingly at the center of scholarly inquiry; when the richness of multidisciplinary, multilingual approaches is steadily more apparent; and when bold mélanges of personal and analytical writing have increasingly displaced the tedious preciousness of "high theory" in the humanities.

In *Borderland/La Frontera,* Gloria Anzaldúa had written that "the future belongs to the New Mestiza." In a book of interviews published in 2000, as the new century dawned, she offered a slightly different vision of who would "own" the future:

We all of us find ourselves in the position of being simultaneously insider/outsider. The Spanish word "nosotras" means "us." In theorizing insider/outsider I write the word with a slash between nos (us) and otras (others). . . . [But the] future belongs to those who cultivate cultural sensitivities to differences and who use these abilities to forge a hybrid consciousness that transcends the "us" versus "them" mentality and will carry us into a nosotras position bridging the extremes of our cultural realities. (*Interviews/Entrevistas* 254)

"How can we learn to live together?" Anzaldúa asked. "What tools, what strategies can we use?" ("Daughter of Coatlicue" 43). Gloria Anzaldúa's books give us tools and strategies that remain vital as we try to learn to live together—in the academy and in the world. May she continue to be a nepantlera—bridging communities, bridging worlds, speaking to us from the grave through her words on the page, inspiring us, challenging us, goading us to break down the barriers that divide us from one another.

CHAPTER 18

Risking the Vision, Transforming the Divides: Nepantlera Perspectives on Academic Boundaries, Identities, and Lives

ANALOUISE KEATING

When Gloria Anzaldúa and I first became writing comadres and friends, I was especially struck by her willingness to take dangerous theoretical and other writing-related risks, her generosity with her own writings, and her enormous curiosity about how people were interpreting and applying her ideas and words. She did not shy away from expressing radically bold ideas—no matter how outrageous or against-the-norm these ideas might appear—if she believed that her insights could be used to increase social justice and develop new communities of almas afines, or like-minded souls.[1] At times, her desire to create new, potentially transformative knowledge inspired her to make provocative (indeed, radical) claims despite the very real possibility that these claims would sometimes be misinterpreted and that she, herself, would be criticized and possibly rejected. She put herself in the service of her visionary ideas and risked her own reputation. Similarly, Anzaldúa rarely expressed a sense of strong ownership about her theories, and she never authoritatively insisted exclusively on her interpretations of her own words. Instead, she was eager to see what kinds of work her theories would do in the world and how they would be changed in the process. Although it sounds paradoxical, given her use of autohistoria and her emphasis on the personal, Anzaldúa detached herself from her work, enacting an almost egoless relationship to her writing. Anzaldúa's bold, generous spirit has inspired me to borrow from and build on her theories of nepantla and nepantlera(s)—two of my all-time favorite Anzaldúan theories—and use them to challenge a few of our most commonly accepted beliefs about academic disciplines and identity categories. As I explain in the following pages, this challenge grows out of my own experiences as an academic formally trained in the humanities but currently working in Women's Studies, which was for several years housed in the social sciences.

Those of us who live skirting otros mundos, other groups, in this in-between state I call nepantla have a unique perspective. We notice the breaches in feminism, the rifts in Raza studies, the breaks in our disciplines, the splits in this country. These cracks show the flaws in our cultures, the faults in our pictures of reality. The perspective from the cracks gives us different ways of defining the self, of defining group identity.

GLORIA E. ANZALDÚA

In Anzaldúa's writings, nepantla—a Náhuatl term meaning "in-between space"—indicates temporal, spatial, psychic, and/or intellectual points of liminality and potential transformation. During nepantla, individual and collective self-conceptions and worldviews are *shattered* as apparently fixed categories—whether based on gender, ethnicity/"race," sexuality, religion, or some combination of these categories and often others as well—are destabilized and slowly stripped away. As Anzaldúa explains, nepantla is "this birthing stage where you feel like you're reconfiguring your identity and don't know where you are. You used to be this person but now maybe you're different in some way. You're changing worlds and cultures and maybe classes, sexual preferences" (*Interviews/Entrevistas* 225–26). Boundaries become more permeable and begin breaking down. This loosening of previously restrictive labels, while intensely painful, can create shifts in consciousness and new opportunities for change; we acquire additional, potentially transformative perspectives, different ways to understand ourselves and our worlds.

Some people who experience these nepantla states choose to become what Anzaldúa calls "nepantleras"—a word she coined to describe radical mediators, "in-betweeners,"—those who "facilitate passages between worlds" ("(Un)natural bridges" 1). Take, for instance, Anzaldúa herself: punished in grade school for her inability to speak English, she went on to obtain a B.A. in English from Pan American University and an M.A. in English and Education from the University of Texas at Austin, where she also completed all coursework for a doctorate in Comparative Literature. At the time of her death she had finished all degree requirements for a doctorate in Literature (which was awarded posthumously) from the University of California, Santa Cruz. Anzaldúa kept up with recent theoretical trends, read widely in academic scholarship crossing numerous fields, and for the last twenty years of her life occasionally taught college-level courses. Despite this close relationship with the academy, she had no tenure-line appointment and did not view herself as a professional academic. Instead, she located herself simultaneously inside and outside the academy. As she asserts in "Transforming American Studies," her 2001 Bode-Pearson Prize acceptance speech, "I am an outsider/insider in academic circles. This allows me to look at American Studies from three points of view: the distance of the outsider, the closeness of the insider, and the in-between zone, the space between worlds I call 'nepantla'" (239). As this statement indicates, Anzaldúa used her outsider/insider perspective to gather insights from multiple locations. By so doing, she developed what I'll describe later in this essay as a nepantlera epistemology and ethics.

Anzaldúa offers one of her most extensive discussions of nepantleras in "now let us shift . . . the path of conocimiento . . . inner work, public acts," in which she draws on her personal experiences at the infamous 1990 Akron, Ohio, National Women's Studies Association (NWSA) conference to develop her theory. She attended this event to publicize her new book, *Making Face, Making Soul/Haciendo Caras: Creative and Critical Perspectives by Feminists of Color;* however, when many women-of-color attendees accused the organization of deep-seated racism and walked out, Anzaldúa made the painful decision to stay and use her conference session to directly address the conflict: "From the eye of the storm you choose to hold fast to the bridge and witness for all camps" (567). She did not align herself with any of the conference groups but instead worked to create a dialogue that included them all.

Nepantleras live within and among multiple worlds and, by so doing, develop a perspective from the cracks. Significantly (and perhaps surprisingly), this altered perspective does not lead to further divisions. *Nepantleras do not pick sides.* Instead, they witness to all sides. In epistemological terms, nepantleras use their views from these cracks-between-worlds to develop holistic, "connectionist" approaches, enabling us to reconceive and perhaps transform the various worlds in which we exist.

"Connectionist" is another Anzaldúan term. As Anzaldúa explains in "now let us shift,"

When perpetual conflict erodes a sense of connectedness and wholeness la nepantlera calls on the "connectionist" faculty to show the deep common ground and interwoven kinship among all things and people. This faculty, one of less-structured thoughts, less-rigid categorizations, and thinner boundaries, allows us to picture—via reverie, dreaming, and artistic creativity—similarities instead of solid divisions. (567–68)

Connectionist thinking is visionary, relational, and holistic. As such, it offers a crucial alternative to conventional Enlightenment-based epistemologies, which generally focus primarily on logical, rational thought, naturalized categories, and other forms of analysis. When we view ourselves and one another from a connectionist perspective, we remind ourselves to look beneath surface judgments, rigid labels, and other divisive ways of thinking; we seek commonalities and move toward individual and collective healing: "Where before we saw only separateness, differences, and polarities, our connectionist sense of spirit recognizes nurturance and reciprocity and encourages alliances among groups working to transform communities" (568).

In this essay I speak as a nepantlera and offer a connectionist perspective on academic boundaries. Typically, we're led to assume that each field of study is a discrete unit with clearly delineated courses and roles. (So, for example, English focuses on English, History focuses on history, Biology focuses on biology, and so on.) I didn't recognize the rigidity of these boundaries until I moved from English—the site of my training and my first two academic positions—to a Women's Studies job that was housed in a Sociology department. Despite the fact that I'd been teaching English and directing graduate work in U.S. American Literature for almost ten years, I was suddenly perceived and treated very differently by my non–Women's Studies colleagues. To me, there should have been no difference between AnaLouise Keating, the professor of English, and AnaLouise Keating, the professor of Women's Studies: I was basically the same person, teaching the same concepts, texts, and ideas I'd been teaching for the previous decade. However, my change in title led to a change in perception and treatment. I was appointed to committees as a representative of the social sciences. I was not permitted to teach English courses or direct English graduate work. Prior to this job change, I paid absolutely no attention to disciplinary boundaries or the underlying institutional structures (budgets, curriculum requirements, and so on) that help to create and reinforce these structures. I just did my work. But the striking differences in how I was perceived led me to reflect on academic disciplinary boundaries, and I began paying more attention to how people (both inside and outside "the academy") talk about disciplinary knowledge structures.

While in some ways interdisciplinary fields are more complex and thus much less rigid, in other ways they, too, are often shaped by the academy's divisive approach to knowledge. In such instances, people make overly simplistic assumptions; for instance, they believe that Women's Studies should focus exclusively on gender, Ethnic Studies should focus exclusively on ethnicity/"race," Queer Studies should focus exclusively on sexuality, and so on. This perception is inaccurate and overlooks the many historical and contemporary interconnections, intersections, and commonalities various identity-based studies (can) share, and such assumptions invite turf wars and battles over shrinking allocations, student loyalties, faculty needs, research priorities, and more.[2] Far too often, these divisions among academic disciplinary and interdisciplinary fields play into the academy's divide-and-conquer approach, an approach that effectively pits potential allies against each other. Rather than attempt to bring about systemic change, academics engage in struggles that inadvertently reinforce the status quo.

This obsession with disciplinary boundaries—or what Herman Daly and John Cobb call "disciplinolatry" (125)—greatly reduces our fields of vision and action. In such instances, progressive scholars cannot use our academic disciplines (or interdisciplinary fields) to further our understanding of the world and create transformative knowledge but instead focus on the discipline itself, working only to reinforce the discipline's organization of knowledge. Rather than using the discipline (or idol) as a vehicle moving us toward something larger (like social justice and increased individual-collective transformation), we narrow our goals and pledge allegiance to the discipline itself. My point here is not that disciplinary academic structures are bad and should be disbanded. I'm simply suggesting that at least occasionally we step back from our daily work, self-reflect on our disciplinary and interdisciplinary alliances, and consider developing a broader, connectionist vision.

Like other forms of idolatry, the worship of academic boundaries stops too soon; it converts potential pathways into solid walls. I build here on Owen Barfield's theories of participatory epistemologies and idolatry. Although we generally think of idols as dead objects, Barfield draws on a prehistorical framework to suggest a different perspective, which he calls "original participation." According to Barfield, for our ancestors long ago, idols had a different meaning and function. They did not represent inanimate things (a chunk of wood or a carved stone, for example); instead, they represented a larger cosmic force, a divine, fluid energy infusing all that exists. Idolatry was not the worship of "dead" objects but rather a celebration of an interconnecting force that moved through these objects, the worshipers, and more.

So here's my question: how might we transform the dead idols of our academic fields into more vibrant, more potent vehicles? This question is, I believe, an important one to ask at this particular moment. As Michele Rowley notes, "The increasing institutionalization of the discipline within academic sites of knowledge production comes with a possible cost: the loss of subversion" (146). Although Rowley refers specifically to Women's Studies, her warning applies to other fields and to individual scholars (especially progressive scholars!) as well. It's difficult to succeed in academic positions without in some ways assimilating into the system. However, as we become more ingrained in the institution, we can lose our transgressive edge.

Like the nepantleras Anzaldúa describes in "now let us shift," my work in English and American, Ethnic, Queer, and Women's Studies has occurred between worlds. During my academic career, I've taught at three fairly different institutions of higher learning: an open-admissions, medium-size, comprehensive university in eastern New Mexico attended by first-generation college students who self-identify as "Hispanic" and "white"; a private Catholic liberal arts college in western Michigan attended by first- and second-generation college students classified by others as "white" but by themselves as "just human"; and a public university in North Texas attended by a racially diverse group of primarily first-generation, primarily female college students. Despite the many differences among them, these schools share several traits: first, they do not have any Ethnic, LGBTQ, or American Studies programs; in fact, they rarely even offer ethnic-specific or sexuality-focused courses. Second, Women's Studies has not fared much better, offering, at best, only an undergraduate minor composed almost entirely of cross-listed courses. Although my current institution offers vibrant M.A. and doctoral degrees in Women's Studies, we have no plans to develop an undergraduate major.

What can these liminal academic situations—when interdisciplinary programs like American, Ethnic, Women's, and Sexuality/Queer Studies either do not exist or occupy (temporary?) space among more established disciplines—teach us about disciplinary boundaries and the intersections between social justice issues and radical change? I have no answers! I simply offer a few Anzaldúan-inspired suggestions to consider as we investigate the possibility of moving beyond disciplinolatry and transforming disciplinary boundaries. More specifically, I suggest three possible directions, or pathways, some of us working in the academy (whether as students, teachers, staff, administrators, or some combination of these positions and perhaps others) might want to explore: first, asking new questions; second, "retribalizing"/liberating identity; and third, moving beyond oppositional politics and energies.

Possible Pathway 1: Asking New Questions

In "Thawing Hearts, Opening a Path in the Woods, Founding a New Lineage," Helene Shulman Lorenz describes what she calls "a theory of reframing and restoration" that she associates with *This Bridge Called My Back: Writings by Radical Women of Color* and other cultural studies texts published (roughly) around the time of Ethnic Studies and Women's Studies development and growth. She describes her theory as follows:

> A theory of reframing asks how margins are created, enforced, justified, denied, challenged, and recentered. It looks for what has been made to appear "natural" or "normal" in every social location; how this naturalization is enacted to create a frame or border pushing out difference; and how difference survives with a life of its own, and can then become a resource either to help strengthen the frame or else to question or rupture it. (497)

In short, theories of reframing enable us to expose and denaturalize status-quo stories.[3] Through self-reflection, we investigate the power dynamics in our (inter)disciplinary fields. The goal here is not to arrive at yet another "master narrative" or "authentic" origin story but rather to open space for "multiple voices," stories, and perspectives enabling us to "build up a many-sided and ongoing dialogue" that leads to relational, contextualized truths, what Lorenz calls "provisional truth-in-perspective-for-the-moment" (597).

Applied to the various intersections we all cross in our academic lives, this theory of reframing invites us to ask questions like the following:

1. What are the status-quo stories, the norms in our disciplines (and in the academy as a whole)?
2. How have these norms functioned to patrol and push out difference?
3. What margins have these norms "created, enforced, justified, denied, challenged, and recentered"?
4. How might we reframe our disciplines if we—as interlocking communities—begin asking ourselves and each other these types of questions and listening deeply to the answers we offer each other?

These questions, and the reciprocal dialogues they can provoke, allow us to transform status-quo stories and thus work our way toward new knowledges, or what Lorenz describes as "a growing, opening edge [in which] the not-yet-voiced could begin to create new myths . . . beyond the limited already-known" (503).

Possible Pathway 2: "Retribalizing"/Liberating Identity

As terms like "Women's Studies" and "Ethnic Studies" imply, these inter-disciplinary fields emerged from and are built around identity categories, interests, and histories. Because these various identities ("women," "black," "Latina," and so forth) represent peoples whose needs and concerns have been located—or, rather, *shoved*—outside the western academic so-called "norm," it has been crucial to focus on these identities. By so doing, we bring careful, nuanced attention to the everyday life challenges, the submerged histories, the subjugated knowledges, the specific oppressions, and other dimensions of the material realities of those who have been dominated for a variety of reasons. We do so be-cause we believe that this overtly politicized scholarship can make con-crete, genuine, positive differences in people's lives. Students, scholars, and teachers in many inter/disciplinary studies have done groundbreak-ing, lifesaving (and I mean this literally: lifesaving) work.

However, the focus on identity, especially when we define identity in narrow terms, can sometimes be too limited: first, identity generally functions through exclusion. We define who and what we are by ex-cluding who and what we are not. Second, conventional identity cat-egories—those based on gender, ethnicity/"race," sexuality, sometimes class, and sometimes ability—are too restrictive and cannot adequately define us. And third, because identity categories have their source in status-quo stories, they often lead to separatist thinking that prevents us from recognizing our interconnectedness with others. All too often, identity categories distort our perceptions and create arbitrary divisions among us. When we hold too tightly to our specific identity-based la-bels, we establish and police boundaries, boundaries that shut us in with those we've deemed "like" "us" and boundaries that shut us out from those whom we assume to be different. We adopt an oppositional "us-against-them" mentality that prevents us from recognizing potential commonalities.

Could we self-define our disciplines in broader terms that go beyond conventional identity-based categories? Anzaldúa illustrates some forms this shift can take in her description of the contributors to *this bridge we call home: radical visions for transformation*. Unlike its "sister volume" (*This Bridge Called My Back*), which was written exclusively by self-identified women of colors, the contributors to *this bridge we call home* are even more diverse and include people who self-identify as "of color" and "white," as "male," "female," and "trans." As Anzaldúa explains, "Many of us identify with groups and social positions not limited to our ethnic, racial, religious, class, gender, or national classifications. Though most people self-define by what they *ex*clude, we define who we are by what we *in*clude—what I call the new tribalism" (3, my emphasis). She explains about a year later that she uses the term "to formulate a more inclusive identity, one that's based on many features and not solely on race. In order to maintain its privileges the dominant culture has imposed identities through racial and ethnic classification. The new tribalism disrupts this imposition by challenging these categories. The new tribalism is a social identity that could motivate subordinated communities to work together in coalition" ("Speaking across the Divide" 283).

I build on Anzaldúa's inclusionary vision to ask: how might our disciplines look if we defined them not by groups and social positions but by actions and goals? Let me emphasize: I am not saying, "Let's *erase* the categories, let's ignore the many differences among us, let's pretend that we're all the same." Rather, I'm suggesting that all of us with our various, multiplicitous identities come together—*not into sameness*—but into commonalities. What commonalities do we share? I won't try to offer a definitive list or pin down possible commonalities with precise labels, but I wonder if these commonalities could include envisioning radical social change or forging more adequate human rights. Under this umbrella of working/theorizing toward transformation, we could adopt and enact—and emphasize in our scholarship and teaching—whatever specific identities seem most appropriate to us and our goals.

I've been thinking about this possibility for a few years—ever since a student suggested to me that my teaching and scholarship could be described as "identity studies." For some reason that at the time I could not understand, this suggestion—while appropriate—made me incredibly uncomfortable. As I lived with and reflected on my extreme discomfort, I realized that "identity studies" stops too soon (like the disciplinolatry I described earlier). While I *do* focus on identity-related issues, this focus occurs in the service of larger goals: envisioning liberation, enacting social change, developing new communities, creating transformative knowledges, and so on. I now like to think of my "discipline" as Transformation Studies.

Possible Pathway 3: Moving beyond Oppositional Politics and Energies

Women's Studies, Ethnic Studies, and LGBTQ Studies—among many other interdisciplinary fields—have relied extensively on oppositional politics. However, because of the marginalized identities on which they are based, these identity-shaped fields have been especially impacted by deeply ingrained forms of oppositionality. As Chandra Mohanty notes in her discussion of Women's Studies and Ethnic Studies, "[Their origins], unlike those of most academic disciplines, can be traced to oppositional social movements. In particular, the civil rights movement, the women's movement, and other Third World liberation struggles fueled the demand for a knowledge and history 'of our own'" (197). I don't want to rewrite these histories or diminish the importance of these desires for an academic "home"—the yearning for scholarly spaces that can more accurately reflect our lives, our interests, our desires, and our concerns. Nor am I suggesting that we should abolish interdisciplinary fields such as Women's Studies, Ethnic Studies, and Queer Studies.[4]

My point here is much smaller, though with potentially large results. I want to suggest that the oppositional energies so crucial to the development of these interdisciplinary fields have (mis)shaped and sometimes harmed us as students, teachers, scholars, and colleagues.

Ironically, our oppositional politics have their source in some of the most negative dimensions of western, eurocentric thought and are themselves a tool in oppressive social and epistemological structures.[5] Flora Bridges notes that in oppositional discourse,

> what becomes normative, "right," and regulatory within the culture is determined by beating down or stamping out various other alternatives. Norms and values are established by way of domination. In this mental framework the possibility for both/and is destroyed. Both/and thinking is basically determined as irrational, primitive, or illogical. What results is a ravaging, hate-filled dogmatic form of establishing cultural values. (71)

I question whether the oppositional energies so crucial to the origins and development of Ethnic, Women's, and LGBTQ Studies are as useful today as they once were. These energies become poisonous when we direct them at each other, as we too often do. In such instances, we enact what Timothy Powell describes as "corrosive exchanges" (168) and embark on a "downward spiral of ever more hostile counter-accusations that tend to irrupt when a multiplicity of contentious and contrasting cultural points of view come into contact" (175). Like Jacqui Alexander, I believe that "our oppositional politic has been necessary, but it will never sustain us; while it may give us some temporary gains. . . . it can never ultimately feed that deep place within us: that space of the erotic, that space of the soul, that space of the Divine" (99).

But how might we move beyond these oppositional politics and energies, given their usefulness and their deeply ingrained status? I'm still trying to live and feel my way toward possible answers to this question. At this point, I believe that adopting a relational worldview and enacting the types of "nepantlera acts" Gloria Anzaldúa describes could offer important and useful clues.[6] As we replace oppositional attitudes and worldviews with broader, connectionist perspectives, we can challenge the status-quo stories about our academic disciplines, identities, and lives. Together, we can reframe our disciplines, ask new, perhaps risky, questions, develop nonoppositional energies and tactics, and envision new possibilities for change. I want to end with Anzaldúa's conclusion to her 2001 acceptance speech for the Bode-Pearson Prize for Outstanding Contributions to American Studies:

It requires courage to carve out a separate distinct eye/perspective from the field we're in. . . . It requires nerve to explore the discipline's unsavory aspects, its unaddressed issues and underlying conflicts. It takes courage to tear the field apart and reconstruct it. Let's challenge each other to examine, in our classrooms, our own inherited or acquired privileges, our social positions, and to take responsibility for our assumptions about people who are different from us. Let's challenge each other to spread conocimiento (knowledge). . . . I invite all of you to become academic activists and join women of color in exploring developing peace, spiritual, and social movements, and in bringing about social change. Let us teach our students to become world citizens and move at ease among diverse cultures, countries, and customs ("Transforming American Studies" 241).

IV

BRIDGING THEORIES:
INTELLECTUAL ACTIVISM
WITH/IN BORDERS

CHAPTER 19

"To live in the borderlands means you"

MARIANA ORTEGA

La mujer del desierto tiene espinas . . .
    To live in the Borderlands means you are neither hispana India negra
Española / ni gabacha, eres mestiza, mulata, half-breed / caught in the
crossfire between camps / while carrying all five races on your back / not
knowing which side to turn to, run from . . .
GLORIA ANZALDÚA, *BORDERLANDS/LA FRONTERA*

Alive always, despite the body having given up at sixty-one, Gloria Anzaldúa remains here in this world as in the next, if there is one. Latina writers, dreamers, border-dwellers, poets, thinkers, queers, cactus-
women, feel that they can write and that there is someone who listens,
who reads their words, words that owe part of their life to this Chicana word-magician who opened the doors to let us in. *Borderlands/La
Frontera: The New Mestiza* continues to shed book skins only to display
new, shiny, lively ones. It is all that Anzaldúa probably wanted it to be:
bridge, crossroads, red and black ink, even shaman and flesh and bone,
Anzaldúa's own flesh and bone, which she so beautifully displayed so
that she could understand herself—so that others could understand her.
*Este libro se viste y se baña; lo vestimos y bañamos nosotras que nos
vemos en él.* Those who feel like her, who walk around sometimes with
a low head, tired of being half and half, in-between, "other," nada, "ni
chicha ni limonada,"[1] but sometimes with heads high up because we
are the New Mestizas with double, triple vision and thus multiple possibilities—those who find themselves living between those bone-carving
pages are no longer alone, are no longer voiceless.
    Borderlands has shaped the past of Chicana/Latina Studies by bring-
ing our voices forth, and if we dare to foresee the future, we can safely

say that this gift in the form of a book will continue to influence Chicana/Latina Studies by not only carrying the legacy of Anzaldúa's vision but also by opening up new possibilities of theorizing. There are many such possibilities, many theories, skins, that this book can shed or wear. Theorizing about self and difference within us is one of these possibilities. Although *Borderlands* has already contributed in this area of the utmost importance—after all, exploring our selves is one of our most meaningful endeavors—it still has much to offer, particularly when we think of diversity within Latinas, as there are not only New Mestizas among us but also mulatas, New Mulatas, whose voices also need to be heard if we are truly to embrace difference.

Thus let those in bright, shiny, paper-clean academic hallways, offices, conferences who continue to dream of the respectable, venerable, unified subject beware. New visions of subjectivity are emerging accompanied and guided by the spirit of Anzaldúa. Perhaps these respectable places will continue to be inhabited by those who trick themselves and appeal to homogeneity—but it gets harder and harder to avoid meeting the New Mestiza, the New Mulata, in those very hallways or in the pages of those who invoke Anzaldúa's words in their own ink.

The New Mestiza theory of self constitutes an alternative to theories that prioritize the unity of the subject, such as the Kantian view, or theories that emphasize the epistemic component of human beings, such as the Cartesian view of subjectivity. It also constitutes an alternative vision to postmodern views of self that criticize traditional views of selfhood or jettison the self. The New Mestiza does not require complete unity; it does not prioritize knowledge—the seven stages of conocimiento go far beyond our connection to the world via knowledge.[2] Nor does it give up the self; it reshapes, restores, and transforms it in order to include the complexity of its life.

Theories of self have to be revised so as to take seriously the in-betweenness, difference, and heterogeneity that Anzaldúa's ink brings forth. We who are in-between need to pay more attention to the in-betweenness within us, and those who may not live the life that Anzaldúa so poignantly describes also must pay attention, hear what she and those who come after her, those whom she has deeply inspired, have to say about the self. The world that Anzaldúa and others have opened needs to be put on our intellectual maps lest we allow ourselves to inhabit only one country, putting blinders on our eyes to block those "others" who continue breathing even as we ignore them. And we can no longer avoid the borders, the margins, territories claimed and unclaimed that human beings cross to play, work, dream, suffer, and change. To avoid these borders, margins, territories that point to difference in us, within us, and for others to avoid us makes for a static world in which the doors to prejudice, discrimination, and misunderstanding open wide.

The future promises much for Anzaldúa's red and black ink. Let us not abuse it, overuse it, think that we know it and understand it while there is much that awaits within it to be discovered. They say Latinos have become the largest minority, but this largest minority still waits for adequate political representation, educational opportunities, safe neighborhoods—and a loud, clear voice. This largest minority does not have enough of our mouths that speak for us, about us, hands that write about our lives, our desires. If there could be more Anzaldúas to bring us to life—yet she remains unique in her ability to describe the lived experience, the life in the flesh, as Moraga would say, of the New Mestizas. More Latinas will take risks, expose themselves, write their lives following Anzaldúa's example. As we do it, let us not forget the border, the Chicana experience from which Anzaldúa writes, but let us also not forget the diversity within us: atravesados, mestizos, mulatos, light, dark, black, brown. There are borders among us and it is time to cross.

CHAPTER 20

A modo de testimoniar:
Borderlands, Papeles, and U.S. Academia

ESTHER CUESTA

Living in a no-man's borderland, caught between being treated as criminals and being able to eat, between resistance and deportation, the illegal refugees are some of the poorest and the most exploited of any people in the U.S. . . . La mojada, la mujer indocumentada, is doubly threatened in this country. Not only does she have to contend with sexual violence, but like all women, she is prey to a sense of physical helplessness. As a refugee, she leaves the familiar and safe homeground to venture into unknown and possibly dangerous terrain.

GLORIA ANZALDÚA, *BORDERLANDS/LA FRONTERA*

Fall 2002: I encountered Gloria Anzaldúa's work in my first semester of an M.A./Ph.D. program in Comparative Literature while experiencing the conflictive reality of sitting in university classrooms as an undocumented migrant in the United States. "La conciencia de la mestiza/ Towards a New Consciousness" was a suggested reading in a feminist theory seminar. Disappointingly, it was merely glossed over, when I had hoped that I could feel more connected to the class discussions and contribute without having to quote other theorists to support my argument. *Borderlands/La Frontera* was one of the few texts I encountered that discussed concrete and worldly matters in a poetico-theoretical language to which I could relate. Anzaldúa's unapologetic historicizing of Chicano/mexicano/indigenous/Anglo cultures and theorizing of psychological/sexual/spiritual/ethnic borderlands provided me with the tools to unpack my heavy luggage of pain and memorias.

I was particularly intimidated in this seminar because almost everyone seemed so familiar with Marx, Freud, Lacan, Foucault, and all the other major male theorists that feminists were critiquing and/or building on.

Most students spoke with authority, confidently entitled to give their opinions. And here I was, una ecuatoriana indocumentada doubting my own interpretations of texts. I found myself piecing together the professor's and students' interventions, as I had little background on the debates, and the academic language seemed too dense, almost incomprehensible. Thinking that I had learned nothing so far and had so much catching up to do, I felt like a real alien among academic feminists. I couldn't connect their discussions on women, womanhood, and femininity with my own struggles as an indocumentada and the frustration, anger, and pain about the type of impoverishment and subordination I had encountered in Ecuador and the United States.

That semester, unable to get a teaching assistantship or other funding that seemed available to "documented" students, I lingered for the U.S. government's "permission" to allow the university to release the funds of a fellowship I had been granted upon my acceptance to the program. Without this, I couldn't study. Working in restaurants in a college area couldn't cover all my graduate school expenses. I remember a migration lawyer who told me that I shouldn't bother with graduate school, as most of the country's population doesn't pursue it; it would be asking too much for an "illegal" with no prospects of "fixing" her status.[1] I missed my family, my ayllu,[2] ever more, constantly planning a return to Ecuador but never deciding on it.

For the 2002 winter break, I went to my grandmother's house in New York—she is my aunt, but I think of her as my grandmother, mi mamá grande. A few years prior, I had left her house to venture out. This time I wanted to stay and forget the anguish of my illegality. In her house, I was her granddaughter, her compañerita, her English translator and interpreter. El no tener papeles didn't matter. Outside, being "illegal" became a mark with which I had branded myself, my identity, almost controlling my decisions and my interactions with people. I feared disclosing too much of myself, being betrayed, reported, and deported, constantly feeling dislocated and estranged from my family and most people. As Anzaldúa wrote, "Your identity is a filtering screen limiting your awareness to a fraction of your reality. What you or your cultures believe to be true is provisional and depends on a specific perspective" ("now let us shift" 542). This lack of papers shaped how I understood this alien-nation.

At my grandmother's I unpacked copies of *Borderlands* and *This Bridge Called My Back* that I had borrowed from the library, and I read them on my own. Anzaldúa, along with the women of color included in *This Bridge,* demonstrated that there were *other ways* of writing, of theorizing and transforming academia from within and without, and I wondered who was writing about undocumented migrants and young ecuatorianas in U.S. higher education. I had moved beyond society's filtering screen, with its huge signs telling me, "Universities are not for you." I resisted this message, mainly because being undocumented does not mean being *unfit* for education.

As the youngest child of a schoolteacher and a college professor, I had always envisaged a university degree. As an indocumentada, I had the privilege of having made it to the United States and being fluent in English. For six years of U.S. higher education I had to move between these two worlds/terrains where borders/checkpoints had been created: not qualifying for scholarships because I had no papers; being asked in job interviews to provide a Social Security number; when offered a job, being required to show a Social Security card, driver's license, passport with visa, work permit, alien card. Beyond the specific physical realm (fronteras: Ecuador/Mexico/United States) that I had crossed, I straddled two seemingly irreconcilable spheres—U.S. academia and my undocumentity. Without fully recognizing or comprehending it, I had straddled my own nepantla.

Geopolitically located in the Texas–U.S. Southwest/Mexican border, *Borderlands* became a webbed metaphorical tool with which I was able to make sense of the "mojada" I became in this country—as I was jokingly called by those to whom I confessed my migratory experience—along with twelve million people without white plastic and paper cards. As an alliance-building, feminist-consciousness strategy, Anzaldúa brought the mexicanas y mexicanos who cross the Río Grande without checking in at U.S. checkpoints to the forefront of the discussion of mexicanas y mexicanos de ambos lados, from both sides of the border, that ever more dangerous border that represents the attempts to divide them (us, all people from the Americas). Working from within and without hegemonic cosmologies, pasando la aguja por dentro y por fuera, Anzaldúa's border-thinking helped me recognize that I had a situated knowledge most people in that feminist theory seminar didn't have, and my migratory experience became a key epistemological standpoint from which I began understanding women's experiences in the United States, Ecuador, and elsewhere. Anzaldúa's marginalized experiences in South Texas also elucidated how being born in U.S. territories and its colonial "dependencies" does not make someone a U.S. sovereign citizen with full rights. The very plurality of *Borderlands* allowed me to expand

Anzaldúa's notion of frontera to other barreras/fronteras/conflicts in the Middle East, the Korean Peninsula, the Caribbean, and the European Union. A site of contradictions, contestation, multiplicity of self, Anzaldúa's mestiza consciousness became a methodology to deconstruct and reconstruct myself, to live with the contradictions in my life. Anzaldúa encouraged me to rethink my experiences as an undocumented immigrant in this country and to search for conocimiento in people and loci I had been taught to ignore. I started to find ways to validate my knowledge, not always coming from books but from lived experiences and histories of Latin Americans.

The pain of institutionalized racism in Ecuadorian schools had taught me to negate Afro-descendants' and indigenous people's knowledges, my ancestors, to other them. I was trained not to inquire who I was. Growing up in La Chala, a marginal neighborhood in the southwest part of Guayaquil, while attending costly bilingual schools with the help of my grandmother, Ecuador's diverse populations and cultures were only folkloric misrepresentations in the curriculum. Having a limited knowledge about Ecuador, I never felt part of that nation, which—one way or another—expelled me . . . or did I expel myself? Even sin papeles, how could I return? I feared feeling trapped again in Ecuador, like twelve years earlier, when I desperately tried to get visas to go anywhere. I couldn't envision life in a system that never held accountable the medical doctors responsible for my mother's overdose of anesthesia, for killing her.

At the age of nineteen, I flew to Mexico City, taking with me all the savings from the office jobs I had had for almost two years. No one knew about my plans to cross the Mexican/U.S. border except one person who helped me along the way. Unlike Mexican immigrants, I did not return to Aztlán. My indigenous roots are not in the U.S. Southwest. I was not among the "ten million people without documents [who] have returned" there (*Borderlands* 33). Still, I crossed that same deadly border on an inflatable raft and felt I had no place to return.

Laredo checkpoint.

San Antonio checkpoint.

In San Antonio, I bought a bus ticket to New York. From Columbus, Ohio, I called my father to tell him I was not returning, and I later heard from my siblings that my call had saddened him. I've never asked him.

Waitress, bartender, factory worker, medical assistant, receptionist, secretary, immigration and tax form preparer were some of the jobs I had in New York while taking English classes. I had learned English in Ecuador, but that did not prepare me for a college education in English. In fall 1998 I was still undocumented, but I was allowed to enroll in a college in New York and pay the city resident's tuition. I obtained my B.A., and three months later I was in graduate school.

In summer 2005, the U.S. system *documented* my existence, after eleven years of undocumented self-exile. Gradually, I was able to get out of the cage into which I had locked myself. While the U.S. government keeps their taxes, immigrants are offered few policy measures para arreglar sus papeles and dim possibilities of returning to their countries of citizenship. This is the privilege I have now: being "legal" in this imperio, when millions remain "undocumented."

Anzaldúa invited me to embark on a transformative process I did not expect to undergo when I left Ecuador: to go back home emotionally, ideologically, and politically while remaining in the United States, working, studying, falling in love. Her vision led me to begin searching/recuperating my own cultural and ethnoracial roots, to understand my multiple identities, my own country, one I didn't really know or care to know when I emigrated. Today, I am reclaiming mis raíces, the indigenous, the African, the European, excavating my fluminense campesino background, my ancestral roots in Ventanas, in the province of Los Ríos, my mother's homeland; mi cuencano and lojano paternal side, those who were part of the Tawantinsuyo and those who have resisted colonizations and colonialities and created alternative ways of existing in capitalist organizations of society. I'm trying to understand my family's migrations and genealogy and how these experiences connect with larger national, regional, and global subalternized histories.

While scholarship on Ecuadorian migration increases and Ecuadorian migrants share their experiences in the online versions of major Ecuadorian newspapers, clear divisions (borders) between subjects of study (or research participants) and researchers continue. As much as our experiences differ, I'm weaving my experiences with the diverse life histories of my relatives and friends abroad, my siblings' yearning to migrate, and the women and men I have met in consulates, airports, restaurant kitchens, hotels, streets in Barcelona, Cologne, New York, Madrid, Rome, Aarhus. As Anzaldúa writes, "Change requires more than words on a page—it takes perseverance, creative ingenuity, and acts of love" ("now let us shift" 574). As I embark on the agonizing and isolating career of the academic, I'm taking with me Anzaldúa's vision of love and social justice to integrate into my work on cultural studies and migration, my teaching, and my long-term commitment to collaborate with Amazonian Kichwa communities.

University walls are very high and difficult to scale; once we're in, it's even harder to get out and make time to share our energy in other struggles, activisms, luchas de resistencia, y urgentes propuestas de re-existencia. A professor once told me that if I want to change the world, I should quit graduate school and become a full-time activist. I considered this option many times, feeling incapable of functioning in this little circle of the "educated," but I'm still here. Despite the systematic individualism that *also* works in U.S. universities and impedes students' deviation from academics to do activist work, I am convinced I can contribute to larger transformations.

I'm building on the legacy of Anzaldúa and other women-of-color feminists as I center my dissertation research on Ecuadorian women migrants to understand how subjectivities shift in different geopolitical spaces and how we resist and transgress multiple forms of violence that global capitalism imposes on our bodies and minds, including death, rape, sexual exploitation, and all kinds of abuses and lies women encounter as we are desperately trying to migrate. The fact that many women are forced to leave their children behind and cannot see them for six or ten years is yet another type of violence poor and working-class people from the Southern Hemisphere and elsewhere have to confront. Anzaldúa's *Borderlands* has taken a transatlantic direction in my research, as I'm documenting and facilitating the creation of oral and written narratives of Ecuadorian women living in Italy and Spain. I cannot let the fears, the pleasures, and the pains of being an undocumented ecuatoriana continue being undocumented. Inspired by Anzaldúa, I envision this ongoing project as a book that will elicit ways of exploring and promoting intellectual activism.

But for whom am I writing this essay? Who will the readers be? What are we going to do with this book? People living in the global North, speaking and reading in English, may run the risk of shearing the possibilities for transformation in a planet that seems less and less viable on which to subsist, if we only keep this book in our hands. Not only will this anthology need linguistic translation but cultural and material ones. In an unequal world where not everyone has access to books, an interest in reading them, or the luxury of literacy, a multi-sited trans-(lation)formation is needed to continue Anzaldúa's vision of challenging the ways knowledges are reproduced.

I learned about Anzaldúa's writings in a university classroom. Had I not been sitting there, my chances to know her work would have been almost nil. Although her work has reached U.S. women's shelters, community centers, activists, and young women in high school, I have a gut feeling that if artists in hip-hop, reggaeton, R&B, and other genres of popular music were exposed to Anzaldúa's work, they might reflect on some of her views and incorporate them into their music; thus, this knowledge may have the potential of reaching unimaginable numbers of people in the United States and beyond. Given the current U.S. hegemony, U.S. artists have great prominence in shifting cultural trends and critiques. Revolutionary thinkers' ideas, reflections, and writings have seldom been translated into popular culture for U.S. youth. We need the interpretations of young people who are not necessarily in academia expanding on Anzaldúa's vision to promote and disseminate a transformation in youth consciousness. If there were more like Taleb Kweli, Immortal Technique, Mos Def, and Dead Prez, to name a few, transformation would be nearer. Because high school is a key component in the experiences of youth, Anzaldúa's work will need to reach those spheres to reach hip-hop artists.[3]

It is also critical to bring Anzaldúa's wisdom in dialogue with cosmologies across the globe, of people who protect life, trees, oceans, the air, and work toward social justice and life outside the page. Life. That word that sounds so banal now, perhaps because it has lost its meaning. Urgency for life is what I have found in Kichwa communities in Ecuador, while I am delearning, desaprendiendo tanto, and committed to return to Amazonian Kichwa communities to teach English to children—for children and adults to teach me. As Gloria Anzaldúa dug in and dismantled and constructed knowledge, she offered novel ways of intellectual activism. Sharing (talking, writing, singing) how we live and envision our interactions with each other in love and solidarity allows us to widen already large webs of potential transformation.

CHAPTER 21

On Borderlands and Bridges:
An Inquiry into Gloria Anzaldúa's Methodology

JORGE CAPETILLO-PONCE

The first time I read *Borderlands/La Frontera,* in 2001, I found myself irresistibly drawn to Gloria Anzaldúa's theory of an emerging borderland culture. She surprised me at each new twist and turn of her text with her probing analysis and methodology of the emergence of a new mestiza consciousness and her tracing of the intercultural bridges that her emergence implies. I read *Borderlands* again and again and also such other works as *this bridge we call home* and *Interviews/Entrevistas.* I attribute this attraction to two central strands in my life's fabric, the personal and the professional.

As for the former, I can say that I have been living in the borderlands all my life. I was born in Havana, the offspring of a Mexican American father from California and of a Mexican mother whose family had been displaced from Yucatán to Cuba by the Mexican Revolution. I arrived in Mexico City in the early 1960s, my family having been displaced by yet another revolution, this one the overthrow of Batista by Castro's freedom fighters. From that day on, my background seemed to me too difficult and messy to try to explain to others. I was Mexican, American, and Cuban, and I felt a certain attraction to all of these nationalities. My understandable desire to fit in, as a schoolboy, led me to make Mexicanness my central cultural idiom, but part of my young adulthood was spent in Nicaragua, and then it was on to New York City and my doctoral studies at The New School. By the time I arrived in the Big Apple, I had become thoroughly comfortable living in the borderlands.

And that brings us to the professional strand. As a trained theorist I am always seeking to make sense of a particular work by tracing its theoretical and methodological influences and thereby situating it within a particular field or tradition. Thus, each new reading of an Anzaldúa work produced a new batch of notes on the various theorists, artists, and methodological approaches that each particular text had brought to my mind. Until 2004 I was glad to read her work and learn from her insights. It was only after Anzaldúa's untimely death that year that I decided to bring my notes together into a more systematic presentation of my thoughts.

My problem then was the incredible number of items I had as-sembled—Marx, Vasconcelos, Said, Freud, dialectics, Gilman, psycho-analysis, Nietzsche, Juan Rulfo, Foucault, Lobsang Rampa, Tomás Ri-vera, Habermas, postmodernism, spirituality, DuBois, Octavio Paz, conflict resolution, Jung, Hillman, Weber, Carlos Castañeda, and Sim-mel. I wondered how on earth I was going to arrive at any categoriza-tion that would make sense of that near-chaos of persons and of influ-ences. And how could such a piecemeal approach possibly do justice to Anzaldúa's theoretical and methodological unity? One can of course speak of her "eclecticism," but that word doesn't even begin to suggest the complexity-within-unity of her method.

Gradually I realized that Anzaldúa's work doesn't fit into the usual critical categories because she follows inclination of interest, as opposed to striving for systematization, shifting continually from analysis to med-itation and refusing to recognize disciplinary boundaries. She intuitively follows her passion while using her autohistoria in creative ways. Indeed, her method is more akin to "style" in art than it is to "analysis" in the social sciences. I suppose the most I can hope for is that the reader who witnesses, in the ensuing pages, my efforts to pin down the methodol-ogy of this unmethodical mind will be inspired to turn from my analyses to her refreshing syntheses.

Anzaldúa is, like Foucault, an archeologist of knowledge. She digs for ideas, symbols, and myths in her own historic and mythic past. This effort allows Anzaldúa to invent new concepts that are inspired in her findings. Such pre-Hispanic concepts and deities as nepantla, Coatlicue, and Coyolxauhqui are refashioned in her work, acquiring the form of new spiritual and psychological theories that can then be applied to the study of identities and society in general. In one particular passage of *Interviews/Entrevistas,* Anzaldúa sounds especially Foucauldian as she poses a question central to all her work: "What is the relationship be-tween power and knowledge, between conocimientos and power? How do they create subjectivities?" (216). The immaterial findings unearthed by the excavations of both these thinkers have struck my mind as being almost palpable methodological tools, of real use in digging up discursive fields. There is also a link between them in the way both are always touching upon postmodern, postnational, postcolonial identities.

Still, in my opinion it is problematic to call Anzaldúa's work merely "postmodernist," especially because the term "postmodernism" has become an empty signifier, one we can fill with almost any content. Thus, even if we were all to agree that Gloria Anzaldúa is a postmodern thinker, we would still have to ask, "Just what *type* of postmodernism are we talking about here?"

Perhaps we can shed light onto Anzaldúa's methodological approach by looking instead at those classical theorists and traditions that made postmodernist thought possible—for example, Marx and his dialectical method. On a superficial level, Anzaldúa's method does seem dialectical. In *Borderlands* she limns the contours of a native, pre-Hispanic Mexican past that can be taken as thesis; explores those Spanish political, economic, and especially cultural conquests that can serve as antithesis; and finally describes the emergence of an implicitly synthetic Mexican culture. Then the whole process plays itself out again in modern times, but now with Mexican culture as thesis, the Anglo politico-economic and cultural conquest of part of Mexico (Anzaldúa's borderland) as antithesis, and as synthesis the new mestiza, a figure born of the dialectic of races and ethnicities. Anzaldúa fruitfully uses dialectics in her exploration of the borderlands, where she finds "the lifeblood of two worlds merging to form a third country—a border culture" (*Borderlands/La Frontera* 25).

Anzaldúa's work does show a Marxist strand in that she makes room for "minor" and alienated voices. For Anzaldúa this does not mean the proletariat but a mixed bag of groups differentiated on the basis of ethnicity, sexual orientation, and cultural alienation: the queer, the mestiza, the "Chicano-mexicanos, people of mixed race, people who have Indian blood, people who cross cultures" (*Borderlands/La Frontera* 52). What sets Anzaldúa apart from Marx, however, is her disinclination to draw any clear-cut distinction between a material world below and ideas hovering above. It is as if she is telling us that ideas and the material world are so intimately intertwined that it is impossible to pry the two apart. And here we encounter a problem, for in the absence of sustained efforts to divide the world into opposing categories by which the thinker can then see the march of events as slowly synthesizing, can a thinker's method truly be called "dialectical"?

While on a superficial level—the *conscious* level, the level cluttered with those socio-political-economic realities that we confront every day—Anzaldúa's method seems dialectical, her root concern is not the interplay between material conditions and ideas but what she calls the "chthonic": the underworld, the unconscious, the domain explored by Freud, Jung, and many others. But whereas Freud's ego and superego are born from every self's negotiation with the external, social world and hence are inherently dialectical and conscious, what fascinates Anzaldúa is the id, which Freud considered the oldest part of the mind, out of which the other structures are derived:

> After each of my four bouts with death I'd catch glimpses of an other-world Serpent. Once in my bedroom, I saw a cobra the size of a room, her hood expanding over me. . . . I realized she was, in my psyche, the mental picture and symbol of the instinctual in its collective impersonal, pre-human. She, the symbol of the dark sexual drive, the chthonic (underworld), the feminine, the serpentine movement of sexual creativity, the basis of all energy and life. (*Borderlands* 57)

This superlatively Anzaldúan passage is just one example of the unique way in which Gloria reshapes those concepts and categories of Freud that are based upon western culture and especially upon the male characters and myths of classical Greece, repeopling them with female characters drawn from her own pre-Hispanic and Mexican mythological past. This is not merely a matter of changing names from Greek to Náhuatl; it is a complete rejection of the dominant phallo-eurocentric methodological approach and the creation of a new interpretive framework of psychic entities.

This methodological innovation allows Anzaldúa to show us how the female archetypes presented in her work—such as the enduring Virgin of Guadalupe, the raped and dishonored La Chingada, and the long-suffering mother La Llorona—have in the past been partitioned and weakened by a violent, divisive, and dominating male ethos. In fact, in one enigmatic passage Anzaldúa alludes to a reality that is "older than Freud" (*Borderlands/La Frontera* 48). I believe she is talking about a unified reality that existed before Freud and other males insisted on seeing the world through lenses distorted by dualism, that is, by the interaction of and conflict between opposites.

In order to get us beyond dualism and create a unified form capable of serving as an analytical tool, Anzaldúa relies on such archetypes as Coatlicue, the Aztec goddess who "depicts the contradictory. In her figure, all the symbols important to the religion and philosophy of the

Aztecs are integrated" (*Borderlands/La Frontera* 69). Coatlicue is not just a primordial archetype, however; she is also a state of consciousness and thereby a method of interpreting reality and implementing change: "When you're in the midst of the Coatlicue state—the cave, the dark—you're hibernating or hiding, you're gestating and giving birth to yourself. You're in a womb state. When you come out of that womb state you pass through the birth canal, the passageway I call nepantla" (*Interviews/Entrevistas* 226). These original insights are not only part of a methodological venture; they offer a bridge to a therapeutical realm, a place where the sojourner can recreate a sense of wholeness, of unity, in a divided world. In this sense Anzaldúa's method, like Freud's, is not merely analytical but also transformative.

At this juncture we begin to perceive the contours of the Anzaldúan methodology. One element is her interest in unity and in decolonizing cultural analysis from its male/dualistic domination. This effort at unification is an aspect of her contributions that makes the traditional theorist's work of disentangling disciplinary strands very difficult. I gradually understood that instead of prying apart her dialectics from her psychoanalysis, we should focus on analyzing how Anzaldúa creates something new when she bridges these two strands together into a more powerful, multilayered analytical tool. Such an effort allows Anzaldúa to build one of her most important contributions to intellectual activism: a bridge between the inner and external worlds, linking "inner reflection and vision—the mental, emotional, instinctive, imaginal, spiritual, and subtle bodily awareness—with social, political action and lived experiences to generate subversive knowledges" ("now let us shift" 542).

Such theoretical innovations make her method an ideal analytical tool to be applied in such diverse fields as feminist theory, migration studies, critical theory, conflict resolution, race and ethnic relations, and sociological research in general. But to further situate her work and envision the areas of possible influence, I want to make a final reflection regarding the evolution of Anzaldúa's work.

In *Borderlands* Anzaldúa presents the new mestiza as a woman who has to "cross over" by "kicking a hole out of the old boundaries of the self and slipping under or over, dragging the old skin along. . . . It is a dry birth, a breech birth, a screaming birth. . . . It is only when she is on the other side and the shell cracks open and the lid from her eyes lifts that she sees things in a different perspective" (71). This is clearly a transformative period (what she calls "threshold nepantla"); it is not, however, a massive, class-consciousness scheme but rather an individualistic and painful—while also synthetic—transformation. It suggests that for Anzaldúa self-change is (or can become) the first step to collective/ social change and that valuable existential knowledge can be acquired only by living amid a multiplicity of realities or borderlands.

While I believe there is no conscious attempt at excluding other groups in Anzaldúa's work, I still do see in the new mestiza an element of uniqueness that sets her apart. This forces me to raise three questions. First, is Anzaldúa really trying to free her methodology from any and every attempt at exclusion and transcend any trace of elitism? Second, would not critics of all political persuasions see in her implicit conception of uniqueness as a highly personalized, identity-through-torment process (the new mestiza's "dry, breech, screaming birth") merely a more refined form of distinction-making? And third, what would Anzaldúa have said about completely different processes of consciousness formation, for example, those that evolve within the homogeneous terrain of white suburbia? Can the new mestiza consciousness find a way to take root even in such a sterile soil?

Part of the answer to these questions lies in the fact that the new mestiza is a theoretical concept that Anzaldúa developed in the 1980s. In later writings she shifted her focus to nepantla—the in-between, unstable, precarious space where the new mestiza was transformed. This evolution in her thought enhanced her methodological balance while allowing her to cast a wider analytical net. For example, in *Interviews/Entrevistas* she maintains that white women are finally theorizing about racism and domination, but "they haven't gotten to the level of hands-on dismantling it" (217). Yet, in *this bridge we call home* she assumes herself the role of nepantlera, refusing to walk the color line and positioning herself between the white world and the world of people of color, underlining that the latter group has sometimes bought into victimhood, becoming "experts on oppression" who don't "have to listen/ learn from whites" (565). Thus Anzaldúa reveals the dualistic nature of the problem, creating a new space where a more holistic solution can be reached.

This takes us to the method's versatility. The various methodological levels I have explored here allow for its successful application to the analysis of personal/individual transformations as well as to conflict resolution at the micro social level (family, neighborhood, conference) or to macro social problems such as the ongoing immigration debate or war in the Middle East. In fact, I believe that Anzaldúa's complexity-within-unity approach is already having an impact on the work of contemporary social scientists, allowing us to arrive at fresh understandings of illegitimate and/or marginalized perspectives and subjugated knowledges imbedded in social life.

There is no question that Anzaldúa's work has a political angle, one that will surely attract the attention of a specific group of social theorists interested in analyzing heterogeneous human interactions that take place within complicated and unstable situations. But isn't that a definition of today's world anyway? Indeed, we are all undergoing shifts in perception at the personal level and "bleed-throughs among different worlds each with its own version of reality" ("now let us shift" 541) at the macro level. The order we have created seems to be one that reproduces unjust hierarchies, control, and alienation. To confront these new situations, full of complexities, multiplicities, instabilities, and contradictions, we need a method like Anzaldúa's that goes beyond analysis and transforms our gaze through what she calls "the Coyolxauhqui imperative" ("(Un)natural bridges" 5), that is, imagining a reality different from what already exists.

CHAPTER 22

For Gloria, Para Mí

MARY CATHERINE LOVING

tomar razón de los poemas

I am suspicious of poets who claim to know the single impetus for any work. I suspect that Gloria, mi tía, la hermana de my mamá, y la hermana de my abuela, también, was similarly predisposed. I imagine her so because it comforts me to suppose that she too experienced seasons of wonder and seasons of little—and without any idea whom to curse or praise for the seasons filled with ripe, fleshy verse. Seasons alive with untamed verse. Or for the seasons barren of rhyme. (Signs: Fragile, bitter, insufficiently bound in punctuation; grammar-less verse.) Or how to tell the two apart. How to know which would yield poetry, which would feed the poet.

I am suspicious. Of poets. Find them often untrustworthy; yet: in their words, I take shelter. To their verse, I run. *I write to restore what has been erased. Made shameful. Obscured.* To celebrate las fronteras of my own existence: to acknowledge the Spanish explorer, conquistador, rapist, slave owner who explored, conquered, raped, and owned my mother's grandmother. Not necessarily in that order. To render carefully the site of her violation—san augustine: the patron saint of grace. To record my great-great-grandmother's voice. *No.* To shout the secret of my continued existence, inscribed in code understood by the women, slaves, whose tongues are not now quiet.

I am. Suspicious of poets. Find them unruly, disorderly, meticulous in their pursuit of disorder. Unfaithful. Unrelentingly so. !Oye¡ porque a todos nos agrada mi tía, la hermana de mis madres: Patron saint of poets, she who nurtures myth, encourages skepticism toward that child's malicious sister, History. Together we (re)cord our daughters' prayers, witness our sisters' miracles; reveal our enemies' lies—retell them all, in verse: Women's stories are mirrors: / their joys and fears, / who we were. / Once. / Who we are. Once again.

I run to her words porque in them I encuentro seguridad. Within her verse I recover a haven—warm fire, bread, wisdom, guidance. Loving guidance. I write. Because she compels me to: her voice, the echo from my mother's mothers and their mothers before, calls me back into the fold. Connects me, bone flesh to bone flesh to la cultura olvidada de mi mamá. The language recently tasted. Another language yet unfamiliar. The aftertaste of Spain; the frightful silence of Africa—both seek shelter in my verse. How many tongues has a poet?

How many lives?

Ars Poetica

For Gloria Evangelina Anzaldúa

The poet is obliged to wait,
on guard,
for the poem out of season—
attentive to vine,
patch of dirt, dwindling
rain, the verse
battling for its life
in that same patch. Bountiful
springs spawn indifference
to the horde of ghosts—Immortal
mistresses, holy slaves. And the poet
turns away;
attends to life,
neglects death, scolds gods
who hold no sway.

Unformed poet! Yet feeble virgin
whose unbleached bones can not
know language,
can not sense the impetus
from her mothers' rhymes, raw
in her fertile belly. Should she persist,
worship once more at sites
scorned in recent plenty, tend steadfast
to sacrament there,
temper barren moments
with expectation—Bear the sting
when poetry erupts, bloodied,
mangled
from her gut; she
may be honed true
in your shade: Broken.
Still.

CHAPTER 23

Chicana Feminist Sociology in the Borderlands

ELISA FACIO AND DENISE A. SEGURA

In this essay we discuss the ways that Gloria Anzaldúa's conceptualization of "borderlands" expanded our sociological imaginations. Trained as qualitative sociologists, we were well versed in feminist methods that emphasized women's voices and experiences as critical analytical starting points. For us, Anzaldúa's writings offered a new language that liberated the "ser" from the "estar"—that "to be" is formed by the politics of place and space in the borderlands. Liberated methodologically and linguistically, more and more Chicana activist scholars in sociology are moving beyond research *about* Chicanas to a *Chicana feminist sociology* dedicated to social change. We examine key theoretical and applied developments in Chicana feminist sociology, including a borderlands community praxis. We argue that a borderlands community praxis that draws theoretical nurturance from Anzaldúa empowers Chicana/o communities. As examples, we discuss two borderlands projects, one in health care, the other in education. We conclude with some thoughts about the ongoing development of Chicana feminist sociology.

Gloria Anzaldúa states, "The U.S.-Mexican border *es una herida abierta* where the Third World grates against the first and bleeds. And before a scab forms it hemorrhages again, the lifeblood of two worlds merging to form a third country—a border culture. Borders are set up to define the places that are safe and unsafe, to distinguish *us* from *them*" (*Borderlands/La Frontera* 25). Anzaldúa's borderlands inhabit physical and spiritual spaces that center on the movement of people, products, and ideas across the United States and Mexico. The borderlands are not confined to geographical spaces but refer to spaces where two or more cultures "edge" each other. These meetings are active and vibrant where social subjects negotiate for position, legitimacy, and place. In the borderlands, "difference" becomes meaningful even as "sameness" is questioned. Marginality is revealed as a social reality marked by moments of transgression from the dominant culture as well as assertions of a unique and valuable "otherness"—or "in-between" subject positions. Understanding otherness as a site of resistance and empowerment is a core concept within a Chicana feminist sociology situated in the borderlands.

Segura and Zavella's recent review of key theoretical and methodological characterization of borderlands in the social sciences found a strong emphasis on transnational social formations, in particular economic, political, or sociocultural activities by individual and collective actors that cross national borders, thereby "deterritorializing" politically drawn international boundaries. Increasingly, researchers who use this approach conduct field research in both "sending" and "receiving" communities, thereby revealing specifics of how deterritorialized processes unfold at micro and macro levels.

Segura and Zavella argue that a second approach to borderlands, centered in cultural studies, "emphasize[s] the ways in which identity formation is linked to multiple sites, both real and imagined, such that new hybridized and creolized identity forms emerge. According to this perspective, identities shift and are negotiated in response to forces from above and below and therefore are never fixed or bounded (Levitt 2001, 237–238)" but are rather fluid (4). One must be familiar with both approaches to get a sense of the multifaceted changes that women negotiate.

Borderlands Feminist Studies

Anzaldúa's discussion of the borderlands disrupts Anglocentric nationalist histories, assimilationist paradigms, and Chicano nationalist agendas regarding the incorporation of Mexicans into the United States. Within the context of feminist ideology, women's narratives expand previous androcentric history texts and deconstruct the heteronormative patriarchal Chicano master narrative. Women-centered analyses expand previous versions of texts politically labeled "neutral" or "objective" by conventional social science that objectify working-class, racial-ethnic, and queer communities.

One critical contribution of the borderlands perspective is its attention to the history of colonization and racialization of Mexicans. The confluence of Mexico and the United States creates specific social conditions for both Mexicanas/Mexicanos and Chicanas/Chicanos. Race, gender, sexuality, and class are negotiated in the daily lives of Chicanas within the context of the borderlands. By using the term "borderlands" we contextualize and substantiate myriad Mexicana/Chicana experiences as forms of adaptation and resistance to linguistic and cultural terrorism. The borderlands is a fertile ground from which individual and collective action has arisen.[1] In a transnational framework, borderlands emphasizes coalitions with other mujeres across the U.S.-Mexican geopolitical border. Hence, a borderlands feminist sociology interrogates and moves beyond a nation-bound discourse. Borderlands feminist research works to develop binational approaches that include structural forces and women's individual and collective agency, incorporating perspectives of women on both sides of the U.S.-Mexican border.[2]

A borderlands feminist project focuses on women's construction of cultural identity and agency in the nebulous space of their lived realities, or what Segura and Zavella refer to as "subjective transnationalism." Women constantly negotiate economic and political space in the geographic and psychic borderlands. This activity disrupts traditional notions of gender within households, local communities, and the state. Rosa Linda Fregoso argues that violence against women in Ciudad Juárez, in the state of Chihuahua, and elsewhere illustrates a male-dominated state's efforts to reclaim women as subordinate objects (3–6). Subjective transnationalism refers to women's spiritual agency and borderless concientización that reclaims their political and sexual subjectivities and rejects all forms of domestic or state-sanctioned violence. Reclaiming women's voices and uncovering their paths to resist violence and assert their sexual subjectivity are critical borderlands feminist projects engaged in by such researchers as Gloria González-López, Yvette Flores-Ortiz, and Enriqueta Valdez Curiel.

Borderlands Community Praxis

Validating connections to our communities that center on women's voices and experiences is integral to Chicana/Latina feminist sociology. Chicana feminist sociology explores how women express complex human agency within the transformations occurring in the borderlands between the United States and Mexico and beyond. Moreover, given the community praxis embodied within Chicana feminist sociology, developing research and policy initiatives or programs to address the economic marginality of women of all races-ethnicities and their families is essential. To illustrate this point, we briefly discuss two community-based projects anchored in a Chicana borderlands praxis: Sisters of Color United for Education, or SISTERS, in Denver, Colorado; and ENLACE (Engaging Latino Communities for Education) at the University of California, Santa Barbara.

SISTERS is a nonprofit, community-based organization established thirteen years ago and dedicated to improving comprehensive health and quality of life for women of color.[3] Through indigenous community leadership, SISTERS develops and conducts culturally proficient models of prevention, empowerment, and information sharing. The fundamental values that guide SISTERS' community work are empowerment, individual growth, social justice, health care as a human right, respect for differences, and a belief that the indigenous community has the strength, wisdom, and ability to navigate in mainstream society. Currently, SISTERS is engaged in a peer-led program to prevent HIV infection among Chicanas and Mexicanas in Denver.

Elisa Facio argues that a Chicana feminist praxis validates how empowerment has a different meaning for Chicanas participating in intervention programs. Generally, empowerment entails accessing power structures rather than dismantling, eradicating, and/or changing structures that are oppressive to their communities. The women desire to institutionalize programs that support their communities' goals in creating healthy and productive environments. Consequently, terminology like "healing and transformation" has replaced the term "empowerment" in teaching materials and implementation strategies. The notions of healing and transformation are influenced by Anzaldúa's theory of a new mestiza consciousness, which illustrates how the new mestiza adopts new perspectives toward dark-skinned people, women, and queers. In other words, we need to understand and interpret our worlds from our own academic indigenous standpoints.

The purpose of ENLACE is to identify "best practices" to improve the academic preparation of Latinos for higher education and to enhance their retention in college.[4] This project's objective is to strengthen families' "funds of knowledge" and build partnerships with the university, schools, families, and community-based agencies.[5] ENLACE has three local sites and has affected the lives of several hundred students in Ventura, Oxnard, and Isla Vista/Santa Barbara. As an educational project within the borderlands, one of its first tasks was to disrupt hierarchical relations between educational professionals and parents (mainly mothers) and situate the parents' experiences and insights into the core of ENLACE. This model assumes value and complexity within Latino cultures—value that is all too often unrecognized. Anzaldúa states: "Within us and within *la cultura chicana,* commonly held beliefs of the white culture attack commonly held beliefs of the Mexican culture, and both attack commonly held beliefs of the indigenous culture" (*Borderlands/La Frontera* 78).

Parents, especially mothers, guided a collaboration that resulted in programs that focused on the needs articulated by the community (for example, in Padres Adelante workshops). Concurrently ENLACE trained undergraduates, 90 percent of whom were first-generation Latino college students, to work with families as mentors and advocates in schools. This program did not assume a hierarchical model of learning but rather emphasized broad inclusion of women's voices into developing programmatic goals and evaluation models. This borderlands community praxis inverts power relationships and respects local ways of knowing. ENLACE's goals included enhancing family involvement in schools, increasing the leadership capacity of students and parents, improving the community's knowledge of schools, developing effective family-school negotiation skills with parents, effecting school-centered systemic change (such as working with the schools to be more flexible in their curricular or "track" assignments), and helping sensitize schools to the needs of local families.

All ninety-five undergraduates who have worked in the program graduated, and about one third have gone on for master's degrees, credential programs, or other graduate programs. These students' backgrounds mirror those of the students and families with whom they worked. They are strong symbols to the community that "¡sí, se puede!" And as Gloria Anzaludúa says: "I change myself, I change the world" (*Borderlands/La Frontera* 92). This is particularly important for Latinas since sometimes their families are reluctant to let them stay after school for enrichment programs; but when Chicana or Latina mentors are assigned, the outcomes tend to be positive. "Community empowerment" is not just about giving information to Latino families or community-based organizations. It's a more organic process that includes strengthening families' funds of knowledge of our own Latino undergraduates and those of the faculty, the schools, and the university. It is a reciprocal process.

The ENLACE y Avance experience leads us to consider how a Chicana feminist praxis can facilitate empowerment of our local communities. And what is empowerment? Empowerment is a process to change the nature and distribution of power in a particular cultural context. Empowerment begins when individuals and communities who lack power in a particular context—the schools, for instance—acquire knowledge and a language that assists them in unpacking institutional settings and power arrangements to change the conditions of their lives. The importance of energizing language to "deconstruct, construct" is an essential part of a borderlands feminist project (*Borderlands/La Frontera* 104).

Since at least the early 1990s, Anzaldúa has used the term "spiritual activism" to describe the transformative potential of borderlands subjects. Drawing on Anzaldúa, Keating argues that spiritual activism "begins with the personal yet moves outward, acknowledging our radical interconnectedness. This is spirituality for social change, spirituality that recognizes the many differences among us yet insists on our commonalities and uses these commonalities as catalysts for transformation" ("Charting Pathways" 18). SISTERS and ENLACE are two borderlands projects that embody three aspects of Anzaldúa's conceptualization of spiritual activism: transformative social change, community building, and a tolerance for ambiguity, that is, possessing mestiza consciousness.

Anzaldúa argues, "The knowledge that we are in symbiotic relationship to all that exists and co-creators of ideologies—attitudes, beliefs, and cultural values—motivates us to act collaboratively" ("(Un)natural bridges" 2). Here she paints a landscape with bold strokes, offering a vision of spiritual activism that bridges the community and the academy. SISTERS and ENLACE are engaged in empowerment anchored in indigenous community leadership that strengthens funds of knowledge and extends the principles of spiritual activism. Inverting power relations and respecting local ways of knowing are "the work of opening the gate to the stranger, within and without" (3). To eradicate hierarchies between the academy and local communities, we must build bridges across groups with different access to power and prestige. Anzaldúa argues that we must take responsibility for changing these social relations, and "we must risk being open to personal, political, and spiritual intimacy, to risk being wounded" (3).

Toward a Chicana Feminist Sociology

Our brief sketches of community empowerment in health care and education deploy a Chicana feminist sociology anchored in an activist interpretation of Anzaldúa's borderlands, or what we refer to as a borderlands community praxis. Chicana feminist sociology in the borderlands reveals the complex representations, experiences, and identities that Chicanas and Mexican women construct in the contexts established by globalization, transnational migration, and social formations and imaginaries that span national borders. The challenge facing Chicana feminist researchers is to establish our own genealogy, that is, to understand and interrogate our own social locations within the borderlands with an eye to learning about women, families, and children presented as "others," with caring and respect that allows us to "risk being wounded" ("(Un)natural bridges" 3).

In addition to operationalizing concepts such as "the borderlands," it is essential to interrogate "a new mestiza consciousness" within Chicana feminist sociology. Anzaldúa argues that the new mestiza consciousness validates Chicana selfhood by confronting traditions of male domination within our own communities, including men and male-identified women, and breaking down dualities of sexuality that promote heterosexism. Recognizing the "indígena" in the new mestiza is essential in the development of a politicized, racialized, feminist Chicana. The new mestiza consciousness is a consciousness of the borderlands, which includes "mental nepantilism" (*Borderlands/La Frontera* 100). "Nepantla" is a Náhuatl term meaning "in the middle," "tierra entre medio," or "in between," a state in which defining space(s) of mitigating and negotiating dualities takes place with the goal of healing and transformation.[6]

Anzaldúa attempts to construct a new activist subject, the new mestiza. Thus, as Chicana sociologists our task is twofold: to continue working in our communities by deploying a borderlands community praxis and to disrupt the master narrative of sociology by interpreting the lives of Chicanas through standpoints that bridge the academic with the indigenous, or as Sonia Saldívar-Hull states, a mestizaje consciousness.[7] Ultimately, "The struggle of the mestiza is above all a feminist one" (*Borderlands/La Frontera* 106).

CHAPTER 24

Embracing Borderlands:
Gloria Anzaldúa and Writing Studies

ANDREA A. LUNSFORD

This e-mail interview between the editors and Professor Lunsford took place in early 2008.

How Did Gloria E. Anzaldúa's work affect you and your work?

When I wrote to Gloria Evangelina Anzaldúa in early 1996 to ask if I might talk with her about the relationship between her work and the disciplines of rhetoric and writing studies and postcolonial studies, she didn't say "No" right away, but she wasn't very enthusiastic, either. After all, rhetoric and writing studies have a long reputation of being deeply complicit with colonizing practices of reading and writing (and speaking, too, for that matter): you must read this, not that; you must write this way, not that way. "Especially in composition," Anzaldúa pointed out, "rules are very strict: creating a thesis sentence, having some kind of argument, having a logical step-by-step progression, [this] goes all the way back to Aristotle and Cicero" ("Toward a Mestiza Rhetoric" 6). She was equally chary of postcolonial studies, saying she had grown impatient with trying to understand Homi Bhabha or Gayatri Spivak and just didn't have time to decipher the codes they and others seemed to depend on and demand that their readers acquire.

I persisted in my request, however, and eventually was fortunate enough to spend a day in face-to-face conversation and engage in many phone calls and back-and-forths as I transcribed and edited an interview that eventually appeared in a special issue of *JAC: A Journal of Composition Theory* called *Exploring Borderlands: Postcolonial and Composition Studies.*

My path toward that remarkable interview was a long one, beginning in the mid-1980s when I first came across *This Bridge Called My Back* and, later, *Borderlands/La Frontera*. I knew instinctively—viscerally—that I had encountered a voice that would be very important to me and to my field of study, and as I read and reread Anzaldúa's work, I began to understand the depth of that instinctive recognition. As a child in the rural hills of Tennessee, I grew up speaking a mountain dialect that I later learned was "incorrect," the language of hillbillies or "ridge runners," as the hill folk were often called. To be sure, I was speaking a form of so-called "standard" English that for the most part followed the "rules" but that bent them through the use of regionalisms and the kind of colorful metaphors and similes that characterized my grandmother's speech (to her, the kitchen cabinets would always be the "upper division" and prices were resolutely "high as a cat's back"). When I got to graduate school, I brought with me a strong southern accent and remnants of my Tennessee dialect, and in my second term a fellow student said, "My goodness, I need to apologize to you. I thought you were not very smart at all—well, you know, because of your accent." So while I certainly never experienced the kind of linguistic terrorism Anzaldúa describes in her work, I resonated strongly with her description of it. In addition, I was drawn, from the moment I first read her, to her voice and to the gorgeous way she worked with words, weaving them into strands that seemed like a lifeline of hope and resilience, of strength and clear-sightedness, of wit and wisdom. From Anzaldúa I learned most directly that all people have a chance to create and re-create themselves and that they can do so best through and with collaborations, those deep interactions with others through which we shape ourselves and our worlds. In 1988, when I had an opportunity as chair of the Conference on College Composition and Communication to address members of the central professional organization in rhetoric and writing studies, I drew on what I'd learned from Anzaldúa for the title and substance of my speech, "Composing Ourselves: Politics, Commitment, and the Teaching of Writing."

I carry many enduring memories from the days I spent with Anzaldúa in 1996 but none with more staying power than this: late in the afternoon, over tea, Anzaldúa turned the tables on me. I'd been asking her questions all day; now she had some for me. Leaning forward, she looked steadily at me in that direct way of hers and said, "So who is the Andrea you want to be seven to ten years from now? It's important to know since you are already creating her." It is now a little over ten years since Gloria Anzaldúa asked me that question. I have thought of it every week or so since and have tried to grow into the person I thought of that day. As you see, I'm still trying to do so in that careful, conscious, deliberate way Anzaldúa often modeled for us.

How did Anzaldúa's work affect your discipline? How did her work redefine your field?

As I've already suggested, so much of what Anzaldúa has to say dwells on coming to voice and on being heard, especially from a position within long-marginalized spaces. Surely this is what first touched a nerve with rhetoric and writing studies, a field that had struggled for recognition and for a hearing since its revival in the late '60s and early '70s. By the time I completed my Ph.D. in the late 1970s, a major flowering of scholarship in rhetoric and writing was well under way as the development of a number of graduate programs drew enthusiastic students to them. But these programs were always marginalized within English studies, always secondary to literary studies in ways that were oppositional when they should have been complementary. This struggle for disciplinary status and recognition was part of the lengthy culture wars within English, and those in rhetoric and writing studies worked determinedly to lay out a rigorous research agenda and then to build graduate programs, found journals and book series, and create conferences worthy of disseminating the new knowledge being developed in the field. In this atmosphere, Gloria Anzaldúa's work sounded a call to which those in rhetoric and writing responded immediately: here was a voice we recognized, one that gave us (and continues to give us) the courage of our convictions.

And what were those convictions? Certainly not the ones Anzaldúa sometimes attributed to the field, the gate-keeping, exclusionary, colonizing principles associated with stereotypical English schoolmarms. While those standardizing tendencies have been evident in the field, they ceased to be defining forces shortly after the mid–twentieth century. Researchers in rhetoric and writing were at the forefront of those calling for increased access to higher education, for closing what K. Patricia Cross and others called the "revolving door" (admit students in large numbers and then drum them out, usually through the introductory English or math classes) and replacing it with a welcome sign accompanied by support services aimed at making sure those who entered college had a good chance of succeeding. The 1974 "Students' Right to Their Own

Language" document, developed over two years and distributed by the Conference on College Composition and Communication, contained a detailed rationale for recognizing and valuing the home literacies of all students while offering them access to the so-called language of power and prestige.

These core principles of the field resonate strongly with Anzaldúa's work, which is one reason her essays and books are so widely taught in rhetoric and writing programs, from first-year writing classes through graduate seminars. Chapter 5 in *Borderlands*, "How to Tame a Wild Tongue," especially the discussion of "Linguistic Terrorism," captures one of the driving forces within the field of rhetoric and writing: giving students the opportunity to explore their own voices, to be heard by a wider community, to take pride in their language and take pride in themselves.

But Anzaldúa's work also raises challenges for the field. The paradigm shift writing studies underwent as it moved from a focus on finished products of writing to the processes that brought those products into being, for example, tended to reify or even essentialize students: for more than a decade researchers worked on "the" writing process, studying it in individual and diverse students, to be sure, but nevertheless slipping all too easily into assumptions about and characterizations of "the" student writer. It is impossible to read Anzaldúa without questioning such assumptions. As a result, I see her and her work as very important to the turn from process to social construction in writing studies and to later "post-process" theories of writing and writers. From ethnographic studies of highly diverse individual learners such as Marilyn Sternglass's longitudinal study *Time to Know Them* to Krista Ratcliffe's *Rhetorical Listening: Identification, Gender, Whiteness* or Cheryl Glenn's *A Rhetoric of Silence*, the best work in rhetoric and writing studies is deeply indebted to Anzaldúa's challenges.

Anzaldúa's work also influenced and underscored writing and rhetoric's view of writing and reading as deeply social activities, a move that led to studying collaboration and practices of co-authorship and group writing. Anzaldúa, of course, collaborated on a number of her projects, working with an architect to design her home, with artists in creating her children's books, with co-editors and co-authors, and with many others. "I think," she says, "that there is no such thing as a single author. I write my texts, but I borrow the ideas and images from other people. Sometimes I forget that I've borrowed them. . . . I do the composing, but it's taken from little mosaics of other people's lives, other people's perceptions. I take all of these pieces and rearrange them. When I'm writing, I always have the company of the reader" ("Toward a Mestiza Rhetoric" 19–20). Scholars of writing and rhetoric were among the first in the humanities to challenge the widespread disregard for texts produced by multiple authors, and Anzaldúa helped to inspire and sustain that work. Today, the digital revolution makes even more vividly clear how much of what we write and read and view is collaboratively produced—and how badly we need robust new theories of writing that will account for, accommodate, and help shape such practices (Laddaga). In pursuing this goal, especially as it calls for collaborating across diverse cultural and linguistic borders, Anzaldúa's work provides a solid foundation on which to build.

How do you envision Anzaldúa's writing and theories influencing the future directions of your discipline?

I have already begun to address this question in terms of Anzaldúa's groundbreaking work on subjectivity and agency. Her insistence that individuals carry many others within themselves is brilliantly illustrated in what she calls her nos/otras concept: "Now there is no such thing as an 'other.' The other is in you, the other is in me. . . . So when I try to articulate ideas, I try to do it from that place of occupying . . . the territory of my past and my ethnic community, my home community, the Chicano Spanish, the Spanglish; and the territory of the formal education, the philosophical/educational ideas I have internalized just by being alive" ("Toward a Mestiza Rhetoric" 8). Scholars of rhetoric and writing are among those working to craft new theories of agency that will accommodate Anzaldúa's vision of a subject that is not constructed wholly from without nor the product of radical individualism but something beyond such dichotomies, something on the mestiza borderlands of Anzaldúa's world.[1]

I also see Anzaldúa's work as foundational for a project that has engaged the field of rhetoric and writing for several decades: the issues surrounding language use mentioned earlier in regard to the "Students' Right to Their Own Language" document and related debates. Certainly this field helped lead the way in insisting that dialects of English are not inherently superior or inferior to one another. For most of the past thirty years this conversation has focused on recognizing and valuing students' home languages and using them as bridges to fluency in the range of English usually referred to as "standard." But Anzaldúa's brilliant mixing of dialects, languages, and genres has helped take this conversation to the next level. Following work such as Geneva Smitherman's *Talkin' and Testifin'*; Jacqueline Jones Royster's "When the First Voice You Hear Is Not Your Own"; Chris Schroeder, Helen Fox, and Patricia Bizzell's *ALT.DIS: Alternative Discourses and the Academy*; and Peter Elbow's "Writing in the Vernacular," scholars have begun a new examination of the hegemony of "standard" English in the academy and, indeed, to publish works written in other discourses, such as Lee Tonouchi's "Da State of Pidgin Address." The next decade will see much more exploration of using mixed dialects and languages within academic discourse, and I am excited by the prospects of further opening up this discourse to new and multiple voices, new and multiple ways of seeing and knowing the world we inhabit together.

At the end of my time with Gloria Anzaldúa, I asked what her "wildest dream" would be for a young girl who wanted to grow up to be a writer. "I would hope," Anzaldúa said, "for her to have a peaceful community in all the different worlds, in all the different cultures, in all the different realities. I would hope for her to be a true mestiza." She went on to say that such a dream didn't seem possible right now. "To live is to struggle. Life hurts," she said. But we can mitigate that hurt in a society where a little girl "can pursue her interests and her dreams without being too much constrained by gender roles or racial law or the different epistemologies that say, 'This is the way reality is.' I don't know if that's ever going to happen. But I hope so. Sometimes I think so." In my estimation, Gloria Anzaldúa's life and work went a good way toward making this dream happen. It is now up to the rest of us to take up the challenge, and it is my hope and my conviction that the field of rhetoric and writing studies will do its share of this most necessary work.

V

TODAS SOMOS NOS/OTRAS: TOWARD A "POLITICS OF OPENNESS"

CHAPTER 25

Hurting, Believing, and Changing the World: My Faith in Gloria Anzaldúa

SUZANNE BOST

I was raised, in part, by my Catholic grandmother, and I grew up caring for her increasingly disabled body.[1] She was a paradox: a feminist (at least in my terms) who went to college and worked full time as a nurse; she quit work after marrying at thirty and spent the rest of her life sitting with her rosary in front of the radio (and, later, television), raising her (and, later, her daughter's) children. She started suffering from rheumatoid arthritis somewhere between the two sets of children, and the disease gradually crippled her. By the time I reached puberty, she was blind from cataracts and crooked, with one leg dead in a brace and the other eight inches shorter with a platform shoe too heavy for her to lift alone. While my parents worked, I sat in Grandma's room and listened to soap operas, clicking rosary beads, and the sound of my grandmother's pain emerging in surprised gasps and throaty exhalations.

I'm still trying to understand my grandmother, and her faith has always been a stumbling block. She believed in miracles. She believed that the crucifix she gave me when I left for college had been buried in Chicago with my grandfather and miraculously reappeared in time for my move from Albuquerque to Austin. My repulsion from Catholic church politics has secularized my thinking, but I miss (*long* for) the seemingly anachronistic faith that my grandmother maintained, the miracles, and the jarring sound of rosaries prayed against the backdrop of *The Price Is Right* and *As the World Turns*.

One of my grandmother's more remarkable acts of faith intersected with her disability. She offered up each of her pains, individually, for particular causes, like the poor in Ireland, the victims of war, or her granddaughter's final exams. Each time she got into or out of her wheelchair, the gasps were articulated into prayers. My initial response was to be

suspicious of this Catholic tendency to romanticize suffering, particularly women's suffering. But lately I've been trying to take seriously my
grandmother's faith that her pain was productive. She examined each
sensation, created a path for it from her body to some other trouble
across the world, and believed in that connection.

Here is where the work of Gloria Anzaldúa comes in. I didn't see it
when I first read *Borderlands* as a student, but later it became increasingly visible to me that pain and faith are both central to Anzaldúa's
mestiza feminist politics. Most critics have avoided these aspects of her
work, likely for the same reasons that I looked away when my grandmother was simultaneously suffering and praying: fear of pain, fear of
vulnerability, and fear of committing the intellectual sin of belief in the
supernatural. My first "serious" encounter with Anzaldúa was in a literary theory course, around 1992, in which "La conciencia de la mestiza"
appeared somewhere between Derrida and Butler. I read the essay with
the same attention to différence, artifice, and ideology as I had applied
to the canon of "high theory," and I recall discussing her comparison of
making tortillas and making identity with the same pose of theoretical
rigor that I had been learning to "master" all semester. We didn't think
about the smells, the feelings, or the physical contortions she inscribes
within mestiza consciousness. I would have been afraid to acknowledge
her personal rituals, her altar to Coatlalopeuh, her belief in magic, and
her confessions of shame and vulnerability. I didn't take these gestures
literally because I assumed that to do so would undermine intellectual
seriousness (hers? my own?) and discredit Chicana feminism. Was I simply unable to *see* her statements of faith and feeling, or did I deliberately
ignore what I had supposed were flaws?

Rereading Anzaldúa's work years later, with the confidence and security of a tenure-track job and with the altered attentiveness of a
teacher called upon to explain her ideas, Anzaldúa's corporeal and intellectual "transgressions" became more visible to me. I couldn't side-
step Anzaldúa's personal confessions after teaching my Women's Studies
students that the personal is political. Discussing these "transgressions"
openly in the classroom stirred our passions and imaginations. Listening
to students' responses to *Borderlands*—both the guarded criticism that
feminists cannot risk such "irrational" discourse and the personal revela-
tions of faith—called up my grandmother's prayers and miracles. But
trying to believe in the supernatural is painful.

As Anzaldúa outlines mestiza consciousness in *Borderlands,* she repeatedly insists that realizing her theoretical ideals *is* a painful process. A
little-noted qualification in a much-discussed section of "La conciencia

de la mestiza" explains that "though it is a source of intense pain, its energy comes from continual creative motion that keeps breaking down the unitary aspect of each new paradigm" (102). "La herencia de Coatli- cue" provides another way of thinking about the corporeal and psycho- logical work of mestiza consciousness: "sweating," with a "headache," "voy cagándome de miedo," Anzaldúa describes "allowing myself to fall apart," dismantling and rebirthing the self to resist rigid identification and fear of the other (70). Though contemporary medicine views pain and vulnerability as unacceptable deviations from the norm—deviations that should be eradicated with "health care" commodities—the affect of Coatlicue states is grounded in ancient Mesoamerican beliefs about the simultaneity of creation and destruction, sacrifice and regeneration, as sacred boundary states. Anzaldúa's understanding of pain as a sacred sen- sation is also derived from Catholic ideology, and *Borderlands* includes a poem, "Holy Relics," that recalls the posthumous dismemberment of the body of Saint Teresa of Avila and imagines the strong faith of those who were cured by "pinched off" pieces of her flesh (178–80). Saint Teresa herself experienced her personal illnesses and the punctures of stigmata alike as ecstasy: "Siempre quería el alma . . . estar muriendo de este mal" (The soul would always want to be dying of this illness) (176). Beyond conventional feminine suffering, Saint Teresa's pain, like that of my grandmother and perhaps of Anzaldúa, was powerful, the sensation of crossing beyond the boundaries of one's own body and mind.[2]

In the more personal medium of her interviews, Anzaldúa revealed how much the pain underlying her theoretical ideas was grounded in her own body's painful menstruation and subsequent hysterectomy; her em- pathy with other bodies, animals, and the environment; and, ultimately, her diabetes.[3] Just as *mestiza consciousness* requires continual openness— "nothing is thrust out, the good the bad and the ugly, nothing rejected, nothing abandoned" (*Borderlands/La Frontera* 101)—Anzaldúa's own body was open to the world around her. "I feel a real unification with people, real identification with someone or something—like the grass. It's so painful that I have to cut the connection. But I can't cut the connection, so instead of putting a shield between myself and you and your pain, I put a wall inside, between myself and my feelings" (*Inter- views/Entrevistas* 26–27). Since eradicating the pain was not possible, Anzaldúa changed the way she experienced the sensation. One of her fi- nal essays, "now let us shift," shows how diabetes led her to reframe her suffering and to reshape her physical being in the world: "You've chosen to compose a new history and self. . . . Your ailing body is no longer a hindrance but an asset, witnessing pain, speaking to you, demanding touch. Es tu cuerpo que busca conocimiento; along with dreams your body's the royal road to consciousness" (558–59).

"Ailing" opens new avenues of consciousness. I find Margrit Shildrick's postmodern, feminist ethic of "leaky bodies" particularly compelling. In resistance to the "illusory closure" defended by biomedical convention, "the experience of illness or disability might itself constitute new subject positions not just resistant but excessive to the norms of the Western logos" (214–15), ones that are fluid, open, intertwined with caregivers and prostheses. Anzaldúa accepted this permeability:

> Although all your cultures reject the idea that you can know the other, you believe that besides love, pain might open this closed passage by reaching through the wound to connect. Wounds cause you to shift consciousness—they either open you to the greater reality normally blocked by your habitual point of view or else shut you down. . . . Using wounds as openings to become vulnerable and available (present) to others means staying in your body. ("now let us shift" 571–72)

Valuing wounds as openings to others defies all conventional wisdom about safety, sensation, and appropriate political/intellectual behavior, but perhaps that is because such "wisdom" has been governed by a competitive, self-defensive, and anesthetic sensibility.

In *Transforming Feminist Practice*, a book Anzaldúa called "the next step" in feminism, Leela Fernandes advocates "using one's suffering as the guide and basis for activism," using the sufferer's experience of oppression to "make a fundamental break from the logic of oppression" (72). Though most sufferers refuse to accept their threatened boundaries and the oppressed sometimes make the most likely oppressors, Fernandes suggests that spirituality is the key to finding interconnections with other people and, thus, to breaking this cycle of oppression:

> Spirituality can serve as a tremendous source of power that can enable us to challenge some of our deepest practices of identification, and can lead us to understand our self as an infinite, unbounded source of divinity, spiritual strength and empowerment. It leads us to question our ingrained assumptions regarding the boundaries of individual autonomy, agency and rationality. (37)

Rather than endorsing or critiquing feminist spirituality, I want to highlight the shape of identity it delineates. Spirituality assumes humans' vulnerability to forces beyond themselves and the incorporation of a "spirit" or "soul" that transcends mortal limits. Those who accept spirituality thus accept some forms of boundary crossing and relational attachments of the ego: acceptances that could reshape human interaction. Unlike rhetorical appeals to "Christian" compassion that are missionary or (neo)colonialist in their intent to reform the rest of the world in the image of western Christianity, Fernandes's notion of spirituality requires a continual relinquishing of one's own sensibilities, questioning of one's own beliefs, and expansion of one's identity to welcome others.

The idealism of spirituality is a powerful theoretical and critical tool. Whether or not one believes in the divine, adopting this practice of thinking beyond everyday perception could expand possibility beyond the status quo. Though many critics avoid Anzaldúa's spiritual writings, this avoidance misses the crux of her thinking about bodies, identities, and politics. Her final essays are almost entirely dedicated to spiritual activism, and her late collaborations with AnaLouise Keating indicate Anzaldúa's belief in the power of "spirit" to expand our vision beyond competitiveness, self-defensiveness, and anesthesia. Anzaldúa writes, "Power comes from being in touch with your body, soul, and spirit, and letting their wisdom lead you" ("now let us shift" 570); and Keating writes:

> Viewed from within the Soul's presence there's no "me" or "you." There's just "us." And yet this "us" has been shattered and fragmented—split into a multiplicity of pieces marked by the many forms our identities take. I believe, with all my heart, that spiritual activism can assist us in creating new ways to move through these boundaries. ("Charting Pathways" 19)

The subject most suited to Anzaldúa's politics of openness cannot be motivated by the boundaries of individual bodies or personal needs. Invoking the spirit enables Anzaldúa, Keating, and Fernandes to push our thinking beyond conventionally assumed boundaries, and the academic reluctance to treat things of the heart or soul signals the productive friction of these "less-structured thoughts, less-rigid categorizations" ("now let us shift" 568) against the rules of rational argumentation. Perhaps there is something wrong with arguments that have no feeling.

The passionate mourning that has followed Anzaldúa's death shows how her lifework bleeds into the words of those who have incorporated her ideas and the strength of her rebellion. Inés Hernández-Ávila describes her grief as a gradual embodiment of Anzaldúa's absence: "My body is reluctantly registering in every cell that you are physically no

longer with us" (in Gonzales and Rodriguez). At http://gloria.chicanas
.com, an online altar of memorials, Alicia Gaspar de Alba writes, "Her
passing is extremely personal and painful to me (as it is, I'm sure, to
many of us), and feels like a loss of a higher part of myself" (*Rest in
Peace Gloria*). These personal responses unravel the boundaries between
bodies. Changing "your relationship to your body, and, in turn, to other
bodies and to the world" ultimately, in Anzaldúa's thinking, changes
the world ("now let us shift" 574). These body-opening gestures are
corporeally risky (painful) and theoretically risky (super-rational), but
they push us clearly beyond the static forms and defended states of patriarchy, racism, and militarism. I believe that Anzaldúa has had such an
impact because she took these risks. The mourners at her online altar
seem to have accepted the risk, this leap of faith, bearing out Anzaldúa's
optimism: "We're going to leave the rigidity of this concrete reality and
expand it. I'm very hopeful" (*Interviews/Entrevistas* 285).

As an academic, I was trained to be skeptical, rational, and critically
distant—not hopeful. Anzaldúa's writing revolutionized my thinking in
many ways, but the most important "shift" is in trespassing boundaries.
This is not so much a "direction for future thought" as it is a relinquishing of direction. Anzaldúa made apparent the power of sensations that
exceed the rules of cultural repression, "health management," and academic neutrality. The intellectual boundaries I had been taught to police
now seem to be false limitations. Rereading Anzaldúa taught me to look
for the unexpected and the illegitimate in the texts I encounter, to read
with the desire to shake up, rather than to confirm, established theories. I've learned how much we lose by using the same rules and rulers
to measure new works. I hesitate to propose a specific methodology—
based on faith, politics, or a new "wisdom"—because it is the unlearn-
ing of assumptions and methodologies that has turned out to be the
most powerful "direction" for my own critical practice. Not following
the directions mapped out by my theoretical and feminist education is
what routed my thinking back to my grandmother. I have been thinking
about the apparent anachronism of my grandmother's faith, her defiance
of dominant modes of thought. Though "faith" seems to be everywhere
in mainstream culture, my grandmother's faith savored pain as a gesture
of love for others, even as *The Price is Right* and *As the World Turns* pro-
jected a very different ethic in the background. This ridiculous, anachronistic, unbelievable faith is the most revolutionary gesture I can think
of (for now, at least). It takes faith and imagination to be hopeful about
changing the world.

CHAPTER 26

Feels Like "Carving Bone": (Re)Creating the Activist-Self, (Re)Articulating Transnational Journeys, while Sifting through Anzaldúan Thought

KAVITHA KOSHY

When I write it feels like I'm carving bone. It feels like I'm creating my own face, my own heart.
GLORIA E. ANZALDÚA, *BORDERLANDS/LA FRONTERA*

At a very critical time in my life, in a graduate Women's Studies classroom in Texas, I was introduced to Gloria Anzaldúa's work. To say the least it was a life-changing encounter of epiphanic proportions. As the epigraph suggests, Anzaldúa made me want to reach into myself and create theory. Since then, throughout my emotional, spiritual, political, and theoretical growth, Anzaldúa's writings have led the way. From articulating and validating my marginalized experiences to ensuring that I do not lose myself in oppositional stances, her words keep me afloat on a sea of in-betweenness—so much so that I have come to claim liminality as my reality.

Coming from a dualistic political standpoint as a social activist in India, the contentious politics that I had come to live and breathe was an endless cyclical conundrum. It was also characterized by an unforgiving, reactionary mindset, which I carried with me into my U.S. Women of Colors class in graduate school. One of our assigned texts was *This Bridge Called My Back: Writings by Radical Women of Color;* listening to animated discussions among my peers made the book come alive. It kindled within me the yearning to "enter into the lives of others," but I did not know how. And then Anzaldúa reached out to me with these words in "La Prieta":

We are the queer groups, the people that don't belong anywhere, not in the dominant world nor completely within our own respective cultures . . . because we do not fit *we are a threat.* [However, our] different affinities are not opposed to each other. In El Mundo Zurdo I with my own affinities and my people with theirs can live together and transform the planet. (209, her italics)

In this passage Anzaldúa refers to an inclusive "we." By not alluding to any identity categories, she invited me, the reader, to join her in creating a place for all queers, a new place of belonging. What grabbed my attention was that she risked talking about a nonbinary politics amid a very polarized U.S. feminist movement of the 1980s, and with that she drew me into her theorizing. Besides, she was addressing all of us who had dared to transgress the lines drawn to separate us from one another. We the misfits finally had a common ground in "in-betweenness" or a shared uncertainty in liminality and the hopeful vision of El Mundo Zurdo to work toward.

An Attempt at "Carving Bone"

Born in India, I inherited and learned to live within a society stratified by gender, class, caste, and religion. Like those in most societies rooted in exclusionary, binary thinking, I grew up conscious of both who I was and who I was not. Hindu meant "not Muslim" and Christian meant "not Hindu." Middle-class meant "not working class." "White-collar" meant "not blue-collar." "Brahmin" meant "not dalit."[1] Man meant "not woman," and so on. In due course, unable to tolerate the injustice and poverty that I saw around me, I earned a social work degree and participated in two social movements in India: the indigenous people's movement and the women's movement. Because of my activism, I was sometimes deemed a leftist or a troublemaker. Herein lie my earliest memories of liminality: the liminal experience of the constant back and forth between a middle-class upbringing and work with people who were mostly dispossessed, displaced from their lands, denied their right to livelihood, often victims/survivors of abuse. Caught in the daily struggles that keep movements going, I was unaware that my politics was firmly entrenched in the distinct center/margin binary: on the left of the slash was the oppressor (usually the government, sometimes capitalist patriarchy) and on the right, the victim.[2] The lines were drawn such that either you are with us/them or you are against us/them. Two simple choices existed between revolution and status quo. My naïve revolution was one in which those on the margins would replace those at the center. Power relations were merely to be switched around without addressing the fact that the naked force of power and the hierarchies that structure our lives would remain unquestioned, despite the "revolution" of my dreams. I also had failed to recognize my own privileged status: that I could "choose" to be a social activist rather than be "forced" by adverse circumstances to become one. In reality, I had the privilege to disengage whenever I wanted to.

I became a "woman of color" from the moment I set foot on U.S. soil. I was thrust into the arms of this pan-identity without warning. And within a few months I was clinging to it as if my life depended on it. I discovered that making alliances would come quite easily to me, and yet these alliances could disappear, in light of our failure to weave into the script the complexity that each person brings to the table. As a matter of fact, for the most part, I did find a sense of community with some "others": a sisterhood built on a loosely shared victimhood based on similar experiences of racism and ethnocentrism within U.S. society. I soon learned that sisterhood was not automatic. There existed barriers bolstered by different historical experiences, gaps between those who grew up relatively free of oppression and those who did not. How does one address the experience and repercussions of different kinds of oppression? We were not in the "Oppression Olympics,"[3] but the wide chasm of racialized experiences that existed between us needed to be recognized and bridged . . . an opportunity, maybe, to theorize differently.

I became an "other-other" overnight. Unidentifiable skin tone. Lighter shade of brown. Untraceable genealogy. I did not quite fit traditional U.S. binaries. In real terms, I did not know which box to check. Thus, my fixation with transnational politics and forms of activism started when I was forced to come to terms with my "othered" status in the United States. Sweeping generalizations and misrepresentations about my many cultures (there is no singular "East Indian culture") and my "otherness" sought to envelop and/or dismiss me, as I discovered the heart of western ethnocentrism. There appeared to be no room for complexity in terms of context, experiences, and affiliations. At first I allowed myself to be tokenized, representing whole cultures to curious outsiders. For someone living for the first time in a foreign country, this meant that at least I would not be invisible. I watched as my experiences were exoticized and only the bizarre happenings in my part of the world made it to U.S. American television.

And then something in me snapped. I chose to retaliate. I wrote furiously, framing a counterattack. As fate would have it, once again Anzaldúa scooped me up while I was hurtling through a righteous rage. She put my excruciating pain into words: "The U.S.-Mexican border es *una herida abierta* where the Third World grates against the first and bleeds. And before a scab forms it hemorrhages again, the lifeblood of two worlds merging to form a third country—a border culture" (*Borderlands/La Frontera* 25). She acknowledged transnational realities and captured my attention through the power of the metaphor of the border, the ruptures, and the wounds. At the same time she pointed to the futility of an oppositional mindset: "All reaction is limited by, and dependent on, what it is reacting against. Because the counterstance stems from a problem with authority—outer as well as inner—it's a step towards liberation from cultural domination. But it is not a way of life" (*Borderlands/La Frontera* 100). Here was another awakening followed by a series of realizations, that reactionary politics has its limits. Anzaldúa cautions us that all rebuttals are locked into a tainted status quo. They may appear as possible starting points for reclaiming our waning subjectivities, but they cannot become our ultimate goals.

Strategically Making Nepantla, the Liminal, the Transnational, "Home"

In my search for alternatives to an oppositional mindset I have found strength in "nepantla," a Náhuatl word that Anzaldúa uses to describe places of ambiguity and change. Nepantla has become the liminal reality that I now occupy between worlds and contradictory stances, the shaky ground I stand on while choosing to perform the role of a "supreme border crosser" (or what Anzaldúa calls a "nepantlera"). Within nepantla lie immense possibilities for transforming transnational spaces through what I call "nepantlera-activism." In this essay, with the intent of "carving bone," I will flesh out a nepantlera-act that specifically relates to a form of activism that can transform the volatile nature of the in-between. This act, risking the personal, political, and spiritual, has been at the core of Anzaldúa's activism, where the visionary meets the pragmatist and a spiritual activism combines with deliberate actions and physical pain to transform material realities.

Risking the Personal, Political, and Spiritual

You distend this more inclusive puente to unknown corners—you don't build bridges to safe and familiar territories, you have to risk making mundo nuevo, have to risk the uncertainty of change.
GLORIA E. ANZALDÚA, "NOW LET US SHIFT"

Being able to critically occupy liminality requires a willingness to take risks. The risk here lies in the uncertainty of in-betweenness and the creativity that must transform it. For example, for feminist theorists, risk taking can be in the form of occupying the precarious ground between oppositional forms of feminist consciousness and nonoppositional stances. In other words, despite being immersed in realities that are devoid of social justice, we respond in nonreactionary ways. These acts may take many forms and may require exposing the complexity of every situation, every person. We choose an alternative course of action or nepantlera-acts that may require something like recognizing our own "complex speaking positions."[4] Or we can take on something as risky as challenging the binary designation of the label "feminist" itself, shaking the very foundations of feminist activism. In other words, the exposure of the taintedness of our reality implicates us all, uncovering a commonality, a possible starting point.

Nepantleras who risk subverting traditional identity categories realize that those who resist change might also resist them. By rejecting labels and yet finding nonbinary ways of identifying, nepantleras are "threats" to the dominant/accepted ways of existence. What was once considered home, too, can become unsafe and dangerous. In fact, nepantleras who question the existence of categories/homes rather than take comfort in them run the risk of being ostracized or driven out. Exposing the falsities and fears within categories can be dangerous, for we jolt those who share/claim this space out of their own complacency. In my own life, in order to transgress the binaries of gender, ethnicity, religion, caste, and so on, my Indian nationality became an inclusive identity that I embraced until that too became insufficient in relation to a growing global consciousness. I could not fathom why Indian meant "not Pakistani" or why during communal riots Indian Muslims were asked time and again to prove their "Indianness." I began to see the limits of all labels despite attempts to make them more expansive and inclusive, the limits to any kind of border policing or cartography.

The danger of occupying the in-between space of nepantla lies not only in being seen as a threat to the dominant discourse but also as being seen as a threat to one's own cultural group. By rejecting and criticizing the hierarchical ways (racist and patriarchal beliefs) that circulate among one's "own," the possibility of being viewed as subversive by family or peers is imminent. As Anzaldúa notes while discussing her decision to critique her mexicano upbringing: "In exposing my family and my culture I'm [seen as] betraying it and them" (*Interviews/Entrevistas* 227). We risk being called "race traitors." Stepping outside of social/cultural roles by refusing to fit in and by choosing not to be blind to internal contradictions, nepantleras risk being attacked, wounded, or even killed. For example, in the transnational space critiquing what one's nation-state does in the name of nationalism or "homeland security" can be viewed as unpatriotic. Yet as a nepantlera I find myself consciously being disloyal to categories such as "nation" or "culture" in my rejection of the restrictiveness of national or cultural boundaries.

The "fear of being different" prevents us from going against the grain (Anzaldúa, *Interviews/Entrevistas* 264) and deters the taking of risks. This fear causes us to fragment the self, revealing what we think might be acceptable to others and keeping the subversive, unacceptable side hidden. Anzaldúa in her writing has risked the personal, political, and spiritual by "disclos[ing] intimate details, beliefs, and emotions" (Keating, "Risking the Personal" 2). Despite knowing that she runs the risk of being dismissed, Anzaldúa claims a politics wherein "spiritual realities," "imaginal realities," and the "inner subjective life" are all incorporated. Her greatness, in my view, in no way diminishes with the vast amounts of self-disclosure in her writing. She neither fragments the mind-body-spirit connection nor prioritizes one over the other. Unlike most political activists/academics, who often fail to acknowledge spirituality or the spiritual commitment/component intrinsic to working for change, Anzaldúa's spiritual activism supports and sustains her political vision. Personal and political change are so intertwined that they occur simultaneously ("now let us shift" 568–74).

While presenting versions of this paper at conferences, self-identified people of color have asked me if I have considered the possibility that those belonging to socially dominant groups (such as the category "white") may find the nonbinary approach that I call for and promote convenient; after all, it appears that people of color are willing to meet them halfway. Am I inviting those with any kind of privilege to occupy the slash that separates them from those with fewer privileges, without their having to give up any power? Do I offer an escape route for those seeking to avoid taking responsibility? It is possible that some people with privilege could misinterpret this invitation to occupy liminality or deliberately bypass the step that goes along with nonbinariness that requires that they radically relinquish, let alone recognize, their powerful locations vis-à-vis their new, less powerful allies. This possibility makes bridging all the more risky. Yet, fully aware of the betrayal and deadlocks, setbacks and fractures, and the likelihood of finding new "others" in nepantla, it becomes imperative that we view alliance making as a process and the taking of risks as an aspect intrinsic to it. One realizes that it is a risk to be open to "others" and that we are vulnerable to the possibility of being hurt again and again. Nonetheless, occupying in-between spaces requires consciously giving up safe spaces and power; that is, we are consciously risking the reality of the bridge.

A Step Closer to El Mundo Zurdo

With Anzaldúa's theories of nepantla and nepantleras that offer alternative approaches to acting in the world, more flexibility, and room for creativity, I have tried to redirect and transform my own activism. Her open style has also made me brave enough to risk divulging my own personal contradictions. Through her example, it is possible to connect the self and the body to the writing and to reach into one's innermost thoughts and "carve bone," so that I/you may "create my/your own face." This is an invitation to an arduous journey during which we can learn to move beyond and above the narrowness of binary thinking.

I dream of more inclusive spaces where the identities I carry with me do not limit my ability to connect with others. Because it is inclusive and nonbinary, nepantlera-activism is seamless and boundless. As scholars continue to apply Anzaldúa's powerful words, the hope is that more concrete and more creative strategies for social change will emerge. The Anzaldúan legacy has made me fearless, open, sensitive, and vulnerable: to inhabit complexity and liminality effectively; to risk disidentification,[5] as a conscious step toward establishing new common ground with others; to live in the space between margin and center, complicating rather than essentializing these so-called "oppositional" positions. Instead of defining what we believe in by what we reject, may we define our reality as immersed in both. This paper is an interpretation of Anzaldúa's legacy, one among many that together channel our collective energies toward making El Mundo Zurdo a palpable reality.

CHAPTER 27

Shifting

KELLI ZAYTOUN

You stop in the middle of the field and, under your breath, ask the spirits—
animals, plants, y tus muertos—to help you string together a bridge of
words.

GLORIA ANZALDÚA, "NOW LET US SHIFT"

I asked Gloria Anzaldúa to help me write this essay. It wasn't the first
time I'd called on her to inspire me, but it was the first as mis muertos.
No difference, really. She always seemed to me to be someone not of
this world, even as she rested her tiny frame in a chair in our class circle,
as real as each of us fervent graduate students. She asked us to introduce ourselves: "Tell me your purpose—not your major or where you're
from—but what your life means." *Motivated by the need to understand,*
you crave to be what and who you are (540).[1] As we revealed ourselves,
it became clear that although each of us participated in a world of individual struggle, we also shared a need to connect, to give back, to
be with each other, to make the world better. Our inner worlds col-
lided when we dared to share our desires and visions. Gloria Anzaldúa
wrote what she lived and lived what she wrote. *Change requires more*
than words on a page—it takes perseverance, creative ingenuity, and acts
of love (574). She offered us her words, her presence, her acts; all were
gifts to help strengthen our interconnectedness. To me, her work was
about extending consciousness, strengthening the foundations of inner,
personal awareness and the knowledge and potential of nos/otras, our
oneness with others.

I have stopped in the middle of a field, a picture in my mind, in yoga
class last Monday during shavasana (calm, relief, after paying attention

to movement, balance, the body). Shavasana, corpse pose. Muerta a muerta. This thought enters my mind: Isn't it uncannily prescient that one of Gloria's last published pieces was titled "now let us shift"? With her death came a shift in responsibility, a call to us younger-generation writers, activists, and cultural theorists, las nepantleras jóvenes. As Gloria Anzaldúa stood for the final time on the edge of this life, she offered us one last glimpse into the way of knowing that brought us *Borderlands* and other gems. "now let us shift" showcases her work on conocimiento, or "that aspect of consciousness urging you to act on the knowledge gained" (577). The path of conocimiento is a bridge between personal and collective consciousness, desire and action, destruction and growth, of our selves and of the world. Part of Anzaldúa's legacy is an under-standing of and calling to this path: *step through the doorways between worlds / leaving huellas for others to follow* (576). She forged the path, and now the work shifts to us; those following in Gloria's footsteps are left to envision and enact the possibilities of conocimiento.

I heard Gloria Anzaldúa speak early in my career as a graduate student as I was floundering to find a way to link my (what seemed very disjointed) interests in developmental psychology, memoir, and feminist theory. I was one of a couple hundred students and faculty who had gathered one night to listen to Anzaldúa present her concept of conocimiento. I watched as she drew a chalked line from the left corner of the board upward to the right. Along the line were small, square breaks, or what she called "way stations," stops along the path, the journey toward con-sciousness. I scribbled notes on the back of my program. Drawing path-ways was not uncommon for me as a student of cognitive development theory, the study of changes in mental abilities across one's lifespan. I had grown skeptical of most approaches for their grounding in western assumptions and one-size-fits-all prescriptions about what constitutes a well-developed decision maker and knower—a distinctive *self* in rela-tion to others. I had read criticisms by feminists of traditional theories for their overvaluing of self-sufficiency and independence and their lack of emphases on relational capacities, like empathy and decision making based on how others are affected. With the emergence of postmodern and postcolonial theorizing, feminist developmentalists also had called for more approaches that reflect how a sense of self and meaning change across social contexts. I, too, was curious about how personal identity develops in cultures that encourage their members to consider not only themselves and other humans but animals, plants, the earth, and the spirits when acting in this world. I had often wanted to know why some people were inspired to activism while others were not. I wondered if certain psychological capacities, such as the ability to be empathetic, to appreciate difference in others, and to act in socially responsible ways, were faculties (facultades) that could be encouraged.

The evening of her talk, Gloria Anzaldúa described her theory of conocimiento. Later, in "now let us shift," she expounded on the details of this seven-stage pathway and offered a nuanced and more expansive perspective on psychological development. Conocimiento illustrates a journey through which the individual engages in the mental and the social dimensions of life, fluctuating their focus from "inner work" to "public acts" and back to inner work again (540). Her stage theory sustains components of traditional developmental approaches, such as the concepts of stability and change, and an examination of how individuals' sense of who they are cycles between differentiating from, then integrating with, their relationships. However, because her trajectory is cyclical (the title of the first stage is "an ending, a beginning"), Anzaldúa avoids a problematic assumption inherent in traditional theories: that development progresses linearly, through invariant, qualitatively different mental capacities. Her theory is unique because it does not lend itself to the ranking of psychological abilities. All tasks and experiences in each stage are equally complex and valuable.

Conocimiento offers a pathway to understanding how a range of individual experiences (emotional, cognitive, spiritual, imaginal, bodily) are linked to the social world.[2] Each informs and influences the others. In the first stage, el arrebato, an upheaval in one's view, in one's comfort with the world, occurs. Forced into the second stage, nepantla, or transition, the awareness that change is necessary is piqued: *yesterday's mode of consciousness pinches like an outgrown shoe* (549). The third stage, the Coatlicue state, represents the debilitating condition brought on by the burden of knowing that change is eminent. The stages that follow—which Anzaldúa names *the call . . . el compromiso . . . the crossing and conversion; putting Coyolxauhqui together . . . new personal and collective "stories"; the blow-up . . . a clash of realities;* and *shifting realities . . . acting out the vision of spiritual activism*—entail a coming out of despair and engaging in the reconstructing of self and connection with others. As reconstruction occurs, identity categories used to describe oneself may change to broader, more inclusive terms. With the understanding that identity categories are temporary and fluid, that which divides us from others begins to dissolve; senses of commonality and empathy are ignited. Within stage seven, shifting realities, one yearns for and learns to work with others in positive social transformation.

Recognizing spiritual inquiry and creative acts (including acts of the body) as forms of knowing, Gloria Anzaldúa contributes new avenues for exploring how self, meaning, and connection are constructed. *Through creative engagements, you embed your experiences in a larger frame of reference, connecting your personal struggles with those of other beings on the planet, with the struggles of the Earth itself* (542). Connection does not end with links to other humans; it includes all material and nonmaterial dimensions of life. With such an awareness of an embodied sense of connection comes the motivation to work toward social change. I believe that this is one of Anzaldúa's most valuable legacies: her focus on how personal and political consciousness are inspired and linked. She offered us new terms to use in theorizing and mobilizing our abilities to act collectively. *You call the function that arouses the awareness that beneath individual separateness lies a deeper interrelatedness "la naguala"* (569). Gloria Anzaldúa's theories and language transform what it means to be an activist into a deeper, more spiritual journey. My sisters and I are nepantleras, spiritual activists, traveling on "this bridge we call home." *May we meet illness, death and adversity with strength / may we dance in the face of our fears* (575).

As we set out into the future with Gloria Anzaldúa's parting words a wind on our backs, we are reminded that change does not happen in stillness; we are reminded to act. By practicing conocimiento we can give birth to our potentials, as individuals and as the collective force we have yet to know. I believe that future social change depends on this deeper awareness of the cycling of the self and its relationships to others and the world; it depends on our willingness to steep in the depths of the Coatlicue state and understand that this inner work, engaging in the personal experience of our emotional, spiritual, and physical states, is integral to the process of social change. Indeed, acknowledging and experiencing these states are what feed the mind. *In the deep fecund cave of gestation lies not only the source of your woundedness and your passion, but also the promise of inner knowledge, healing, and spiritual rebirth (the hidden treasures) waiting for you to bear them at the surface* (554).

Part of Anzaldúa's legacy is the consistent reminder (particularly to academics!) that social consciousness is *more than intellectual;* it's *bodymindsoul* work (554). Discovering our connectedness to others and, later, our potential to act means facing our inner work, bringing down the walls of fear, anger, and other defense mechanisms (that may have been useful at one time but are now outworn) in order to trust others. She reminds us that each time we emerge from Coatlicue, each time we put Coyolxauhqui together, we revise our identities and rigid ways of being and knowing and expand our potential to see the similar pain and processes that others experience as well. *This faculty, one of less-structured thoughts, less-rigid categorizations and thinner boundaries, allows us to picture—via reverie, dreaming, and artistic creativity—similarities instead of solid divisions* (568). This faculty leads to the development of la naguala, the ability to sense the potential for connection to others. La naguala will guide our future collective journey.

Social change depends on our truly being willing to encounter the depths of our interrelatedness and, without fear, embracing the power and potential of la naguala. *Las nepantleras envision a time when the bridge will no longer be needed—we'll have shifted to a seamless nosotras* (570). In order to make this shift, the future must include our engagement in the complicated tasks of simultaneously working on, and eventually moving beyond, the goals of our particular identity groups and forming larger, more inclusive communities. *You wonder when others will, like nepantleras, hand themselves to a larger vision, a less-defended identity* (571). This hope for how conocimiento will be revealed may seem like a far-reaching one, but it is necessary nonetheless. It will require much strength, work, and resilience, personally and collectively. Acting on Gloria Anzaldúa's vision, it's up to us to demonstrate that we *can* reach through our wounds to know the other; through collective acts of love and our willingness to be in constant transition, that is, to make the bridge "home," social harmony becomes more than a vision—it too becomes home.

Another Monday has passed, another shavasana. I came to yoga to dwell in a moment when I can be acutely aware of the relationship between my mind and body, when I can sense the energy of the person next to me even with my eyes closed. Our teacher reminds us to breathe, to emanate and absorb wishes for peace. We are, in a sense, "dancing in the face of our fears." Reading Anzaldúa's work is like this for me too—like being reminded to breathe, to pay attention to that which cannot be seen but only felt. In shavasana tonight I listen with my whole body to all the shifts occurring around me. Summer to fall, day to night, inhale to exhale, lessons offered to lessons learned. I think of all my teachers, see their faces, hear their voices. I recall Gloria Anzaldúa's final words "in now let us shift," a prayer for transformation:

> We are ready for change.
> Let us link hands and hearts
> together find a path through the dark woods
>> step through the doorways between worlds
>> leaving huellas for others to follow,
>> build bridges, cross them with grace, and claim these puentes our
>> "home"
>> sí se puede, que asi sea, so be it, estamos listas, vámonos.

Gloria, you asked us to remember *nuestros muertos,* our dead, *those whose backs served as bridges* (576). Now we remember you. Each time we read your words, *tus huellas,* your footprints, whether for the first time or the tenth, you come to life, calling us to persist through the insecurity of change. You offer us your back to cross over to that which we have yet to know, that which will bring us closer to peace, wisdom, unity, to home. Now it is our turn to build bridges to new possibilities. Namaste, Gloria.

Now let us shift.

CHAPTER 28

"Darkness, My Night": The Philosophical Challenge of Gloria Anzaldúa's Aesthetics of the Shadow

MARÍA DEGUZMÁN

In ancient times the Mexican Indians made mirrors of volcanic glass known as obsidian. Seers would gaze into a mirror until they fell into a trance. Within the black, glossy surface, they saw clouds of smoke which would part to reveal a vision concerning the future of the tribe and the will of the gods.

GLORIA ANZALDÚA, *BORDERLANDS/LA FRONTERA*

Night-Reading in Cambridge, November 1990

I first came across Gloria Anzaldúa's work in the fall of 1990, my fourth year in graduate school at Harvard University. The book was *Making Face, Making Soul/Haciendo Caras: Creative and Critical Perspectives by Women of Color,* edited by Anzaldúa. Published in 1990, it contained pieces by Latina, Asian American, African American, and Native American women. Anzaldúa had written the introduction and included her essay "La conciencia de la mestiza: Towards a New Consciousness" from the earlier *Borderlands/La Frontera.* November 3, 1990, was the exact date I finished reading *Haciendo Caras.* I have a habit of penciling these kinds of markers, cryptic signs to myself of letters and numbers, to be interpreted later on. What did it mean that I read this and other Anzaldúa work then? More than sixteen years later, the place where the book was purchased—New Words, a premier feminist bookstore founded in 1974 in the Cambridge/Boston/Somerville area—has closed as a bookstore. Unlike many other feminist bookstores, it has reinvented itself as the Center for New Words, running literacy, reading, and writing programs for women, producing and selling written materials (a new bookstore), and promoting civic exchange. And I? I became a Latina/o Studies scholar and teacher even though Harvard had no Latina/o Studies program. What I learned I had to teach myself, inspired by texts such as *Haciendo Caras* and *Borderlands/La Frontera*. Anzaldúa's writings communicated permission to synthesize analysis and creativity, vision and action, scholarship and political activism. This is not to say that I had not encountered such permission elsewhere as a young graduate student. After all, it was to be found in feminism and womanism, lesbian and gay studies (Queer Studies was still coming into its own), Chicana/o scholarship and activism, ethnic studies more generally, and the intersection of all of these. However, Anzaldúa's prose and poetry were especially powerful—particularly her ability to illustrate her ideas, commitments, in a gut-haunting, mind-bending form. With regard to Queer Theory, though too rarely credited, Anzaldúa should be claimed as a founding figure based on her model of "tolerance for ambiguity" (*Borderlands/La Frontera* 100), her confrontations with shame and abjection, and her call for Chicanos to listen to "their queer," their jotería (107).

I remember sitting in Cambridge, Massachusetts, in my then-partner's apartment on Cambridge Street.[1] She either found *Borderlands* with or for me. Yes, "identity is a relational process" (*Interviews/Entrevistas* 239). I would absorb myself in Anzaldúa's prose and poetry. Accompanied or alone, my skin tingled as I read and night fell beyond the windows, parabolas of lamplight brooding on the apartment's white walls. Immersed in those pages, I was so far from South Texas and yet so close to the Southwest's conflicts as I sat in the Northeast, in a town and beside an institution that saw itself, despite its complex ethnoracial history, in the mirror of its British and Puritan legacies. What burned before me were the images, "faces of feelings" (*Borderlands/La Frontera* 60), and ideas from Anzaldúa's words and the fiery colors—blue, mauve, purple, orange, turquoise, yellow, white, and amber brown—of Judy Baca's "Triumph of the Heart" image from her participatory mural project *The World Wall: A Vision of the Future without Fear,* an image that appeared on *Haciendo Caras*'s cover.[2] This image of four women—three of them holding candles with which to illuminate the darkness, tears coursing down their cheeks, one with a large turquoise eye and another with a blue eye aimed directly at the viewer—transfixed me there in the Cambridge night.

As I write from Chapel Hill, North Carolina, six years into the new thousand years (2006), Anzaldúa's images and Chicana muralist Judy Baca's public artwork of four Llorona visionaries transport me horizontally and vertically into a wider, deeper night.³ They draw me to ponder the relation between all these nights and space-times: the long socio-economic, political, legal, and spiritual struggle of the indio, the mestizo (as identity and philosophy), and the disenfranchised against the frightened homogeneity of a white-supremacist, heterosexist, classist, patriarchal status quo; the shaping force of region on interpretations of U.S. history and of the Americas; the five-hundred-year history of conquest and survival in the Americas and the pressure of this history on the late 1980s, early 1990s, and first decade of the twenty-first century; the connections to be discerned among the experiences of the women in *Haciendo Caras,* Anzaldúa's varied life experience and multidimensional production that spanned the rural poverty of South Texas and the Rio Grande Valley to the intellectual and financial opportunities of elite institutions such as the University of Texas at Austin, the University of California at Santa Cruz, and Georgetown; and my own life and academic/artistic goals and commitments as a scholar, teacher, and conceptual photographer.

Everything about Anzaldúa's life and writings prompts a response in her readers that involves the awakening of la facultad. Anzaldúa defined la facultad as "the capacity to see in surface phenomena the meaning of deeper realities, to see the deep structure below the surface. . . . The one possessing this sensitivity is excruciatingly alive to the world" (*Borderlands/La Frontera* 60). Being alive to the world involves a horizontal as well as vertical journeying—a transversal more than two-dimensional traveling of perception and action that contemplates and acts on interrelations among things beyond accepted or enforced borders and boundaries. Throughout *Borderlands/La Frontera* Anzaldúa associates la facultad with night, shadows, and various kinds of darkness—with a willingness to face "the dark, chthonic (underworld)" (61), to be "a creature at home in the dark" (209). In Anzaldúa's work, this darkness is never divorced from a vertical exploration of the psyche nor from a horizontal movement out into the world of social relations (contemporary and historical) and the factors entailed in these: gender, sexuality, ethnicity, religion, philosophy, geopolitics, and socioeconomics.

I return to re-sensing those hours of night-reading in Cambridge, fall 1990. Silently, I enter the front door and turn diagonally left into the living room of that apartment where a former self is seated cross-legged on the carpet at a low black lacquer coffee table. . . . I am a ghost from the future haunting my past. I step into this former self; the future and the past meet at this glossy black table with these books that abrieron el camino to my present life as a Latina/o Studies scholar and teacher. Again I take up the pen lying beside the books. I have been writing this analytical testimonio . . .[4]

Of Night and Shadows

My analytical testimonio on behalf of Anzaldúa's intellectual legacy focuses on the representation of "the negative" and the dialectic of absence/presence and projection through absence in the aesthetics and politics of nepantilism, a Náhuatl term meaning "torn between ways." This nepantilism involves a tactical embrace of insecurity, uncertainty, and the indeterminate (or what I call "a dreaded non-identity of the night") in the essays and poems of *Borderlands/La Frontera*. Anzaldúa's concept of nepantilism combines a topography of displacement with the lived experience of colonization, persecution, subordination, self-imposed limitations or internalized colonization, and past and present resistance in the Americas and in the Mexico-Texas borderlands (*Borderlands/La Frontera* 43).[5] I would like to take a closer look at nepantilism in terms of the Shadow and darkness.

To explain this consciousness of resistance, Anzaldúa calls on the theories about the collective unconscious of the Swiss psychiatrist and philosopher Carl Jung (1875–1961). Jung is widely discussed by depth psychologists, among them James Hillman, with whose archetypal psychology Anzaldúa was familiar.[6] To describe a consciousness that subverts or does not countenance the subject/object mind/body dualities of so-called "western culture" and its frightened rationalism, she invokes Jung's concept of the Shadow self (*Borderlands/La Frontera* 59). The Shadow self is the "unacceptable" aspects of ourselves, the unsocialized, supposedly animal-divine ones that rebel against man-made rules and categories. According to Anzaldúa following Jung, this Shadow self is connected to the unrepressed drives and instincts. It thinks and feels through the body and the sensual world as much as through the intellect. As the Shadow self is a shadowy concept, she concretizes it with images drawn from Jung's and her own understandings of Mesoamerican lore: snakes, serpents, the dark earth, Llorona wailing for her lost children in the night, night dreams, sexuality and latent sexual forces, the black glossy surface of obsidian mirrors, the darkness of night, and the association of night and darkness with the maternal, as in the womb of night, mother night.

Anzaldúa focuses on "this first darkness" (*Borderlands/La Frontera* 71) as she substitutes it for what she implies has become a western and ethnocentric (as in "white") equivalent of light with goodness and dark with evil. She elaborates her associational constellation "Shadow," "shadow," the "shadow-beast," "dark," "diosa de la noche," and "creature of darkness." The insistence on Shadow/shadow and "darkness, my night" out of which the new mestiza is born functions to tinge neptantilism's tactical embrace of insecurity, uncertainty, and the indeterminate with color. This color, while containing within it the traces of certain ethnoracial coordinates (as in "darkskinned people," Anzaldúa's phrase in *Borderlands/La Frontera*, 71), is not confined to them or to bodily phenotype. Anzaldúa honors "darkskinned people" and yet moves beyond physical traits in her journey to transform the mind, the imagination, the spirit, and, with them, social reality. All people may be included in darkness or could opt to include themselves in darkness rather than stake an investment in whiteness and light, the hegemonically valued side of the "dark/light" binary.

Darkness of many sorts becomes the standard we are invited to revalue positively, where "positively" is not to be confused with easily but, rather, entails the hard work of transforming consciousness and action by embracing the terms of abjection. Hence the emphasis on the negative, the unacceptable, that which oppressive structures (imposed and internalized) have taught us not to accept. "Darkness, my night" encompasses numerous other factors besides ethnoracial ones. Some of those factors pertain to gender ("maternal" night) and sexuality. Anzaldúa mentions "loquería" (*Borderlands/La Frontera* 41). This term connotes not only craziness or madness but also an altered consciousness in a dialectical relationship with libidinal choices besides heteronormative ones. The term "queer" covers not only "homosexual" but also the absurd, crazy, atypical, deviant, exceptional, extraordinary, preternatural, strange, and uncanny.

The qualities of absence and negativity accompanying and attributed to "darkness, my night" are the parts of nepantilism that are not colored in an ethnoracial manner and that are not socially categorizable even as the breaking of conventional categories. These qualities are more philosophically ontological or existential than specifically phenotypic and social. Thus, "darkness, my night" connotes a gamut of conditions, from the ethnoracial to the marginal to the existentially alienated—in fact, from the recognizably identitarian (as in darkskinned people or people of color) to the seemingly anti-identitarian, those states of dreaded non-identity. By "states of dreaded non-identity" I mean situations and states of mind, feeling, in which known language/code fails to adequately convey the experience one is having, when conceptual and linguistic categories are revealed to be insufficient. Anzaldúa, in the tradition of many mystics, saw, in such often terrifying states, a potential for the actual remaking of consciousness and for growth toward social change.

Anzaldúa's deployments of the shadow and of night are capacious and even contradictory. These aspects lie at the crux of her nepantilism. Shadow and night are well suited in their particularities and in their generalities to signify both visibility (darkskinned people) and invisibility (an absorption into the night of people, identity markers, and territorial boundaries). *Borderlands/La Frontera* deploys shadow and night to argue for particularity (the particular struggle of politicized Chicanas, for instance) and universalism at the same time. This double movement plays the particular against the universal to spotlight difference and the hierarchical power dynamics of societies in which darkskinned people are subordinated and considered lesser in every way. And yet, at the same time, her work universalizes the particular. She turns shadow and night into the touchstones of sensibility, ethics, and a coalitional politics of the marginalized and the oppressed. Anzaldúa's shadow darkness presents a decolonizing challenge to some of the most fundamental assumptions within the binaries "dark/light" and "absence/presence" in dominant western epistemology. I say "dominant" because western epistemology does have its heretics. The shadow darkness is decolonizing in the way that it frees darkness from the reservation of shame to which it has been confined and brings forth a way for us to identify with what has been historically devalued, persecuted.

Anzaldúa borrows Jung's concept of the Shadow with a capital "S" to address the "unacceptable" and/or unsocialized aspects of ourselves. In doing so, she grants the Shadow more than ground. She converts it into a space of (in)habitation, a place where we are invited to dwell. The Shadow, while signaling some aspect of the corporealized or embodied personality, refers not merely to an alter ego but to another world—un otro mundo, something akin to the inframundo (an Aztec concept for a world lying within, amidst, and still beyond this world or social order). This formless form entails the fearful and fearlessly passionate act of living at the crossroads, on the border. It means confronting our fears, our insecurities, our defensiveness, our vulnerabilities, and recognizing in ourselves and the other what exceeds social categories and ingrained ways of thinking/feeling/acting, particularly when what exceeds has been negatively valued or stigmatized. It entails a terrifying openness to possibility and the willingness to act on possibility against the socio-economic, historical, and psychological odds that largely spell injustice and harm for the many for the sake of the few who manage to acquire privilege and "security" in their social system.

The Dark Night of the Body-Mind-Spirit

Anzaldúa's concepts of nepantla and la facultad lend themselves to an understanding of her work in relation to a recuperation of melancholia for the cause of self-transformation and political change. This recuperation needs to be understood in the context of the rise of depression worldwide over the past decade and a concurrent interest in the humanities, social sciences, and medical sciences in studying "depression." Art historian and cultural studies scholar Christine Ross observes, "According to the National Institute of Mental Health, major depression is the leading cause of disability worldwide" (xvi). She adds that "melancholia is the main notional ancestor of depression" and that "the melancholy tradition" is "a disappearing aesthetic strategy in an era when melancholia has been absorbed by the category of depression" (xxvii). Ross's study makes a strong case for refusing this "foundational debasement of the melancholy attachment to loss" (200). The book validates much of contemporary art for being "still attached to the creativity traditionally associated with melancholic insight" (200).

Anzaldúa's work can be understood in terms of melancholic insight related to "deep depression" (a phrase she uses in "now let us shift," 551) or melancholia not containable by a clinical definition. Nepantla—which Anzaldúa defined in "now let us shift" as the difficult "overlapping space between different perceptions and belief systems" (541)—involves being torn from security, comfort, complacency. It implies a willingness to confront darkness and declare oneself its creature. And confronting darkness means confronting loss and, moreover, the possibility of profound loss. Christine Ross notes that depression results not only from loss but also from anticipated loss: "The depressed numbs himself in relation to an anticipated loss" (3). That numbing expresses itself in art as an aesthetics of disengagement—for instance, in contemporary performance art, standing or sitting impassively and not looking at spectators. Anzaldúa's work manifests an aesthetics of engagement rather than detachment or disengagement. Her melancholia or constellation of

Shadow, darkness, shadows, and night does not proceed from or result in numbing. Rather, she calls for and embodies "excruciating aliveness." Her "black sun of melancholy" (to borrow French Romantic Gerard de Nerval's image) shines full of passionate intensity. Fiery warmth radiates from the dark night of the soul.

The Radiant Alterity of Darkness:
Anzaldúan Precepts for Latina/o Studies

The Anzaldúan constellation has much to offer people struggling with melancholia and depression. Mental health professionals and researchers who follow traditional models of psychotherapy tend to treat patients/clients as if their emotional conditions were rooted in their inadequate coping strategies or their brain chemistry, ignoring economic, ethnoracial, gender, sexual, national, international, and transnational conflicts and injustices that contribute to emotional challenges. Anzaldúa's exploration of alterity and darkness dignifies their/our experience of loss, pain, marginalization, disorientation, and the anguish of those "excruciatingly alive to the world." She empowers those who feel pain, shame, anguish, and sorrow to understand the strength, energy, and creativity latent in those "negative" emotions and, therefore, to use these emotions to effect social change.

Her conceptual constellation suggests basic precepts for Latina/o Studies, which is often characterized by institutional marginalization and invisibility. Thus, a Latina/o Studies scholar must seek to create a distinction between Lacanian lack and the productive potentiality of loss. For instance, I am learning to build alliances with and bridges across disciplines, including, but not limited to, African American and African Diaspora Studies, Native American/Meso American Studies, Pacific Rim Studies, Women's Studies, LGBTQ Studies, Civil and Human Rights Studies, and Audio/Visual/Media Culture Studies. This alliance building requires a willingness to negotiate different frames of reference and more than several critical languages and a plurality of political agendas—a humbling experience. I have to relinquish illusions of mastery and continually challenge myself and be challenged by others. Loss of mastery casts a daring shadow of inquiry that deepens into the radiant possibilities of reciprocity and collaboration.

CHAPTER 29

The Simultaneity of Self- and Global Transformations: Bridging with Anzaldúa's Liberating Vision

MOHAMMAD H. TAMDGIDI

I am a wind-swayed bridge, a crossroads inhabited by whirlwinds. Gloria, the facilitator, Gloria the mediator, straddling the walls between abysses. "Your allegiance is to La Raza, the Chicano movement," say the members of my race. "Your allegiance is to the Third World," say my Black and Asian friends. "Your allegiance is to your gender, to women," say the feminists. Then there's my allegiance to the Gay movement, to the socialist revolution, to the New Age, to magic and the occult. And there's my affinity to literature, to the world of the artist. What am I? A third world lesbian feminist with Marxist and mystic leanings. *They would chop me up into little fragments and tag each piece with a label.*

GLORIA ANZALDÚA, "LA PRIETA"

"Bridging" is different from what Paulo Freire critiqued as the "banking system" of transmitting knowledge (57–74). The "banking system," in which one person "deposits" information into another person or people, is a one-directional, hierarchical monologue. In contrast, bridging is dialogic and assumes the existence and equal value of "banks" of knowledge on two (or more) sides of a conversation. Bridging is about sharing knowledges that are also independently growing. Bridging involves further dialogue arising from inner conversations. How could one truly appreciate the labors of another if one has not already tasted their liberating effects?

Sadly, I did not come to know about Gloria Anzaldúa until she had died, in 2004. I first heard the news of her passing from a colleague and later noted that several conferences or newsletters dedicated special sessions or columns to remembering her legacy. In the course of my own involvement in planning and organizing the third annual meeting of the Social Theory Forum (STF) at the University of Massachusetts, Boston, I became more acquainted with Anzaldúa's writings. Reading her work was deeply cathartic, for I found in her—in unimaginably lucid, creative, vivid, caring, and highly refined expressions—what I have discovered in a different way as a sociologist of Middle Eastern, specifically Iranian, descent. The hybrid meetings of the East and the West, of the traditional and the modern, of diverse worldviews, knowledges, and spiritualities, are not uncommon to this other region of the world. Like Anzaldúa, we too have been perpetually bridging, personally and world-historically, what appear to be incompatible ways of knowing and making our lives and histories. Borderland consciousness is not regional; it is a global phenomenon that took a most lucid form in Anzaldúa's writing and life as a mestiza intellectual and spiritual activist.

Anzaldúa experienced the violence of dualistic paradigms in deeply personal, sensual, emotional, intellectual, political, and historical ways. I emphasize this point because the significance of her "borderlands" theory cannot be fully appreciated without recognizing its development from her efforts to understand and overcome dualistic modes of knowing and living in the self and in the world. Dualism is the fundamental breeder of alienation, oppression, imperiality, and violence.[1] Dualisms have sedimented as habitual formations in the remotest recesses of our thoughts, feelings, and sensations. These habits are *the* enemy within, Anzaldúa tells us:

> The borders and walls that are supposed to keep the undesirable ideas out are entrenched habits and patterns of behavior; these habits and patterns are the enemy within. Rigidity means death. Only by remaining flexible is she able to stretch the psyche horizontally and vertically. *La mestiza* constantly has to shift out of habitual formations; from convergent thinking, analytical reasoning that tends to use rationality to move toward a single goal (a Western mode), to divergent thinking, characterized by movement away from set patterns and goals and toward a more whole perspective, one that includes rather than excludes. (*Borderlands/ La Frontera* 101)

But how can one become aware of (let alone transform and heal!) these world-historically constituted dualisms, given their deeply embedded structure in our lives? We live these dualisms, day in and day out, in the here and now. Borderlands, as I interpret Anzaldúa, represent those moments where the absurdities of dualistic knowledges and constructions are not only directly known but also most immediately experienced— for some in a flash of insight and gut feeling, for others as an enduring, often quite painful, lifelong experience. Shaman writers like Anzaldúa (*Borderlands/La Frontera* 88) who live the borderlands are especially able to tell us not only how things are but how they can or should be— and this, the dualism of what is and what should be, is itself a confusing borderland to live in, a dualism to heal and transform, in favor of the radical changing of existing conditions. As she writes in her early essay "La Prieta":

> *The pull between what is and what should be.* I believe that by changing ourselves we change the world, that traveling El Mundo Zurdo path is the path of a two-way movement—a going deep into the self and an expanding out into the world, a simultaneous recreation of the self and a reconstruction of society. And yet, I am confused as to how to accomplish this. (208, her emphasis)

The pull between knowing what is and what should be can take many forms, including the pull between science and utopia. Those who see a dichotomy, a dualism, between them, have long abandoned living in the borderlands of the two. Even Karl Marx and Friedrich Engels sought, when founding their worldview, to construct an artificial dualism between science and utopia.[2] But Anzaldúa is not satisfied with a schism that deprives both of their meaning and purpose. Astonishing in her synthesis, in fact, is her comparative appreciation of cross-cultural differences in the paths sought toward the good life. Aware of the distinction between mystical and utopian ways of knowing, she critically embraces both. She is not ready to abandon the mystical and the utopian in favor of academic reputation and credibility, for she has sensed, in the deeply entrenched recesses of her own mestiza consciousness, the validity and the usefulness of alternative mystical and utopian insights into the nature of self and world. Abandoning the best her native culture and movement has offered her is not on the agenda; she doesn't sell out to the powers inhabiting academic disciplinarity's fragmented landscapes.

Anzaldúa is deeply aware of the simultaneity of self- and global knowledge and transformation. This insight permeates every single word of her prose and poetry. Seeking the good life in the self and the world cannot be divorced from one another; in pursuing this insight she breaks genre with stereotypical and rigid versions of both mystical and utopian pursuits that, alienated from one another for centuries, have not been adequately equipped with the simultaneous tasks of self- and global understanding and change. Significantly, the scientific spirit is not alien to Anzaldúa's mestiza consciousness, as we note in the uncommonly self-critical way in which she observes and confronts biases both in her adversaries' views and in her own collective and personal ideologies. By so doing she sets a refreshing example for the more genuine Mannheimian practices of the sociology of knowledge, in which the debunking of adversaries' ideologies transitions to the awareness of the biases in one's own collective conscious and unconscious mentalities.[3] Anzaldúa subjects everything, including the most taken-for-granted assumptions of her own culture and personal life, to severe criticism, for her acknowledgment of habitual dualism as *the* enemy within is not purely a theoretical conjecture but a highly applied and precise scientific endeavor.

Most astonishing to my mind is the seriousness with which Anzaldúa engages in her work with the dualism of conscious and un/subconscious behavior. In many ways, she already has sensed subconscious habituation's significance as a fundamental challenge to utopian, mystical, and scientific endeavors in favor of the good life. No matter to what extent one may become aware of and theorize the most intricate human experiences, Anzaldúa would argue, the challenge posed by habits is a fundamental one to overcome—for it permeates everything, everywhere. The most radical and revolutionary ideas and practices, in other words, can turn to dogmas and carceral practices if they lose sight of the need for perpetual inner self-criticism and renewal that are necessary to break down the habitually formed borders and walls of dualism:

> The work of *mestiza* consciousness is to break down the subject-object duality that keeps her a prisoner and to show in the flesh and through the images in her work how duality is transcended. The answer to the problem between the white race and the colored, between males and females, lies in healing the split that originates in the very foundation of our lives, our culture, our languages, our thoughts. A massive uprooting of dualistic thinking in the individual and collective consciousness is the beginning of a long struggle, but one that could, in our best hopes, bring us to the end of rape, of violence, of war. (*Borderlands/La Frontera* 102)

Anzaldúa's liberating social theory is thereby highly fluid, "shape-shifting," and unclassifiable. It is a snake that constantly bites its own tail and swiftly swerves in the "wind-swayed" sands of turbulent world-historical events. Transcending the artificial dualism of self- and global transformation, Anzaldúa also proclaims an unusual and at the same time innovative and highly plausible strategy to bring about radical change— one that is based on perpetual efforts in self-knowledge and self-transformation as an inner strategy for global liberatory praxis. Radical inner change, for Anzaldúa, is simultaneously an effort in radical global— and, depending on its depth, world-historical—transformation.

> The struggle is inner: Chicano, *indio*, American Indian, *mojado, mexicano*, immigrant Latino, Anglo in power, working class Anglo, Black, Asian—our psyches resemble the bordertowns and are populated by the same people. The struggle has always been inner, and is played out in the outer terrains. Awareness of our situation must come before inner changes, which in turn come before changes in society. Nothing happens in the "real" world unless it first happens in the images in our heads. (*Borderlands/La Frontera* 109)

Anzaldúa left a rich legacy for advancing hybrid sociological visions in theory and practice. We could use her work to propose "borderlands sociology" as one concerned with the radical understanding and transcendence of dualistic structures of knowing and living in the self and the world in favor of a just global society. "Borderlands" is plural, thus signifying the sociological imagination's global and world-historical stretch. Anzaldúa's writings are gold mines of alchemical insights into her highly creative and contagious sociological imagination in the tradition of C. Wright Mills. In many ways the richness, dialecticity, and power in her sociological imagination far exceeds those found in Mills. Anzaldúa does so well what Panagiota Gounari has counterposed as the need to turn personal issues into public troubles and what one may add in terms of turning public issues into personal troubles.

Anzaldúa's writings are rich reservoirs of examples for phenomenological sociological research that advocates problematization of taken-for-granted and habituated knowledges and practices of everyday life, both inner and interpersonal, in order to better understand how they perpetuate (and can, alternatively, transform) larger social structures. Her prose and poetry are creative exercises in experimental breaching and disturbing of our comfort zones in the midst of everyday living in class, race, gender, sexuality, age, and other borderlands. Anzaldúa brings symbolic interactionist theorizing and practice to an innovative and liberatory height. She has long transcended the border walls of prose and poetry, of linguistic dichotomies, of meaning and imagery, of substance and style, of theory and practice. It is no wonder that she has found a highly successful way to tap into the depths of her readers' psyches and subconscious minds. And she is fully aware of what she does in this regard; it is her not-so-secret "alchemy" at work (*Borderlands/La Frontera* 103). As an "Eastern intellectual," she intentionally transgresses and crosses boundaries of knowledge, experience, in favor of ever more holistic modes of knowing and doing.[4]

Anzaldúa's social theory reflects keen awareness of social conflict and hope for finding and seeking alternatives to the dysfunctional orders of patriarchy, imperialism, and colonialism. Her postmodern pursuits in problematizing her readers' habituated beliefs are tinged with hopeful, constructive, and proactive pursuits of self- and world knowledge in favor of a better world. Anzaldúa's sociology bridges and transcends fragmented borderlands of various micro and macro social theorizing; it also breaks down habituated border walls of academic disciplines, of the sciences and the humanities, of on- and off-campus lives, of classes, genders, "racial" and ethnic groups, of ages, of abilities, and all borders that have helped for millennia to perpetuate the oppressive dualistic architecture of human experience.

Anzaldúa's work gives me tremendous affirmation of what I have been discovering and pursuing in my own work. Encountering her was highly transformative for me, for it gave credence and validity, in the public stage of social and cultural theorizing, to my own thinking and interests. Her comparative pursuit of diverse cross-cultural modes of transformative theorizing and practice is highly inspiring for my own interest in utopystics as an applied borderlands sociological research across utopian, mystical, and scientific paradigms. Borrowed from and further transforming Immanuel Wallerstein's invented term "utopistics" into "utopystics,"[5] by way of insertion of an East-West comparative interest in utopian, mystical, and scientific modes of knowing and doing, utopystics is an integrative research endeavor that seeks to bridge cross-cultural insights in favor of a saner world. The sociology of self-knowledge and human architecture, two fields initiated in my work and pursued via *Human Architecture,* a journal devoted to the long-term project, are research and pedagogical strategies in utopystics for understanding and transcending dualistic world-historical structures constituting our everyday lives. The sociology of self-knowledge fosters liberating autobiographical research in increasingly global and world-historical contexts, while human architecture seeks to tear down walls of human alienation and build integrative human realities designed to further a just global society.

One trajectory of my work has focused on distinguishing between Newtonian and quantal sociological imaginations. Based on a conception of society in terms of the interaction of individual or group bodies in which the singularity of the individual is assumed, conventional sociology is Newtonian. Quantal sociology views society as a world-system of self-relations within and across bodies and in relation to their natural or built environments. Newtonian sociology defines society in terms of rigid and predictable interactions of presumably singular persons; quantal sociology conceives and experiences society in terms of chaotic, indeterministic, unpredictable, and creative relations of selves. Newtonian sociology frames the various forms of oppression in terms of conflicts among persons; quantal sociology frames oppressions in terms of conflicts among selves, giving rise to diverse forms of oppression of self and other. Anzaldúa's conceptions of society, social conflict, and social change are deeply quantal, fluid, unpredictable, creative, and unusual.[6] For her, it is not about whites or blacks, males or females, rich or poor, but about whiteness and blackness, maleness and femaleness, richness and poorness. Indeed, her work goes even further, "question[ing] the terms *white* and *women of color* by showing that whiteness may not be applied to all whites, as some possess women-of-color consciousness, just as some women of color bear white consciousness" ("(Un)natural bridges" 2, her italics). Would it be surprising to note that my own attraction, as a male, to Anzaldúa's work is one that arises—I am certain—from the struggles, the stubborn feminism, and the mystical leanings of a mother who experienced an absurd lifelong dualism between tradition and modernity, between her pride as a woman and the absurd expectations of an allegedly "progressing" culture under the shah?

Organizing (with colleagues) the April 2006 conference of the Social Theory Forum in honor of Anzaldúa was for me a small step toward understanding her life and work in association with those who knew her long before and more deeply than I.[7] Bold visions for the future in light of Anzaldúan insights are already emerging across the disciplines through conscious incorporation of borderlands thinking that targets dualistic and fragmented constructions of the self and the world. Quantal sociological imagination advocates a bold vision of society and a paradigm shift in sociology, envisioning society as a world-system of self (rather than presumed "individual") interactions. It seeks alternative forms of social organization in favor of a just global society conceived as a world-system of self-determining individualities. Self- and global transformations for Anzaldúa are part of the same interconnected process; breaking down their dualism is the ultimate goal of the bold vision advanced in her thinking.[8] Her life's work will therefore continue in borderlands everywhere, in the lives of those who have sensed the absurdity of dualistic paradigms and have hopes for the possibility of a transformed world.

In Newtonian sociological imagination, Anzaldúa has passed away. In quantal sociological imagination she lives and works in any self that cares to house and nourish her memory. Anzaldúa's legacy will continue to the extent the living remember and continue her work. The future will tell to what extent Anzaldúa succeeds in transcending the dualism of her life and death. For me, her death has involved a spiritual rebirth. She now lives in me, growing every day and night. Her call significantly validated my own finding, as well, that self-inquiry and self-transformation are simultaneous efforts with—and most effective exercises in—global transformation. The boldest Anzaldúan vision for the future ironically involves radical efforts at self-knowing and self-transforming in the here and now. If there is a will to pursue it, what vision could be bolder—perhaps more difficult, yet more readily attainable and practical—than that!

CHAPTER 30

For Gloria Anzaldúa . . . Who Left Us Too Soon

GLORIA STEINEM

When I first heard of Gloria Anzaldúa's death, I had already lived nine years longer than she had. Now as I write this, I've had fourteen more years—and her death seems all the more unjust.

The last words of hers I read were in a major essay she had written for *this bridge we call home: radical visions for transformation,* the anthology she co-edited with AnaLouise Keating. She described and acted on her fierce determination to live and to write. Indeed, she was already angry at her body for betraying her with its need for constant blood balancing due to a diagnosis of diabetes, but she had no choice if her mind was to stay clear and her own. Still, she ended that essay with a prayer for change that seemed to say she would be with us in the future.

It wasn't only illness that limited her time to write but also the community work that she loved. She held workshops to help others tell their stories, she spread poetry and possibilities through her lectures, and she listened to the voices of the voiceless, then mixed languages and cultures as they did when she co-created anthologies that were portable communities in themselves. All this was rarely balanced by time to express the Self. *Borderlands/La Frontera,* her own best-known book, had taken her eight years to complete.

At the time, I, too, was eight years into an overdue book yet kept leaving it to go on the road for the movement work I loved. Her message felt very personal to me, as her searingly honest words often did. I vowed I would learn a lesson from the memento mori of her essay—as I had not from my own diagnosis of breast cancer years before—and strive for a better balance in my life. Though I knew her only from her writing plus mutual friends and the many women I met as I traveled who told me her work and example had saved their creativity and even their lives, I imagined her working in her room by the sea. She was as real to me as I was sitting at my own desk.

And then she was gone.

I felt anger on her behalf. Was there a moment between sleep and diabetic coma when she knew no more words would ever come? She seemed peaceful when she was found in her bed by a friend and former neighbor, yet passing from dream to coma to death was exactly the fate she feared and had written about.

I felt anger on my own behalf. I had lost a teacher who led me into worlds that were both strange and familiar to me, like a cellular memory. I had lost a rare woman who insisted that balancing community with exploring the Self was our right. In *this bridge we call home,* poet Deborah Miranda perfectly phrased the nature of the anger I felt: "My question here, then," she wrote, "is not only *who has been silenced?* but *whose ears have been denied sound and song?*" (193).

I had been denied not only Anzaldúa's songs but the living example of another writer trying to balance activism and solitude, being useful to others and diving deep into the Self, persuading and expressing, listening outside and listening within. It was a poor substitute, but on my bulletin board I pinned the photograph of her smiling under her black hat and another of her sitting contentedly in front of her own fireplace. I had always imagined we would meet one day when she was living in New York (but I was often on the road) or when I was in California (but never in the right place at the right time). And now it was too late.

I don't have any words of comfort here. All of us who have been denied Gloria Anzaldúa's future songs have a right to be angry. We also have a right to guard what she has left us, to keep it always in print, in libraries, in classrooms, so her words can be heard if not the sound of her voice.

But given Anzaldúa's willingness to admit hard truths, even to and about herself, to tell painful things about those whose voices are heard and those who are silenced, we also must ask ourselves: Would she have had to struggle so hard to write if she had not been born into a campesino/working-class community? How much more and earlier could she have created if she had not felt she had no place as a Chicana, a lesbian, a worker in many jobs that left her too tired at night to write a word? Would she have been more acceptable in academia if she had been less emotional; if she had kept to existing religions instead of exploring all-inclusive spirituality; if she had used academic words like "problematize" and "deconstruction" instead of the everyday magic of Tex-Mex and mestiza and working-class English and all the code-switching and verbal inventions of nepantla, that indigenous and irreplaceable word for an in-between and overlapping space? Would she have been more valued by those at the center if they had understood that, in cultures as in trees, growth happens at the margins?

Might she still be alive if she had not had a disease encouraged by the cheap and unnatural diet inflicted by food stamps that sometimes were her only recourse, so common among the poor that "genocidal diabetes" has become a common phrase? Wouldn't diagnosis have come sooner and treatment been safer with consistent health insurance? Would she have been able to survive as a solitary writer if she'd been able to pay a companion to keep watch on her and make her sleep and her solitude safer?

I don't ask these questions to give anyone pain, nor do I pretend to know the answers. I only know that I am living and she is not; that inequalities of poverty and race and language *do* matter, though they need not and should not; that I am writing this now in the only advanced democracy in the world with no national system of health care. I do know that she was sometimes refused where the less popular and populist were not, that she was given adjectives to wear by white women and men who thought they needed none themselves. I do believe in my heart that she could and should be with us still.

Like Malcolm X toward the end of his life, she put off even some of her own supporters by moving from a cherished identity (in her case, Chicana, which included "indigenous, Mexican, Basque, Spanish, Berber-Arab Gypsy"), toward "an emerging planetary culture" in which "national boundaries dividing us from 'others' (nos/otras) are porous and the cracks between worlds serve as gateways" ("now let us shift" 561). She was beginning to believe that labeling was the enemy of linking.

By definition, injustice affects us differently. Yet by definition, injustice affects us all. I think this is what Gloria Anzaldúa was telling us in her last and most universal words: "Only when those of us whose ears are denied the song become as angry as the silenced singer will we—as she wrote as her last blessing—'together find a path through dark woods.'" ("now let us shift" 576)."

"Closure" is something that is supposed to follow death and loss, but in my own experience, there is no such thing. Relationships don't disappear, they just change. We lose a physical presence in our lives and gain a presence in our minds and hearts.

Because I never said "Thank you" to Gloria Anzaldúa in person, I now imagine us walking by the sea—as she so often did in her last years—watching the surf carve solid rock into openings that might eventually become bridges. At last, there is time for me to say:

- Thank you for turning your anger at what happened or failed to happen three decades ago for women of color at a feminist retreat into *This Bridge Called My Back*. Because of you and your co-creator Cherríe Moraga, it became one of the most mind- and heart-changing books of my generation. Like the women a decade earlier who used anger at inequality inside the peace and civil rights movements to forge important feminist beginnings, you took your anger and turned it into hope.
- Thank you for the first two poems of yours that I read almost thirty years ago. I nearly passed by "Holy Relics" because of the title but then discovered that you had subverted religious imagery to show a woman's body carved into relics; you offered the last hopeful lines: "We are the holy relics . . . we seek each other." In "Cervicide," the young girl forced by fear to kill with her own hands a much-loved pet fawn—a symbol of herself—is every suffering wrapped into one.
- Thank you for your adventures in language that allow the monolingual to become almost bilingual and remind us that each language speaks in many tongues, from street to academe. Thank you for a sense of wordplay that makes me laugh now when I discover that my computer spell-check includes "Chicano" but not "Chicana" but, by underlining "Chicana" in red, turns it into a thing of beauty.
- Thank you for your true, painful, self-exposing accounts of conflict and what it means to try to become a bridge across it; for admitting that conflict gives you stomach cramps; that you fear it, as I do, but nonetheless, you stay with it, knowing that its energy is like the surf that carves openings in the rock.
- Thank you for your own writing and for the anthologies that you created, now in more classrooms and libraries and back pockets of jeans than you could ever guess. They bridge from field to campus, from mind to heart, and help keep women's studies rooted in lived experience.
- Thank you for your images that show us borders as openings and bridges as homes.
- Thank you for a spiritual activism that strives for a whole world and so makes each of us whole.

CHAPTER 31

She Eagle: For Gloria Anzaldúa

BECKY THOMPSON

This bridge called my back
cradles Latina Black Asian Native
women, hearts chanting

feminism explodes
shape shifts, renews its vows
voices sin fronteras

mestiza consciousness
to stand on both sides of the shore
at once, making bridges

speaking in tongues
Tejana lesbiana enamorada
ideas estrellas

el mundo zurdo
enfrente atrás las lenguas
de vida, tu alma

your eyes the color
of puddles made deep by your
words, the earth's sadness

altars in the sky
the priestess time travels, we
light velas, reaching high

Notes

Introduction. Building Bridges, Transforming Loss, Shaping New Dialogues

1. As we explain in more detail later in this introduction, we will refer to Gloria Anzaldúa as "Anzaldúa" rather than as "Gloria."

2. As Suzanne Bost demonstrates, pain is a recurring theme in Anzaldúa's work; see her essay in this volume. For additional information on Anzaldúa's life see *Interviews/Entrevistas* and the timeline in *The Gloria Anzaldúa Reader.*

3. In her latest writings, Anzaldúa often describes this recursive process, which enfolds self-reflection with externally directed transformation, as "conocimiento." As Kelli Zaytoun explains in this volume, "Conocimiento offers a pathway to understanding how a range of individual experiences (emotional, cognitive, spiritual, imaginal, bodily) are linked to the social world."

4. For a definition of status-quo thinking see AnaLouise Keating, *Teaching Transformation: Transcultural Classroom Dialogues.*

5. The tribute, "surviving the battles, shaping our worlds: honoring the life and work of Gloria Evangelina Anzaldúa," was sponsored by the Center for Mexican American Studies (CMAS) and the Center for Women's and Gender Studies (CWGS) at the University of Texas at Austin, ALLGO, the Austin Commission for Women, Resistencia Books, Red Salmon Arts, and BookWoman.

6. As we explain later in this introduction, *Bridging* does not follow the standard practice of italicizing non-English words.

7. Anzaldúa's theory of nepantla grows out of her earlier theories of the Borderlands and the Coatlicue state; for more on this theory see Anzaldúa's *Interviews/Entrevistas*, "now let us shift," and the glossary to this volume.

8. For more on my (AnaLouise's) interest in challenging disciplinary boundaries see my essay in this volume.

9. See my (Gloria's) essay in this volume.

10. Given Anzaldúa's own deep relationship to occult (defined as "hidden" and esoteric) knowledges, I find it highly symbolic that I first encountered Anzaldúa at The Occult Bookstore.

11. For additional discussions of spiritual activism see AnaLouise's "Shifting Perspectives: Spiritual Activism, Social Transformation, and the Politics of Spirit" and Karina Céspedes's essay in this volume.

12. See AnaLouise Keating, "From Intersections to Interconnections: Lessons for Transformation from *This Bridge Called My Back: Radical Writings by Women of Color.*"

13. This discussion of nos/otras is taken, almost verbatim, from AnaLouise Keating, "Shifting Worlds, una entrada."

14. Thanks to Layli Phillips Maparyan, one of our external reviewers, for calling our attention to this shift from conventional intersectionality.

15. For Anzaldúa's earliest published reference to her theory of El Mundo Zurdo see her poem "The coming of el mundo surdo" in *The Gloria Anzaldúa Reader.*

16. For additional discussion of El Mundo Zurdo see Keating, "Shifting Worlds, una entrada."

3. Deconstructing the Immigrant Self

1. See González-López, "Epistemologies of the Wound."

6. Making Face, Rompiendo Barreras

1. This and other e-mail excerpts are included with permission of the authors.

2. Thanks to Edén Torres for allowing me to include this poem, which has also been published in "Homenaje Humilde," *La Voz* (July/August 2004), San Antonio: Esperanza Peace and Justice Center.

3. Velma Perez's e-mail was published on the website http://gloria.chicanas .com.

4. On January 13, 2010, I received permission from Marcos Andrés Flores to include in this essay his poem titled "Making Face."

8. "May We Do Work That Matters"

1. UNAM was founded in 1600.

2. See my "don't paint yourself invisible," 51.

3. See my "Apuntes de colores"; "Cuando los textos cruzan fronteras"; and "(Re)Mapping mexicanidades."

4. *Cantar de Espejos/Singing Mirrors. Poesía de Chicanas/Poetry by Chicanas* (bilingual edition), ed. Claire Joysmith, under review.

5. 25–26 June 2003, Facultad de Filosofía y Letras and CISAN/UNAM.

6. The U.S.-backed coup in Chile was on 11 September 1973.

7. *Esta puente, mi espalda. Voces de mujeres tercermundistas en los Estados Unidos,* a Spanish-language adapted edition of *This Bridge Called My Back: Writings by Women of Color* (in which Gloria Anzaldúa did not appear as co-editor), published in the United States, was at one time available at the UNAM bookstore. It raised criticism in the chilango-centric academic circles it reached because of the

"incorrect" gendering in the title ("Esta puente") and because the translation needed polishing; this did little to promote Gloria Anzaldúa's work.

8. "Patlache" is a Náhuatl term that, Anzaldúa explains, "served to name women who loved other women" (in Joysmith "Ya se me quitó la vergüenza").

9. A Call to Action

1. See Gloria Anzaldúa, "now let us shift," and AnaLouise Keating, "Forging El Mundo Zurdo" and "Shifting Perspectives."

2. Souza, "Disidentification," personal communication.

10. Gloria Anzaldúa and the Meaning of Queer

1. This professor was Ricardo Aguilar-Melantzon†, to whose memory I dedicate this essay.

2. "Hegemony" is here defined as the discourse that is favored by the consensus, in this case the dyad oppressor/oppressed in which the politics of identity is based.

3. Most critiques of Anzaldúa's work have underlined this multilayered identity and the conception of border as a wound as one of her most important contributions to the humanities. Among them we can mention those by Renato Rosaldo (216–17), Debra Castillo and Socorro Tabuenca (3), David E. Johnson and Scott Michaelsen (11), and Benjamín Alire Sáenz (84).

4. Considering the autobiographical character of the text, Coatlicue can be interpreted as the representation of Anzaldúa's painful transformation: her constant fleeing from given identities.

5. AnaLouise Keating observes that Anzaldúa "transforms essentialized conceptions of identity into transcultural, transgendered models of subjectivity. By positing the non-duality of self and other, they construct multilayered discourses recognizing both the diversities *and* commonalities between and among apparently dissimilar people" ("(De)Centering the Margins" 31).

11. Breaking Our Chains

1. By "postcolonial" I refer to the era after the political independence of most colonized lands, roughly after World War II. I include China in this discussion of postcolonialism even though it was not colonized to the extent that many other countries and territories were.

2. This embracing of western ideology is not limited to the Chinese. I have read newspaper articles about how Asian women and men have gone through plastic surgeries to look more western. On my sister's computer desk I noticed a brochure for a well-known Japanese cosmetic company, Shiseido International. All the models in the brochure were western, blond, and blue- or green-eyed.

3. Major western cosmetic companies provide whitening products for Asian

markets. My sister bought the L'Oreal whitening facial wash in Thailand. Her Estée Lauder Cyber White facial care products were bought in Singapore. Estée Lauder's Chinese website sells fourteen whitening products, such as Cyber White Intensive Nighttime Brightening Series and Powder Whitening Essence. Olay's White Radiance series lists eleven products on its Chinese website.

4. The term "whiteness" encompasses not just skin color but also eye shape and color, hair color, and other physical traits such as thinness and larger breasts. The concept of "whiteness" also implies material wealth and political and military power.

5. For more information on the notion of action and motion see Kenneth Burke's book *A Grammar of Motives,* first published in 1945.

6. It is universally acknowledged that every country is "developing." Yet "developing countries" has been used in political discourses to designate those countries that are not as economically advanced as the western countries, setting up another binary against "developed countries."

7. Admittedly, this new type of colonization does not restrict its influence to China. Arguably it is a worldwide phenomenon.

12. Conocimiento and Healing

All quotations are from Gloria E. Anzaldúa's "now let us shift . . . the path of conocimiento . . . inner work, public acts."

1. In 1994 the events surrounding Proposition 187 led me to give up my stubborn resistance to becoming a U.S. citizen after many years of enjoying the benefits of having a permanent residence (a green card).

2. A key concept in Mahayana traditions of Buddhism, bodhicitta promotes the idea of compassion for and interconnectedness among all sentient beings while questioning the inherent existence of a separate self.

3. See my "Epistemologies of the Wound" for my in-depth reflections on the incest project.

13. Letters from Nepantla

1. This passage is a paraphrase of information in Narada, *The Buddha* (284).

2. In April 2004, after reading Gloria Anzaldúa's letter to third-world women writers, students replied to her with letters of their own. These now belong to the Gloria Evangelina Anzaldúa Papers, Benson Latin American Collection, University of Texas at Austin. The quotes here are excerpts from a second set of letters sent to Gloria Anzaldúa in June 2006. I have permission from all students I refer to in this essay to include their actual statements.

15. Living Transculturation

1. The coconut oracle is consulted using four pieces of coconut thrown (dropped) that upon landing reveal the answer to questions generally phrased

in a "yes," "no," or "maybe" format determined by the ratios of dark to white sides of the coconut turned up. See Lele's *Obí: Oracle of Cuban Santería* for a detailed exposition of the mechanics and uses of this oracle.

2. Fernando Ortiz developed this idea, which values the cultures of Afro-Cubans that all Cubans share. He did so out of his dissatisfaction with the notion of "acculturation," which he saw as implying a unidirectional process of acquisition of a dominant culture by dominated or subaltern groups.

3. The Sociology of Religion, an established subdiscipline, leans in the direction of the "church-sect continuum," typing religions according to their dominance and/or formalization, with churches occupying the center ground and pushing more dissenting or minority heterodox types to the periphery. This very language slants the focus of the observer toward a majority perspective.

4. In this regard my recent work on the sociologist Charles Horton Cooley, an early maverick who took his cues from literature, art, and his own spiritual work, suggests how work on oneself can be integrated into intellectual-scholarly life.

16. Acercándose a Gloria Anzaldúa to Attempt Community

1. On this I wrote in "Conflitto e genere," in *Conflitto e libertà femminile* 15–33.

2. I am thinking of the Mediterranean Sea as a point of conjunction between the Magna Grecia–western culture and the Balkan, Turkish, and Moorish cultures.

3. In Anzaldúa's vision, la frontera is a figuration and a locality very different from another peculiar U.S. American figuration, the wilderness, which alludes to borderlessness as primitivism and absence of polis, as boundlessness—which immediately calls for its contrary, the limit, the (de)fence.

4. The Italian version was finally published in 2000, as *Terre di confine/La frontera* (Bari: Palomar).

5. In her preface to *this bridge we call home* Anzaldúa describes bridges as "thresholds to other realities, archetypal, primal symbols of shifting consciousness. They are passageways, conduits, and connectors that connote transitioning, crossing borders, and changing perspectives" (1).

18. Risking the Vision, Transforming the Divides

I am, as always, indebted to Gloria Anzaldúa for her bold words. I'm very grateful to Gloria González-López and Carrie McMaster for comments on various versions of this essay.

1. To get a sense of Anzaldúa's boldness see her *Interviews/Entrevistas*. For an example of her willingness to make radical statements despite the possibility of misunderstanding see her "La Prieta" and "En rapport, In Opposition: Cobrando cuentas a las nuestras."

2. These identity-based assumptions also can lead to an extreme focus on each identity category's norm, so that Women's Studies becomes conflated with

the study of "white"-raced women; Ethnic Studies focuses primarily on men, and so on.

3. I define "status-quo stories" as worldviews that normalize and naturalize the existing social system, values, and standards and thus subtly deny the possibility of change. Status-quo stories contain "core beliefs" about reality—beliefs that shape our world, though we rarely (if ever) acknowledge their creative role. Generally, we don't even recognize these beliefs *as* beliefs; we're convinced that they offer accurate factual statements about reality. Status-quo stories train us to believe that the way things are is the way they always have been and the way they must be. This belief becomes self-fulfilling: we don't try to make change because we believe that change is impossible to make.

4. Unless, of course, we were to totally transform the academy and the idea of disciplinary fields . . . which might not be a bad idea!

5. I intentionally do not capitalize "eurocentric" because I believe that to do so participates in eurocentric thinking.

6. I borrow the term "nepantlera acts" from Kavitha Koshy. See her essay in this volume.

19. "To live in the borderlands means you"

1. This Nicaraguan saying means "neither this nor that," neither chicha, a traditional native drink made out of corn, nor lemonade.

2. For an account of the stages of conocimiento see Anzaldúa's "now let us shift."

20. A Modo de Testimoniar

An earlier version of this essay was presented at the Homage to Gloria Anzaldúa at the Political Economy of the World System (PEWS) Section of the American Sociological Association (ASA) Conference, World-Systemic Crisis and Contending Political Scenarios, University of Massachusetts, Amherst, April 14–17, 2005. Thanks to Gloria González-López, AnaLouise Keating, Juan G. Ramos, and Alejandro Pérez for reading previous drafts and encouraging me to go deep into my memory and heart.

1. I use the verb "fix" to convey the meaning of the Spanish word "arreglar," the way many undocumented immigrants refer to the process arising from lacking the required documents of residence in the country where they reside to becoming "legal aliens."

2. "Ayllu" is a political and economic form of social organization and a way of family life in pre- and post-Tawantinsuyo societies.

3. Most hip-hop artists only attain a high school education, as is also the case with most of the population in the United States and elsewhere. These messages ought to be disseminated in those sites where larger and more diverse groups can be reached. While I acknowledge that translating Anzaldúa's work into popular culture might in some ways maintain the current power structures,

we should also remember that Anzaldúa's work emerges from her experiences in peripheral locations. A crucial aspect of her legacy is to return these knowledges, these analytics, to similar locations, so that subalternized people will have additional tools to better understand their own colonialities; these tools can open up spaces for self-transformation.

23. Chicana Feminist Sociology in the Borderlands

The authors' names are ordered alphabetically. We would like to thank Gloria González-López for encouraging us to submit this essay and acknowledge both Gloria's and AnaLouise's work to create "a conscious rupture with all oppressive traditions of all cultures and religions" (*Borderlands/La Frontera* 82).

1. Mary Pardo's work on the Mothers of East Lost Angeles is a key text on Chicana/Mexicana collective action. In education, the work of Concha Delgado-Gaitán highlights the role of women to engage in collective advocacy for their children's education.

2. For more than three decades, Chicanas and Latinas have been involved in international and transnational political efforts through solidarity movements and documenting women's activism outside the United States. As Chicanas and Latinas continue to do empirical research in transnational sites, the conditions under which they conduct their work lead to important questions. For example, how are Chicana and Latina scholars contributing to and critiquing the "globalization discourse"? As Chicanas and Latinas engage in transnational scholarship and activities, what are the implications with respect to theory, epistemology, methodology, and activism in Chicana and Latina Studies? And how do we define the globalization discourse as Chicanas and Latinas?

3. Elisa Facio has been a consultant for SISTERS since 2004.

4. ENLACE was funded by the W. K. Kellogg Foundation from 2000 to 2005 at the University of California, Santa Barbara, under the direction of two co-principal investigators, Denise A. Segura and Richard Durán.

5. "Funds of knowledge" refers to various forms of home literacy practices, home discourse styles, and familial/cultural resources; see Moll et al.

6. AnaLouise Keating states that nepantla is an expansion of borderlands theory. It is a site she defines as "in-between space involving psychic and emotional healing" ("Remembering Gloria").

7. Sonia Saldívar-Hull argues that "mestizaje" is the key theoretical framework for Chicanas ("Recuerdos de Gloria").

24. Embracing Borderlands

1. Toward this end see Karlyn Kohrs Campbell's analysis of agency in the texts and person of Sojourner Truth: "Agency: Promiscuous and Protean," a keynote address presented at the 2003 Association of Rhetoric Societies meeting.

25. Hurting, Believing, and Changing the World

1. I dedicate this essay to my grandmother, Marian Cassidy (1910–1994), and to Gloria Anzaldúa.
2. See my article "Gloria Anzaldúa's Mestiza Pain: Mexican Sacrifice, Chicana Embodiment, and Feminist Politics" for a more extended discussion of the Aztec and Catholic "pain cultures" Anzaldúa invokes as well as critics' avoidance of the pain in *Borderlands*.
3. See, in particular, the interviews with Linda Smuckler (1982), Christine Weiland (1983), and AnaLouise Keating (1998–99), collected in *Interviews/ Entrevistas*.

26. Feels Like "Carving Bone"

In this paper I have attempted to build on the theories of Gloria E. Anzaldúa by applying them to my own journey as a social activist–student and, I dare say, theorist. Thanks to the editors, AnaLouise Keating and Gloria González-López, for being patient with me throughout this process. A special thanks to AnaLouise Keating for her thoughtful comments on multiple drafts of this paper; without her encouragement, support, and unflinching belief in me, this piece of writing would never have seen the light of day. And finally, my thanks go out to Gloria E. Anzaldúa for emboldening me through her writing to challenge myself to dig deep and write from the very core of my being.

1. "Dalit" is the word claimed by people of a lower-caste status in India to refer to themselves.
2. Zillah R. Eisenstein coined the term "capitalist patriarchy" in the late 1970s to draw attention to the nexus between patriarchal relations and capitalism.
3. For a discussion on "Oppression Olympics" see Elizabeth Martinez.
4. For an analysis see AnaLouise Keating's essay "Transforming Identity Politics" in *Women Reading Women Writing*.
5. For a thorough discussion of what "disidentification" may look like see Leela Fernandes's *Transforming Feminist Practice*.

27. Shifting

1. The italicized passages are from Anzaldúa's "now let us shift." I use this documentation style to emphasize how Anzaldúa's teachings guided my thinking in this essay and lie at the foundation of its messages.
2. I provide a detailed analysis of Anzaldúa's stages of conocimiento as a developmental theory in "New Pathways toward Understanding Self-in-Relation: Anzaldúan (Re)Visions for Developmental Psychology."

28. "Darkness, My Night"

1. My partner from 1990 to 2003 was Jill H. Casid. Among other things, we created the photo-text collaborative SPIR: Conceptual Photography and worked together on text-image projects for twelve years. Our mutual interests extensively informed each of our individual scholarly and pedagogical projects.

2. To date, the mural has seven basic parts or panels to it, each one engaging social issues relevant to our time: Triumph of the Heart, Dialogue of Alternatives, Nonviolent Resistance, The End of the Twentieth Century, Balance, Triumph of the Hands, and Israeli/Arab/Palestinian.

3. The Llorona figure in Mexican mythology is a complicated one, variously interpreted and rendered. The persistent theme regarding Llorona is that she is a dishonored and/or conquered woman, even a goddess, crying for her lost children. Significantly, Judy Baca's mural converts Llorona into visionary women holding candles of light in the darkness.

4. "Analytical testimonio" is my term for analysis that does not maintain the illusion of objective distance but rather places the writer, the scholar-critic, into an engaged relationship with her subject matter and material. For example, in this essay I bear witness to Anzaldúa's enormous intellectual and ethical impact on an entire generation of scholars in Ethnic, Gender and Queer, Feminist, Chicana/o, Latina/o, Border, and Postcolonial Studies at the same time that I am analyzing some of the key elements of her rhetoric. The two acts—analyzing and witnessing—are not assumed to be antithetical to one another. Furthermore, I also bear witness to the time of my own life, to the "momentousness" of the moments that have composed it, and to the connection of those space-times with other space-times as well as the space-times of other people.

5. About that resistance Anzaldúa writes, "My Chicana identity is grounded in the Indian woman's history of resistance" (*Borderlands/La Frontera* 43). This statement suggests that she thought of resistance to patriarchal, colonial, ethnoracially stratified oppression as grounded in the history of the indigenous people of the Americas and of the Southwest in particular.

6. See the 1982 interview with Linda Smuckler titled "Turning Points" in *Interviews/Entrevistas* (23).

29. The Simultaneity of Self- and Global Transformations

1. See my "Mysticism and Utopia" and "Toward a Dialectical Conception."

2. See my "Open the Antisystemic Movements," "Advancing Utopistics," and "De/Reconstructing Utopianism."

3. See Karl Mannheim, *Ideology and Utopia*, and my "Mysticism and Utopia."

4. See my "Orientalist and Liberating Discourses."

5. "What I mean by utopistics, a substitute word I have invented, is something rather different. Utopistics is the serious assessment of historical alternatives, the exercise of our judgment as to the substantive rationality of alternative

possible historical systems. It is the sober, rational, and realistic evaluation of human social systems, the constraints on what they can be, and the zones open to human creativity. Not the face of the perfect (and inevitable) future, but the face of an alternative, credible, better, and historically possible (but far from certain) future. It is thus an exercise simultaneously in science, in politics, and in morality" (Wallerstein 1–2). For more on utopistics see my *Advancing Utopistics*.

6. See my publications "Freire Meets Gurdjieff and Rumi" and "Decolonizing Selves."

7. The conference theme was Human Rights, Borderlands, and the Poetics of Applied Social Theory: Engaging with Gloria Anzaldúa in Self- and Global Transformations. This conference was held on 5–6 April 2006 at the University of Massachusetts, Boston.

8. See my "'I Change Myself.'"

She Eagle

The title is from Gloria Anzaldúa, "Last Words? Spirit Journeys," in *Interviews/Entrevistas*, 284.

Glossary

An earlier version of this glossary appeared in *The Gloria Anzaldúa Reader*.

autohistoria. Anzaldúa developed this term as well as the term "autohistoria-teoría" to describe women-of-color interventions into and transformations of traditional western autobiographical forms. Involved with the search for personal and cultural meaning, or what Anzaldúa describes in her post-*Borderlands* writings as "putting Coyolxauhqui together," both autohistoria and autohistoria-teoría are informed by reflective self-awareness employed in the service of social justice work. Autohistoria focuses on the personal life-story but, as the autohistorian tells her own life-story, she simultaneously tells the life-stories of others.

autohistoria-teoría. Theory developed by Anzaldúa to describe a relational form of autobiographical writing that includes both life-story and self-reflection on this storytelling process. Writers of autohistoria-teoría blend their cultural and personal biographies with memoir, history, storytelling, myth, and/or other forms of theorizing. By so doing they create interwoven individual and collective identities. Personal experiences—revised and in other ways redrawn—become a lens with which to reread and rewrite existing cultural stories. Through this lens Anzaldúa and other autohistoria-teóricas expose the limitations in the existing paradigms and create new stories of healing, self-growth, cultural critique, and individual/collective transformation. Anzaldúa described *Borderlands/La Frontera* as an example of one form autohistoria-teoría can take.

borderlands. When Anzaldúa writes this term with a lower-case "b" it refers to the region on both sides of the Texas-Mexico border.

Borderlands. For Anzaldúa, "Borderlands" with a capital "B" represents a concept that draws from yet goes beyond the geopolitical Texas/Mexico borderlands to encompass psychic, sexual, and spiritual Borderlands as well. These B/borderlands—both in their geographic and metaphoric meanings—represent intensely painful yet also potentially transformational spaces where opposites converge, conflict, and transform.

Coatlicue. According to Aztec mythology, Coatlicue (kwat-LEE-kway), whose name means "Serpent Skirts," is the earth goddess of life and death and mother of the gods. As Anzaldúa explains in *Borderlands'* fourth chapter, Coatlicue has a horrifying appearance, with a skirt of serpents and a necklace of human skulls. According to some versions of the story, after being impregnated by a ball of feathers, Coatlicue was killed by her daughter Coyolxauhqui and her other children.

Coatlicue state. An important element in Anzaldúa's epistemology; she coined this term to represent the resistance to new knowledge and other psychic states triggered by intense inner struggle that can entail the juxtaposition and the transmutation of contrary forces as well as paralysis and depression. She associates the Coatlicue state with a variety of situations, including creativity and her own writing blocks. These psychic conflicts are analogous to those she experienced as a Chicana; she explains that the opposing Mexican, Indian, and Anglo worldviews she has internalized lead to self-division, cultural confusion, and shame. Anzaldúa first discussed the Coatlicue state in *Borderlands/La Frontera* and developed it in her later writings.

conocimiento. A Spanish word for "knowledge" or "consciousness," Anzaldúa uses this term to represent a key component of her post-*Borderlands* epistemology. With her theory of conocimiento, she elaborates on the potentially transformative elements of her better-known *Borderlands* theories of mestiza consciousness and la facultad. Like mestiza consciousness, conocimiento represents a nonbinary, connectionist mode of thinking; like la facultad, conocimiento often unfolds within oppressive contexts and entails a deepening of perception. Conocimiento underscores and develops the imaginal, spiritual activist, and radically inclusionary possibilities implicit in these earlier theories.

conocimientos. While "conocimiento" refers to the theory in general (see above), "conocimientos" refers to specific insights acquired through the process of conocimiento.

Coyolxauhqui. According to Aztec mythology, Coyolxauhqui (Ko-yol-sha-UH-kee), also called La Diosa de la Luna (goddess of the moon), was Coatlicue's oldest daughter and the instigator of her murder. After her mother was impregnated by a ball of feathers, Coyolxauhqui encouraged her four hundred brothers and sisters to kill Coatlicue. As they attacked their mother, the fetus, Huitzilopochtli, sprang fully grown and armed from Coatlicue. He tore Coyolxauhqui into more than a thousand pieces, flung her head into the sky, and killed her siblings.

Coyolxauhqui imperative. Drawing from the story of Coyolxauhqui, Anzaldúa developed this concept to describe a self-healing process, an inner compulsion or desire to move from fragmentation to complex, multiplicitous wholeness. As she explains in "Speaking across the Divide": "The path of the artist, the creative impulse, what I call the Coyolxauhqui imperative is basically an attempt to heal the wounds. It's a search for inner completeness" (292, her emphasis). Anzaldúa often associated this imperative with her desire to write.

El Mundo Zurdo. One of Anzaldúa's earliest, least discussed concepts, El Mundo Zurdo (the left-hand world) has various ethical, epistemological, and aesthetic definitions. Most generally, El Mundo Zurdo represents relational difference. Applied to alliances, it indicates communities based on common-alities, visionary locations where people from diverse backgrounds, often with very different needs and concerns, co-exist and work together to bring about revolutionary change. In the late 1970s Anzaldúa initiated a reading series and writing workshops called "El Mundo Surdo." (She intentionally spelled "zurdo" with an "s" to honor the South Texas pronunciation.) These read-ings and workshops, while grounded in women-of-color perspectives, were di-verse and open to progressive people of any identity. For more on El Mundo Surdo see *The Gloria Anzaldúa Reader*.

Guadalupe. Also known as La Virgen de Guadalupe, she appeared to Juan Diego in 1531 with a message. Generally viewed as a more recent version of the indigenous goddess Tonantzín, Guadalupe represents a synthesis of mul-tiple traditions, as well as the conquest of the Americas. In *Borderlands/La Frontera* Anzaldúa describes her as "the single most potent religious, political, and cultural image of the Chicano/mexicano."

La Chingada. Literally translated to English as "the fucked one," this term is often associated with Malinche, the indigenous woman given to Hernán Cortés upon his arrival on the continent and, as such, the symbolic mother of the Mexican people.

la facultad. Anzaldúa's term for an intuitive form of knowledge that includes but goes beyond logical thought and empirical analysis. As she explains in *Borderlands/La Frontera*, it is "the capacity to see in surface phenomena the meaning of deeper realities, to see the deep structure below the surface. It is an instant 'sensing,' a quick perception arrived at without conscious reason-ing . . . an acute awareness mediated by the part of the psyche that does not speak, that communicates in images and symbols which are the faces of feel-ings" (60). While la facultad is most often developed by those who have been disempowered (or as Anzaldúa puts it, "pushed out of the tribe for being dif-ferent"), it is latent in everyone.

La Llorona. Sometimes referred to as the Weeping Woman, Llorona is a cen-tral figure in Mexican, Mexican American, and Chicano/a folklore as well as an important presence in Anzaldúa's work. There are many versions of the story, but in most versions Llorona is the ghost of a beautiful young woman who, after being seduced and abandoned by a man, kills (usually by drowning) her children. She is destined to wander forever crying for her lost children.

mestiza consciousness. One of Anzaldúa's best-known concepts, this "con-sciousness of the Borderlands" is a holistic, both/and way of thinking and acting that includes a transformational tolerance for contradiction and am-bivalence. Anzaldúa develops this theory in *Borderlands/La Frontera*.

mestizaje. The Spanish word for "mixture," mestizaje, as Anzaldúa generally uses it, refers to transformed combinations.

nagual. The Náhuatl word for "shape-shifter."

nagualismo. Shamanism.

nepantla. Náhuatl word meaning "in-between space." Anzaldúa used this term to develop her post-*Borderlands* theory of process, liminality, and potential change that builds on her theories of the Borderlands and the Coatlicue state. For Anzaldúa, nepantla represents temporal, spatial, psychic, and/or intellectual point(s) of crisis. Nepantla occurs during the many transitional stages of life and describes both identity-related issues and epistemological concerns. See her "now let us shift" and *Interviews/Entrevistas*.

nepantleras. A term coined by Anzaldúa to describe a unique type of mediator, one who "facilitate[s] passages between worlds" ("(Un)natural bridges" 1). Nepantleras live within and among multiple worlds and, often through painful negotiations, develop what Anzaldúa describes as a "perspective from the cracks"; they use these transformed perspectives to invent holistic, relational theories and tactics, enabling them to reconceive or in other ways transform the various worlds in which they exist.

new mestiza. Anzaldúa's theory of the new mestiza, which she develops in *Borderlands/La Frontera*, represents an innovative expansion of previous biologically based definitions of mestizaje. For Anzaldúa, new mestizas are people who inhabit multiple worlds because of their gender, sexuality, color, class, bodies, personalities, spiritual beliefs, and/or other life experiences. This theory offers a new concept of personhood that synergistically combines apparently contradictory Euro-American and indigenous traditions. Anzaldúa further develops her theory of the new mestiza into an epistemology and ethics she calls "mestiza consciousness" (see above).

new tribalism. Anzaldúa develops this theory to describe an affinity-based approach to alliance making and identify formation. This post-*Borderlands* theory offers provocative alternatives to both assimilation and separatism.

nos/otras. A theory of intersubjectivity Anzaldúa developed in her post-*Borderlands* writings. "Nosotras," the Spanish word for the feminine "we," indicates a type of group identity or consciousness. By partially dividing "nosotras" into two, Anzaldúa affirms this collective yet also acknowledges the sense of divisiveness so often felt in contemporary life ("nos" implies "us," while "otras" implies "others"). Joined together, nos + otras holds the promise of healing: we contain the others; the others contain us. Significantly, nos/otras does not represent sameness; the differences among "us" still exist, but they function dialogically, generating previously unrecognized commonalities and connections. Anzaldúa's theory of nos/otras offers an alternative to binary self/other constellations, a philosophy and praxis enabling us to acknowledge, bridge, and sometimes transform the distances between self and other. See her "now let us shift."

spiritual activism. Although Anzaldúa did not coin this term, she used it to describe her visionary, experientially based epistemology and ethics. At the epistemological level, spiritual activism posits a metaphysics of interconnectedness and employs nonbinary modes of thinking. At the ethical level, spiritual activism requires concrete actions designed to intervene in and transform existing social conditions. Spiritual activism is spirituality for social change, spirituality that recognizes the many differences among us yet insists on our commonalities and uses these commonalities as catalysts for transformation.

Yemayá. According to Yoruban beliefs, Yemayá is the orisha associated with the oceans and other waters.

Works Cited

Alexander, M. Jacqui. "Remembering *This Bridge*, Remembering Ourselves: Yearning, Memory, and Desire." *this bridge we call home: radical visions for transformation.* Ed. Gloria E. Anzaldúa and AnaLouise Keating. New York: Routledge, 2002. 81–103.

Alires Sáenz, Benjamin. "In the Borderlands of Chicano Identity, There Are Only Fragments." *Border Theory: The Limits of Cultural Politics.* Ed. David E. Johnson and Scott Michaelsen. Minneapolis: University of Minnesota Press, 1997. 68–96.

Andric, Ivo. *Na Drini cuprija.* Belgrade: Prosveta, 1945. Translated as *The Bridge on the Drina.* Chicago: University of Chicago Press, 1977.

———. *Racconti di Bosnia.* Rome: Newton Compton, 1995.

Anzaldúa, Gloria. *Borderlands/La Frontera: The New Mestiza.* San Francisco: Spinsters/Aunt Lute, 1987.

———. "Daughter of Coatlicue: An Interview with Gloria Anzaldúa." Interview with Irene Lara. *EntreMundos/AmongWorlds: New Perspectives on Gloria Anzaldúa.* Ed. AnaLouise Keating. New York: Palgrave Macmillan, 2005. 41–55.

———. "Exploring Nepantla, El Lugar de la Frontera." *NACLA Report on the Americas* 27.1 (1996): 37–42.

———. *The Gloria Anzaldúa Reader.* Ed. AnaLouise Keating. Durham: Duke University Press, 2009.

———. "Haciendo caras, una entrada." *Making Face, Making Soul/Haciendo Caras: Creative and Critical Perspectives by Women of Color.* Ed. Gloria Anzaldúa. San Francisco: Aunt Lute, 1990. xv–xxviii.

———. *Interviews/Entrevistas.* Ed. AnaLouise Keating. New York: Routledge, 2000.

———. "Let us be the healing of the wound. The Coyolxauhqui imperative—la sombra y el sueño." *One Wound for Another/Una herida por otra. Testimonios de Latin@s in the U.S. through Cyberspace (11 de septiembre de 2001–11 de marzo de 2002).* Ed. Claire Joysmith and Clara Lomas. 2005. 9–13.

———. "El Mundo Zurdo: The Vision." *This Bridge Called My Back: Writings by Radical Women of Color.* Ed. Cherríe Moraga and Gloria Anzaldúa. New York: Kitchen Table, Women of Color, 1983. 195–96.

————. "now let us shift . . . the path of conocimiento . . . inner work, public acts." *this bridge we call home: radical visions for transformation.* Ed. Gloria E. Anzaldúa and AnaLouise Keating. New York: Routledge, 2001. 540–78.

————. "La Prieta." 1981. *This Bridge Called My Back: Writings by Radical Women of Color.* Ed. Cherríe Moraga and Gloria Anzaldúa. New York: Kitchen Table, Women of Color, 1983. 198–209.

————. "Speaking across the Divides." *The Gloria Anzaldúa Reader.* Ed. AnaLouise Keating. Durham: Duke University Press, 2009. 292–94.

————. "Speaking in Tongues: A Letter to 3rd-World Women Writers." 1981. *This Bridge Called My Back: Writings by Radical Women of Color.* Ed. Cherríe Moraga and Gloria Anzaldúa. New York: Kitchen Table, Women of Color, 1983. 165–73.

————. "Toward a Mestiza Rhetoric: Gloria Anzaldúa on Composition and Post-Coloniality." Interview with Andrea Lunsford. *JAC: A Journal of Composition Theory* 18 (1998): 1–28.

————. "Transforming American Studies." 2001 Bode-Pearson Prize acceptance speech. *The Gloria Anzaldúa Reader.* Ed. AnaLouise Keating. Durham: Duke University Press, 2009. 239–41.

————. "(Un)natural bridges, (Un)safe spaces." *this bridge we call home: radical visions for transformation.* Ed. Gloria E. Anzaldúa and AnaLouise Keating. New York: Routledge, 2002. 1–5.

————, ed. *Making Face, Making Soul, Haciendo Caras: Creative and Critical Perspectives by Women of Color.* San Francisco: Aunt Lute, 1990.

———— and AnaLouise Keating, eds. *this bridge we call home: radical visions for transformation.* New York: Routledge, 2002.

Barfield, Owen. *Saving the Appearances: A Study in Idolatry.* Middletown, CT: Wesleyan University Press, 1988.

Barthes, Roland. *Camera Lucida: Reflections on Photography.* Trans. Richard Howard. New York: Hill and Wang, 1981.

Booth, Wayne C. *The Rhetoric of RHETORIC: The Quest for Effective Communication.* Malden, MA: Blackwell, 2004.

Bost, Suzanne. "Gloria Anzaldúa's Mestiza Pain: Mexican Sacrifice, Chicana Embodiment, and Feminist Politics." *Aztlán* 30.2 (Fall 2005): 5–34.

Braidotti, Rosi. *Metamorphoses. Towards a Materialist Theory of Becoming.* Cambridge, England: Polity, 2002.

Bridges, Flora Wilson. *Resurrection Song: African-American Spirituality.* Maryknoll, NY: Orbis, 2001.

Buck-Morss, Susan. *Origen de la dialéctica negativa.* Mexico City: Siglo XXI, 1981.

Burawoy, Michael. "For Public Sociology." *American Sociological Review* 70 (2005): 4–28.

Burke, Kenneth. *A Grammar of Motives.* Los Angeles: University of California Press, 1945.

Campbell, Karlyn Kohrs. "Agency, Promiscuous and Protean." *Communication and Critical/Cultural Studies* 2.1 (March 2005): 1–19.

Castillo, Debra, and Socorro Tabuenca. *Border Women. Writing from La Frontera.* Minneapolis: University of Minnesota Press, 2002.

Coronil, Fernando. "New Introduction." *Cuban Counterpoint: Tobacco and Sugar*. Fernando Ortiz. Durham: Duke University Press, 1995.

Cross, K. Patricia. *Beyond the Open Door*. San Francisco: Jossey-Bass, 1971.

Daly, Herman E., and John B. Cobb Jr. *For the Common Good: Redirecting the Economy toward Community, the Environment, and a Sustainable Future.* Boston: Beacon, 1994.

Djebar, Assi. *Queste voci che mi assediano*. Milan: il Saggiatore, 2004. Translation of *Ces voix qui m'assiegent*. Paris: Albin Michel, 1999.

Elbow, Peter. "Should We Invite Students to Write in Home Languages? Complicating the Yes/No Debate." *Composition Studies* 31.1 (March 2007): 25–42.

———. "Writing in the Vernacular." Conference on College Communication and Composition. Denver, 16 March 2001.

Fanon, Franz. *Black Skin, White Masks*. Trans. Richard Philcox. New York: Grove, 1967.

Fernandes, Leela. *Transforming Feminist Practice: Non-Violence, Social Justice, and the Possibilities of a Spiritualized Feminism*. San Francisco: Aunt Lute, 2003.

Fisher Fishkin, Shelley. "The Borderlands of Culture: Creative Experimentation in American Nonfiction Narrative." *Literary Journalism in the Twentieth Century*. Ed. Norman Sims. New York: Oxford University Press, 1990.

———. "Crossroads of Cultures: The Transnational Turn in American Studies—Presidential Address to the American Studies Association, November 12, 2004." *American Quarterly* 57.1 (March 2005): 17–57.

———. "Interrogating 'Whiteness,' Complicating 'Blackness': Remapping American Culture." *American Quarterly* 47:3 (September 1995): 428–66.

———. *Lighting Out for the Territory: Reflections on Mark Twain and American Culture*. New York: Oxford University Press, 1997.

———. *Was Huck Black? Mark Twain and African American Voices*. New York: Oxford University Press, 1993.

Fisher Fishkin, Shelley, and David Bradley, eds. *Encyclopedia of Civil Rights in America*. New York: M. E. Sharpe, 1997.

Fregoso, Rosa Linda. *meXicana Encounters: The Making of Social Identities on the Borderlands*. Berkeley: University of California Press, 2003.

Freire, Paulo. *Pedagogy of the Oppressed*. Trans. Myra Bergman Ramos. New York: Seabury, Continuum, 1970.

Freud, Sigmund. "Mourning and Melancholia." *The Standard Edition of the Complete Works of Sigmund Freud*, vol. 14: *1914–1916*. London: Hogarth, 1957.

Frye, Marilyn. "White Woman Feminist 1983–1992." *Race and Racism*. Ed. Bernard Boxill. New York: Oxford University Press, 2001. 83–100.

Geertz, Clifford. *Local Knowledge: Further Essays in Interpretive Anthropology*. New York: Basic Books, 1983.

Glenn, Cheryl. *Unspoken: A Rhetoric of Silence*. Carbondale: Southern Illinois University Press, 2004.

Godayol, Pilar. *Spazi di frontiera. Genere e traduzione*. Bari: Palomar, 2002. Translation of *Espais de frontera. Génere i traducció*. Eumo Editorial, 2000.

Gonzales, Patricia, and Roberto Rodriguez. "The Crossing of Gloria Anzal-dúa." October 2004. http://findarticles.com/p/articles/mi_km2912/is _200406/ai_n6905400/.

González-López, Gloria. "Epistemologies of the Wound. Anzaldúan Theories and Sociological Research on Incest in Mexican Society." *Human Architecture: Journal of the Sociology of Self-Knowledge* (2006): 17–24.

Gounari, Panagiota. "Intellectuals Rethinking Politics of Difference: A Pedagogical Project." *Discourse of Sociological Practice* 7.1–2 (2005): 175–86.

Gramsci, Antonio. *Selections from the Prison Notebooks.* New York: International, 1971.

Habell-Pallán, Michelle. "'Don't Call Us Hispanic': Popular Latino Theater in Vancouver." *Latino/a Popular Culture.* Ed. Michelle Habell-Pallán and Mary Romero. New York: New York University Press, 2002. 174–89.

Hedges, Elaine T., and Shelley Fisher Fishkin, eds. *Listening to Silences: New Essays in Feminist Criticism.* New York: Oxford University Press, 1994.

Hurtado, Aída. *Voicing Chicana Feminisms: Young Women Speak Out on Sexuality and Identity.* New York: New York University Press, 2003.

Jacobs, Glenn. *Charles Horton Cooley: Imagining Social Reality.* Amherst: University of Massachusetts Press, 2006.

Johnson, David E., and Scott Michaelsen. "Border Secrets: An Introduction." *Border Theory: The Limits of Cultural Politics.* Ed. David E. Johnson and Scott Michaelsen. Minneapolis: University of Minnesota Press, 1997. 1–42.

Joysmith, Claire. "Apuntes de colores: (Re)Writings and (Re)Translations." *Tameme: New Writing from North America/Nueva Literatura de Norteamérica* 2 (2001): 186–96.

———. "Crossing Ethnic and Cultural Boundaries: Translated Mexicanidades." *Raizes e rumos. Perspectivas interdisciplinares em estudos americanos.* Niteroi, Brazil: 7 Letras, Asociação Brasileira de Estudos Americanos, Universidade Federal Fluminense, 2001. 427–34.

———. "Cuando los textos cruzan fronteras: Consideraciones en torno a la traducción de la literatura chicana." *Las nuevas fronteras del siglo XXI: Dimensiones culturales.* Ed. Alejandro Álvarez, Pedro Castillo, Norma Klahn, and Federico Manchón. Mexico City and Santa Cruz: UNAM, UAM, *La Jornada,* and UC Santa Cruz, 2001. 135–47.

———. "don't paint yourself invisible." *Voices Without Borders,* vol. 2. Ed. Robert L. Girón. Arlington: Gival Press, 2009.

———, ed. *Las formas de nuestras voces: Chicana and Mexicana Writers in Mexico.* Mexico City and Berkeley: CISAN-UNAM and Third Woman, 1995.

———. "'Let us be the healing of the wound': Escribiendo desde la herida." *Debate Feminista* (Mexico City) 17 (34 October 2006): 331–41.

———. "(Re)Mapping *mexicanidades:* (Re)Locating Chicana Writings and Translation Politics." *Chicana Feminisms. A Critical Reader.* Ed. Gabriela Arredondo, Aída Hurtado, Norma Klahn, Olga Nájera-Ramírez, and Patricia Zavella. Durham: Duke University Press, 2003. 146–54.

———. "Sol y luna." *Tameme: New Writing from North America/Nueva Literatura de Norteamérica* 2 (2001): 108–11.

———. "Ya se me quitó la vergüenza y la cobardía. Una plática con Gloria Anzaldúa." *Debate Feminista* 8.4 (September 1993): 3–18.

————. "Ya se me quitó la vergüenza y la cobardía. Una plática con Gloria Anzaldúa." *Fronteras y cruces: Cartografía de escenarios culturales latinoamericanos.* Coord. Marisa Belausteguigoitia and Martha Leñero. Mexico City: Programa Universitario de Estudios de Género and Facultad de Ciencias Políticas Y Sociales, UNAM, 2005. 215–29.

Joysmith, Claire, and Clara Lomas, eds. *One Wound for Another/Una herida por otra. Testimonios de Latin@s in the U.S. through Cyberspace (11 de septiembre de 2001–11 de marzo de 2002).* Mexico City, Colorado Springs, and Whittier, California: Centro de Investigaciones sobre América del Norte (CISAN)–Universidad Nacional Autónoma de México (UNAM), Colorado College, and Whittier College, Colorado College, and Whittier College, 2005.

Keating, AnaLouise. "Charting Pathways, Marking Thresholds. . . . A Warning, an Introduction." *this bridge we call home: radical visions for transformation.* Ed. Gloria Anzaldúa and AnaLouise Keating. New York: Routledge, 2002. 6–20.

————. "(De)Centering the Margins? Identity Politics and Tactical (Re)Naming." *Other Sisterhoods. Literary Theory and U.S. Women of Color.* Ed. Sandra Kumamoto Stanley. Urbana: University of Illinois Press, 1998. 23–43.

————, ed. *EntreMundos/AmongWorlds: New Perspectives on Gloria Anzaldúa.* Palgrave Macmillan, 2005.

————. "Forging El Mundo Zurdo: Changing Ourselves, Changing the World." *this bridge we call home: radical visions for transformation.* Ed. Gloria Anzaldúa and AnaLouise Keating. New York: Routledge, 2001. 518–30.

————. "From Borderlands and New Mestizas to Nepantlas and Nepantleras: Anzaldúan Theories for Social Change." *Human Architecture: Journal of the Sociology of Self-Knowledge* 4 (2006): 5–16.

————. "From Intersections to Interconnections: Lessons for Transformation from *This Bridge Called My Back: Radical Writings by Women of Color.*" *The International Approach: Transforming Women's and Gender Studies through Race, Class, and Gender.* Ed. Michele Tracy Berger and Kathleen Guidroz. Durham: University of North Carolina Press, 2009.

————. "Remembering Gloria." MALCS (Mujeres Activas en Letras y Cambio Social) Annual Summer Institute, 6 August 2004. Seattle.

————. "Risking the Personal: An Introduction." *Interviews/Entrevistas.* Gloria E. Anzaldúa. New York: Routledge, 2000. 1–15.

————. "Shifting Perspectives: Spiritual Activism, Social Transformation, and the Politics of Spirit." *EntreMundos/Among Worlds: New Perspectives on Gloria Anzaldúa.* Ed. AnaLouise Keating. Palgrave Macmillan, 2005. 241–54.

————, ed. "Shifting Worlds, una entrada." *EntreMundos/Among Worlds: New Perspectives on Gloria Anzaldúa.* Palgrave Macmillan, 2005. 1–12.

————. *Teaching Transformation: Transcultural Classroom Dialogues.* New York: Palgrave Macmillan, 2010.

————. "Transformational Identity Politics: Seeing 'Through the Eyes of the Other.'" *Women Reading Women Writing: Self-Invention in Paula Gunn Allen, Gloria Anzaldúa, and Audre Lorde.* Philadelphia: Temple University Press, 1996. 60–92.

Laddaga, Reinaldo. "From Work to Conversation: Writing and Citizenship in a Global Age." *PMLA* 122.2 (March 2007): 449–63.

Lele, Ócha'ni. *Obí—Oracle of Cuban Santería*. Rochester, VT: Destiny Books, 2001.

Levins Morales, Aurora. "The Historian as Curandera." *Medicine Stories: History, Culture, and the Politics of Integrity*. Cambridge, MA: South End, 1998. 23–38.

Levitt, Peggy. *The Transnational Villagers*. Berkeley: University of California Press, 2001.

Lichtenberg Ettinger, Bracha. "Matrix and Metamorphosis." *Differences: A Journal of Feminist Cultural Studies* 4.3 (1999): 176–208.

Lorenz, Helene Shulman. "Thawing Hearts, Opening a Path in the Woods, Founding a New Lineage." *this bridge we call home: radical visions for transformation*. Ed. Gloria E. Anzaldúa and AnaLouise Keating. New York: Routledge, 2002. 496–506.

Lugones, María. "Playfulness, 'World' Traveling, and Loving Perception." *Making Face, Making Soul/Haciendo Caras: Creative and Critical Perspectives by Women of Color*. Ed. Gloria Anzaldúa. San Francisco: Aunt Lute, 1990. 390–402.

Lunsford, Andrea A. "Composing Ourselves: Politics, Commitment, and the Teaching of Writing. *College Composition and Communication* 41.1 (1990): 71–82.

Madsen, William. *Mexican-Americans of South Texas*. New York: Holt, Rinehart, and Winston, 1964.

Mannheim, Karl. *Ideology and Utopia: An Introduction to the Sociology of Knowledge*. New York: Harcourt Brace, 1936.

Moll, Luis C., Cathy Armanti, Deborah Neff, and Norma Gonzalez. "Funds of Knowledge for Teaching: Using a Qualitative Approach to Connect Homes and Classrooms." *Theory into Practice* 31 (1992): 132–41.

Moraga, Cherríe, and Ana Castillo, eds. *Esta puente, mi espalda: Voces de mujeres tercermundistas en los Estados Unidos*. Trans. Ana Castillo and Norma Alarcón. San Francisco: Ism Press, 1988. Spanish adaptation of *This Bridge Called My Back: Writings by Women of Color*.

Moraga, Cherríe, and Gloria Anzaldúa, eds. *This Bridge Called My Back: Writings by Radical Women of Color*, 1981. Expanded and revised 3rd edition. Berkeley: Third Woman, 2002.

Moreiras, Jorge. *The Exhaustion of Difference: The Politics of Latin American Cultural Studies*. Durham: Duke University Press, 2001.

Morgan, Robin. *Sisterhood Is Global: The International Women's Movement Anthology*. New York: Anchor/Doubleday, 1984.

Naples, Nancy. *Feminism and Method: Ethnography, Discourse Analysis, and Activist Research*. New York: Routledge, 2003.

Narada, Maha Thera. *The Buddha and His Teachings*. 4th edition. Kuala Lumpur: Buddhist Missionary Society, 1988.

O'Neill, Eugene. *Long Day's Journey into Night*. New Haven: Yale University Press, 1956.

Ortiz, Fernando. *Cuban Counterpoint: Tobacco and Sugar*. 1947. Trans. Harriet de Onís. Durham: Duke University Press, 1995.

Pérez, Emma. "Gloria Anzaldúa: La Gran Nueva Mestiza Theorist, Writer, Activist-Scholar." *NWSA Journal* 17.2 (2005): 1–10.

Powell, Timothy B. "'All Colors Flow into Rainbows and Nooses': The Struggle to Define Academic Multiculturalism." *Cultural Critique* 55 (2003): 152–81.

Ratcliffe, Krista. *Rhetorical Listening: Identification, Gender, Whiteness.* Carbondale: Southern Illinois University Press, 2006.

Razack, Sherene. *Looking White People in the Eye: Gender, Race, and Culture in Courtrooms and Classrooms.* Toronto: University of Toronto Press, 1998.

Rest in Peace Gloria. Ed. Susana L. Gallardo. http://gloria.chicanas.com. June 2004.

Rosaldo, Renato. *Culture and Truth. The Remaking of Social Analysis.* Boston: Beacon, 1989.

Ross, Christine. *The Aesthetics of Disengagement: Contemporary Art and Depression.* Minneapolis: University of Minnesota Press, 2006.

Rowley, Michelle. "Rethinking Interdisciplinarity: Meditations on the Sacred Possibilities of an Erotic Feminist Pedagogy." *Small Axe* 12.2 (2007): 139–53.

Royster, Jacqueline Jones. "When the First Voice You Hear Is Not Your Own." *College Composition and Communication* 47.1 (1996): 29–40.

Rubin-Dorsky, Jeffrey, and Shelley Fisher Fishkin, eds. *People of the Book: Thirty Scholars Reflect on their Jewish Identity.* Madison: University of Wisconsin Press, 1994.

Said, Edward. *Culture and Imperialism.* New York: Vintage, 1994.

Saldívar-Hull, Sonia. "Recuerdos de Gloria, Return to the Homeland." MALCS (Mujeres Activas en Letras y Cambio Social) Annual Summer Institute, 6 August 2004. Seattle.

Sandoval, Chela. "U.S. Third World Feminism: The Theory and Method of Oppositional Consciousness in the Postmodern World." *Genders* 10 (1991): 1–25.

Schroeder, Christopher, Helen Fox, and Patricia Bizzell. *ALT/DIS: Alternative Discourses and the Academy.* Portsmouth, NH: Heinemann, 2002.

Sedgwick, Eve Kosofsky. *Epistemology of the Closet.* Berkeley: University of California Press, 1990.

Segura, Denise A., and Patricia Zavella. "Introduction." *Women and Migration in the U.S.-Mexico Borderlands: A Reader.* Ed. Denise A. Segura and Patricia Zavella. Durham: Duke University Press, 2007.

Shildrick, Margrit. *Leaky Bodies and Boundaries: Feminism, Postmodernism, and (Bio)ethics.* London: Routledge, 1997.

Shiva, Vandana. *Earth Democracy: Justice, Sustainability, and Peace.* London: Zed, 2005.

Smitherman, Geneva. *Talkin' and Testifyin': The Language of Black America.* Houghton Mifflin, 1977.

Souza, Caridad. "Disidentification." Lecture. Latina Feminism(s) course. Rutgers University, New Brunswick, NJ. Spring 1996.

———. Personal communication to Karina L. Céspedes. May 2006.

Spivak, Gayatri Chakravorty. "Can the Subaltern Speak?" *Marxism and the In-*

terpretation of Cultures. Ed. Lawrence Grossberg and Gary Nelson. Chicago: University of Chicago Press, 1988. 271–313.

Sternglass, Marilyn. *Time to Know Them: A Longitudinal Study of Writing and Learning at the College Level*. New York: Routledge, 1997.

"Students' Right to Their Own Language." Special issue of *College Composition and Communication* 25 (October 1974): 1–45.

Tamdgidi, Mohammad H. *Advancing Utopistics: The Three Component Parts and Errors of Marxism*. Boulder: Paradigm, 2009.

———. "Decolonizing Selves: The Subtler Violences of Colonialism and Racism in Fanon, Said, and Anzaldúa." *Fanon and the Decolonization of Philosophy*. Ed. Elizabeth A. Hoppe and Tracey Nicholls. Lanham, MD: Lexington Books, forthcoming.

———. "De/Reconstructing Utopianism: Towards a World-Historical Typology." *Human Architecture: Journal of the Sociology of Self-Knowledge* 2.2 (2003/4): 125–41.

———. "Freire Meets Gurdjieff and Rumi: Toward the Pedagogy of the Oppressed and Oppressive Selves." *Discourse of Sociological Practice* 6.2 (2004): 165–85.

———. "'I Change Myself, I Change the World': Gloria Anzaldúa's Sociological Imagination in *Borderlands/La Frontera: The New Mestiza*." *Humanity and Society* 32.4 (2008): 311–35.

———. "Mysticism and Utopia: Towards the Sociology of Self-Knowledge and Human Architecture (A Study in Marx, Gurdjieff, and Mannheim)." Ph.D. dissertation, State University of New York at Binghamton, 2002.

———. "Open the Antisystemic Movements: The Book, the Concept, and the Reality." *REVIEW: Journal of the Fernand Braudel Center for the Study of Economies, Historical Systems, and Civilizations* 24.2 (2001): 299–336.

———. "Orientalist and Liberating Discourses of East-West Difference: Revisiting Edward Said and the Rubaiyat of Omar Khayyam." *Discourse of Sociological Practice* 7.1–2 (2005): 187–201.

———. "Toward a Dialectical Conception of Imperiality: The Transitory (Heuristic) Nature of the Primacy of Analyses of Economies in World-Historical Social Science." *REVIEW: Journal of the Fernand Braudel Center for the Study of Economies, Historical Systems, and Civilizations* 29.4 (2006): 291–328.

Teresa de Jesús. *Obras completas*. Madrid: Aguilar, 1988.

Tonouchi, Lee. "Da State of Pidgin Address." *College English* 67.1 (2004): 75–82.

Turner, Victor. *Dramas, Fields, and Metaphors: Symbolic Action in Human Society*. Ithaca: Cornell University Press, 1974.

Wallerstein, Immanuel. *Utopistics: Or, Historical Choices of the Twenty-First Century*. New York: New Press, 1998.

Zaccaria, Paola. *La lingua che ospita. Poetica, politica, traduzioni*. Rome: Meltemi, 2005.

———, ed. *Transcodificazioni*. Rome: Meltemi, 2005.

Published Writings by Gloria E. Anzaldúa

Books

Borderlands/La Frontera: The New Mestiza. San Francisco: Spinsters/Aunt Lute, 1987.
Friends from the Other Side/Amigos del Otro Lado. Ill. Consuelo Méndez. San Francisco: Children's Book Press, 1993.
The Gloria Anzaldúa Reader. Ed. AnaLouise Keating. Durham: Duke University Press, 2009.
Interviews/Entrevistas. Ed. AnaLouise Keating. New York: Routledge, 2000.
Prietita and the Ghost Woman/Prietita y La Llorona. Ill. Maya Christina Gonzalez. San Francisco: Children's Book Press, 1995.

Edited Collections

Making Face, Making Soul/Haciendo Caras: Creative and Critical Perspectives by Women of Color. San Francisco: Aunt Lute Foundation, 1990.
This Bridge Called My Back: Writings by Radical Women of Color. Co-edited with Cherríe Moraga. Persephone Press, 1981.
This Bridge Called My Back: Writings by Radical Women of Color. Expanded and revised 3rd edition. Co-edited with Cherríe M. Moraga. Berkeley: Third Woman, 2002.
this bridge we call home: radical visions for transformation. Co-edited with AnaLouise Keating. New York: Routledge, 2002.

Essays

"Border Arte: Nepantla, El Lugar de la Frontera." *La Frontera/The Border: Art about the Mexico/United States Border Experience*. Museum of Contemporary Art, San Diego, 1993. 107–203.

"Bridge, Drawbridge, Sandbar or Island: *Lesbians-of-Color Hacienda Alianzas.*" *Bridges of Power: Women's Multicultural Alliances.* Ed. Lisa Albrecht and Rose M. Brewer. Philadelphia: New Society, 1990. 216–31.

"counsels from the firing . . . past, present, future." Foreword to *This Bridge Called My Back: Writings by Radical Women of Color.* Ed. Cherríe M. Moraga and Gloria E. Anzaldúa. Berkeley: Third Woman, 2002.

E-mail interview. *Studies in American Indian Literature* 15 (Fall 2003): 7–22.

"En rapport, In Opposition: Cobrando cuentas a las nuestras." *Sinister Wisdom* 33 (1987): 11–17.

Foreword to *Encyclopedia of Queer Myth, Symbol, and Spirit.* Ed. Randy Conner, David Sparks, and Moira Sparks. New York: Cassell, 1996.

"Let us be the healing of the wound: The Coyolxauhqui imperative—la sombra y el sueño." *One Wound for Another/Una Herida por Otra: Testimonios de Latin@s in the U.S. through Cyberspace (11 septiembre 2001–11 marzo 2002).* Ed. Claire Joysmith and Clara Lomas. Mexico City, Colorado Springs, and Whittier, CA: Centro de Investigaciones sobre América del Norte (CISAN)/ Universidad Nacional Autónoma de México (UNAM), Colorado College, and Whittier College, 2005.

"Metaphors in the Tradition of the Shaman." *Conversant Essays: Contemporary Poets on Poetry.* Ed. James McCorkle. Detroit: Wayne State University Press, 1990. 99–100.

"now let us shift . . . the path of conocimiento . . . inner work, public acts." *this bridge we call home: radical visions for transformation.* Ed. Gloria E. Anzaldúa and AnaLouise Keating. New York: Routledge, 2002. 540–78.

"La Prieta." *This Bridge Called My Back: Writings by Radical Women of Color,* 1981. Ed. Cherríe Moraga and Gloria Anzaldúa. New York: Kitchen Table, Women of Color, 1983. 198–209.

"Putting Coyolxauhqui Together, A Creative Process." *How We Work.* Ed. Marla Morris, Mary Aswell Doll, and William F. Pinar. New York: Peter Lang, 1999.

"Speaking in Tongues: A Letter to 3rd-World Women Writers." *This Bridge Called My Back: Writings by Radical Women of Color.* Ed. Cherríe Moraga and Gloria Anzaldúa. New York: Kitchen Table, Women of Color, 1983. 165–74.

"To(o) Queer the Writer—*Loca, escritora y chicana.*" *Inversions: Writing by Dykes, Queers, and Lesbians.* Ed. Betsy Warland. Vancouver: Press Gang, 1991. 249–64.

"(Un)natural bridges, (Un)safe spaces." *this bridge we call home: radical visions for transformation.* Ed. Gloria E. Anzaldúa and AnaLouise Keating. New York: Routledge, 2002. 1–5.

Fiction/Autohistorias

"Ghost Trap." *New Chicana/Chicano Writing* 1. Ed. Charles Tatum. Tucson: University of Arizona Press, 1992. 40–2.

"La historia de una marimacha." *Third Woman* 4 (1989): 64–68.

"Lifeline." *Lesbian Love Stories,* vol. 1. Ed. Irene Zahava. Freedom, CA: Cross-ing Press, 1991. 1–3.

"Ms. Right, My True Love, My Soul Mate." *Lesbian Love Stories,* vol. 2. Ed. Irene Zahava. Freedom, CA: Crossing Press, 1991. 184–88.

"El paisano is a bird of good omen." *Conditions* 8 (1982): 28–47.

"People Should Not Die in June in South Texas." *My Story's On: Ordinary Women, Extraordinary Lives.* Ed. Paula Ross. Berkeley: Common Differences, 1985. 280–87.

"Puddles." *New Chicana/Chicano Writing* 1. Ed. Charles Tatum. Tucson: University of Arizona Press, 1992. 43–45.

"She Ate Horses." *Lesbian Philosophies and Cultures.* Ed. Jeffner Allen. New York: State University of New York, 1990. 371–88.

"Swallowing Fireflies/Tragando Luciérnagas." *Telling Moments: Autobiographical Lesbian Short Stories.* Ed. Lynda Hall. Madison: University of Wisconsin Press, 2003. 3–12.

Contributors' Biographies

SUZANNE BOST is associate professor of English at Loyola University, Chicago. She has written two books, *Mulattas and Mestizas: Representing Mixed Identities in the Americas, 1850–2000* (University of Georgia Press, 2003) and *Encarnación: Illness and Body Politics in Chicana Feminist Literature* (Fordham University Press, 2009), as well as a number of articles published in journals (including *African American Review, MELUS, Postmodern Culture, Nepantla,* and *Aztlán*) and edited collections (most recently, *Material Feminisms*).

NORMA E. CANTÚ is a daughter of the U.S.-Mexican borderlands whose work for the past thirty years has focused on that geographical region. As a folklorist, scholar, and creative writer she seeks to decolonize the spaces, wherever they may be, that keep people in chains. Author of the award-winning *Canícula: Snapshots of a Girlhood en la Frontera* and co-editor of *Chicana Traditions: Continuity and Change* and *Telling to Live: Latina Feminist Testimonios,* she is working on a novel titled *Champú, or Hair Matters* and an ethnographic work, *Soldiers of the Cross: Los Matachines de la Santa Cruz.*

JORGE CAPETILLO-PONCE is presently director of Latino Studies and associate professor of Sociology at University of Massachusetts, Boston. Dr. Capetillo-Ponce is the editor of two books: *Images of Mexico in the U.S. News Media* and *A Foucault for the 21st Century.* His latest publications are "Deciphering the Labyrinth"; "The Influence of Georg Simmel on the Sociology of Octavio Paz"; "Politics, Ethnicity, and Bilingual Education in Massachusetts"; "From 'A Clash of Civilizations' to 'Internal Colonialism': Reactions to the Theoretical Bases of Samuel Huntington's 'The Hispanic Challenge'"; "Framing the 'Taxes and Undocumented Workers' Debate"; and "Foucault, Marxism, and the Cuban Revolution."

KARINA LISSETTE CÉSPEDES was born in Havana, Cuba. She immigrated to the United States with her family in 1980 and grew up in Elizabeth, New Jersey. Karina received her B.A. from Rutgers University, where she majored in Puerto Rican and Hispanic Caribbean Studies, and then received both her master's and Ph.D. from the University of California, Berkeley, in Ethnic Studies. Currently Karina is an assistant professor at the State University of New York College at Oneonta in the Women's and Gender Studies Department and the Africana and Latino Studies Department. She has published in a number of journals and anthologies and is finishing a manuscript on Cuban tourism and sex work during the 1990s. Karina divides her time between upstate New York and Santa Fe, New Mexico.

SEBASTIÁN JOSÉ COLÓN-OTERO is a Boricua poet, performer, and activist. He has a master's degree in Social Work from the University of Michigan and is a nationally recognized public speaker. Sebastián is a radical transqueer feminist of color with an evolving sense of gender identity and self-definition. He has identified as female to something else, genderqueer, and after physically transitioning, as a muchacho-transman. Sebastián believes in the struggle for libertad y autodeterminación and considers Gloria Evangelina Anzaldúa la gran clarividente: una luciérnaga guiando pasos en el camino oscuro.

ESTHER CUESTA. By birth, guayaquileña. By choice (and in loose translation), mashi (friend), wayna (lover), killkakatik (reader), killkak (writer), yachachik (teacher), yachakuk (learner), and Ph.D. candidate in Comparative Literature at the University of Massachusetts, Amherst. She is currently consul of Ecuador in Genoa, collaborating with diasporic Ecuadorians living in the regions of Liguria and Emilia Romagna, Italy. (E-mail: esthercita108@yahoo.com.)

MARÍA DEGUZMÁN is associate professor of English and Comparative Literature and director of Latina/o Studies at the University of North Carolina at Chapel Hill. She is the author of *Spain's Long Shadow: The Black Legend, Off-Whiteness, and Anglo-American Empire* (University of Minnesota Press, 2005). Among her publications are articles and essays on the work of Achy Obejas, on Mariana Romo-Carmona (in *Cen-*

tro: Journal of the Center for Puerto Rican Studies), Ana Castillo (in *Aztlán*), Graciela Limón (in *Revista Iberoamericana*), on Rane Ramón Arroyo, John Rechy, and Floyd Salas. She also writes on the relationships among various kinds of photographic practice and literature. Some of that scholarship is being published in *Word and Image: A Journal of Verbal/Visual Enquiry* (Routledge). Currently, she is working on a second book project, concerning Latina/o aesthetics of night, and is continuing to produce photo-text work as Camera Query (http://www .cameraquery.com), both solo and in collaboration with colleagues and friends.

HÉCTOR DOMÍNGUEZ-RUVALCABA is an associate professor in the Department of Spanish and Portuguese at the University of Texas at Austin. He has published *La modernidad abyecta. Formación de discurso homosexual en Latinoamérica* (Universidad Veracruzana, 2001) and *Modernity and the Nation in Mexican Representations of Masculinity: From Sensuality to Bloodshed* (Palgrave Macmillan, 2007), as well as numerous articles on homosexuality, masculinities, and violence. His areas of academic interest are: masculinity and queer studies in Latin America, Mexican-U.S. border violence, and cultural and political implications of organized crime in Mexico.

BETSY EUDEY is associate professor of Gender Studies and director of the Faculty Center for Excellence in Teaching and Learning at California State University, Stanislaus. She holds a Ph.D. in Cultural Studies in Education from Ohio State University and engages in teaching and research related to gender and education, inclusive pedagogies, feminist activism, and civic engagement. The voices of Gloria Anzaldúa, bell hooks, Paulo Freire, John Dewey, and Robert J. Nash are ever present in her mind, providing guidance as she strives to support her students and faculty colleagues.

ELISA FACIO is associate professor in the Department of Ethnic Studies at the University of Colorado, Boulder, where she teaches courses on Chicana Feminist Thought; Critical Issues on Age, Aging, and Generations; Chicana-Indígena Spiritualities; and globalization and transnational issues related to gender, race, and sexuality. Elisa's publications include a book on older Mexican women titled *Understanding Older Chicanas: Sociological and Policy Perspectives* (Sage, 1996). Elisa is co-editing an anthology on Chicana, Indígena, and Latina spirit and spirituality/ies with Irene Lara and completing a manuscript on female sex workers in Havana.

SHELLEY FISHER FISHKIN is a professor of English, director of American Studies at Stanford University, and the author, editor, or co-editor of more than forty books, including *Was Huck Black? Mark Twain and African American Voices; Lighting Out for the Territory; People of the Book: Thirty Scholars Reflect on Their Jewish Identity; Listening to Silences: New Essays in Feminist Literature;* and most recently, *Feminist Engagements: Forays into American Literary And Culture* (Palgrave/Macmillan 2009). She is a past president of the American Studies Association and is a founding editor of the *Journal of Transnational American Studies.*

LORENA M. P. GAJARDO is a Chilean Canadian scholar whose work focuses on Latina/o identity in Canada and who is very interested in helping develop the emerging field of Studies of Latinidad in Canada. She is also a founding member of the Latina Feminist Writing Collective LETRAS and is editing a book on Latina/o Canadian youth and practices of representation. Muchas gracias Gloria por recordarnos que todas somos mujeres mágicas. (E-mail: lorena.gajardo@utoronto.ca.)

GLORIA GONZÁLEZ-LÓPEZ is an associate professor of Sociology at the University of Texas at Austin. She was born and educated through undergraduate years in Monterrey, Mexico, before she migrated to the United States; she received a Ph.D. in Sociology from the University of Southern California in 2000. She conducts sexuality research with Mexican and Mexican immigrant populations and teaches graduate and undergraduate courses on sexuality, gender and society, and qualitative methods and sexuality research. She is the author of *Erotic Journeys: Mexican Immigrants and Their Sex Lives* (University of California Press, 2005). She is currently conducting sociological research on the sexual, romantic, and life experiences of adult women and men with histories of incestuous relationships and who currently live in the largest urbanized areas in Mexico.

JESSICA HEREDIA was born and raised in the borderlands of San Diego, where the courageous women of her family (Mom, Nana, tías) taught her the ways of the world. With their encouragement, she pursued education as a way to challenge and nourish her bodymindspirit.

Gloria Anzaldúa's writing inspired Jessica while working with her mentor, Dr. Irene Lara. Because of their heart-to-heart chats, Jessica has been able to embrace the nepantlera within her. Now she looks forward to the new transitions and transformations in her life as a violence prevention educator, a friendwifepartner to D, and mama to her son, Dominick Isaiah.

AÍDA HURTADO is chair of the Department of Chicana and Chicano Studies at the University of California, Santa Barbara. A psychologist by training, her books include *Voicing Chicana Feminisms: Young Women Speak Out on Sexuality and Feminism* and *Relating to Privilege: Three Blasphemies on Race and Feminism.* Aída Hurtado recently ended a two-year term as chair of the National Association for Chicana and Chicano Studies. In 2007 she was awarded the Distinguished Contributions to Gender Equity Award from the American Educational Research Association. For a number of years, she has collaborated with a GEAR UP program in South Texas, assisting it with long-term program evaluation.

GLENN JACOBS is an associate professor of Sociology at the University of Massachusetts, Boston. He has published a book on a founding U.S. sociologist, *Charles Horton Cooley: Imagining Social Reality* (University of Massachusetts Press, 2006), and has researched and written scholarly articles on educational privatization and Latino issues and on Afro-Cuban religion and music. Currently he is researching and writing about Latino immigrant community-based organizations. He heads a research consortium for the William Monroe Trotter Institute studying immigration in the Boston metropolitan area.

CLAIRE JOYSMITH was born and raised in Mexico; she works at the UNAM. Her research focuses on Mexico/Latin America cross-border transculturation, Chicana/Latina Literature, and cultural/linguistic translation. Her publications include *Cantar de Espejos/Singing Mirrors. Poetry by Chicanas* (bilingual edition, 2008), *Speaking desde las heridas. Cibertestimonios Transfronterizos/Transborder* (2008), *One Wound for Another/Una herida por otra* (2005), and *Las formas de nuestras voces: Chicana and Mexicana Writers in Mexico* (1995). Her articles and translations have appeared in *Chicana Feminisms: A Reader* and *Debate Feminista,* among other journals; her interviews include one with Gloria Anzaldúa in Mexico; and she participated in the collective introduction to the twentieth-anniversary edition of *Borderlands/La Frontera.*

ANALOUISE KEATING is a professor of Women's Studies and the director of the Doctoral Program in Women's Studies at Texas Woman's University; the author of *Women Reading, Women Writing: Self-Invention in Paula Gunn Allen, Gloria Anzaldúa, and Audre Lorde* and *Teaching Transformation: Transcultural Classroom Dialogues;* co-editor of *Perspectives: Gender Studies* and *this bridge we call home: radical visions for transformation;* and editor of Anzaldúa's *Interviews/Entrevistas, EntreMundos/AmongWorlds: New Perspectives on Gloria Anzaldúa* (Palgrave Macmillan, 2007), and *The Gloria Anzaldúa Reader* (Duke University Press, 2009). AnaLouise has also published articles on Latina authors, African American literature, queer studies, multiculturalism, eighteenth- and nineteenth-century American writers, feminist theory, Anzaldúa, and pedagogy.

C. MICHELLE KLEISATH was born in California in 1981. She received a bachelor's degree in Spanish and Gender Studies from the University of California, Davis, in 2003. From 2003 to 2007 she taught Sociology in Xining, China, where she co-founded and directed Shem Women's Group. She is currently pursuing a doctoral degree in Anthropology at the University of Washington.

KAVITHA KOSHY was born and raised in India. She is currently working on a Ph.D. in Sociology at Texas Woman's University. She also holds a master's in Women's Studies and a master's in Social Work. She worked as a social activist in India from 1997 to 2003. Kavitha's current research focuses on processes of racialization and the experiences of nonwhite immigrants to the United States. Her other areas of interest include critical "race" theories, transnational feminist theorizing, whiteness studies, and globalization studies.

MARY CATHERINE LOVING is currently on leave from her position as an associate professor of English at New Jersey City University. She is also a project girl, a daughter, a mother, a sister, a friend—sometimes all at once, often intermittently. She is a poet, a student, a believer in things she has not seen, a seer of things she does not believe.

ANDREA A. LUNSFORD is the Louise Hewlett Nixon Professor of English and Humanities and director of the Program in Writing and Rhetoric at Stanford University. She has designed and taught undergraduate and graduate courses in writing history and theory, rhetoric, literacy studies, and women's writing and is the author or co-author of many books and articles, including *The Everyday Writer; Essays on Classical Rhetoric and Modern Discourse; Singular Texts/Plural Authors: Perspectives on Collaborative Writing; Reclaiming Rhetorica: Women in the History of Rhetoric; Everything's an Argument; Exploring Borderlands: Composition and Postcolonial Studies;* and *Writing Matters: Rhetoric in Private and Public Lives.*

MARIANA ORTEGA is professor of Philosophy at John Carroll University, University Heights, Ohio. Her research focuses on questions of self and sociality in existential phenomenology, in particular Heideggerian phenomenology. Her other interests include U.S. third world feminism, latina feminism, and race theory. She co-edited with Linda Martín-Alcoff the anthology *Constructing the Nation: A Race and Nationalism Reader* (SUNY, 2009).

ARIEL ROBELLO is a mother/writer/educator who lives on poetry and random acts of kindness. She has taught ESL/creative writing/composition workshops for a host of nonprofits and colleges as both adjunct faculty and guest lecturer stateside and abroad. She holds an MFA from Antioch University and is at work on her MA in TESOL. Her book of poems, *My Sweet Unconditional,* was published by Tía Chucha (distributed by Northwestern University Press) in 2005. She is at work on a collection of short stories, *Love Letters from Miss America,* that emphasize the international pandemic of immigrant rights abuses.

DENISE A. SEGURA is a professor of Sociology and an affiliated professor in the Department of Chicana/o Studies, Program in Latin American and Iberian Studies, and the Department of Feminist Studies at the University of California, Santa Barbara. She has published numerous articles on Chicanas and Mexican immigrant women workers and Chicana/Latina feminisms. She is the co-editor with Patricia Zavella of *Women and Migration in the U.S.-Mexico Borderlands: A Reader* (Duke University Press, 2007).

GLORIA STEINEM is a writer who has been traveling as a feminist organizer since the late 1960s. A co-founder of *Ms. Magazine,* the Ms. Foundation for Women, and the Women's Media Center, her books include *Outrageous Acts and Everyday Rebellions, Revolution from Within,* and *Moving Beyond Words.*

MOHAMMAD H. (BEHROOZ) TAMDGIDI is associate professor of Sociology teaching social theory at the University of Massachusetts, Boston. He is the founding editor of *Human Architecture: Journal of the Sociology of Self-knowledge,* a publication of OKCIR: The Omar Khayyam Center for Integrative Research in Utopia, Mysticism, and Science (Utopystics) (http://www.okcir.com), which serves to frame his research and teaching initiatives. Most recently he is the author of *Gurdjieff and Hypnosis: A Hermeneutic Study* (Palgrave Macmillan, 2009) and *Advancing Utopistics: The Three Component Parts and Errors of Marxism* (Paradigm, 2007; softcover edition 2009). His writings have appeared or are forthcoming in *REVIEW: Journal of the Fernand Braudel Center for the Study of Economies, Historical Systems, and Civilizations; Sociological Spectrum; Humanity and Society; Contemporary Sociology;* and several edited collections.

BECKY THOMPSON is a writer, teacher, and activist living in Jamaica Plain, Massachusetts. Her books include *Fingernails across the Chalkboard: Poetry and Prose on HIV/AIDS from the Black Diaspora,* co-edited with Randall Horton and Michael Hunter (2007); *When the Center Is on Fire,* co-authored with Diane Harriford (2008); *A Promise and A Way of Life* (2001); *A Hunger So Wide and So Deep* (1994); and *Mothering without a Compass* (2000). She has been awarded fellowships from the NEH, the Rockefeller Foundation, the American Association for University Women, the Ford Foundation, and Political Research Associates, and she received the Gustavus Myers Award for Outstanding Books on Human Rights in North America. Her recent poems appear in *Harvard Review, We Begin Here: For Palestine and Lebanon, Warpland: A Journal of Black Literature and Ideas, Amandla, Illuminations, The Teacher's Voice,* and *Margie* (forthcoming). She is currently director of Women's and Ethnic Studies at the University of Colorado at Colorado Springs. (E-mail: bthompso@uccs.edu.)

ANAHÍ VILADRICH is a medical anthropologist and sociologist of Argentine origin. She has widely published on gender, immigration, and health in Argentina and in the United States. She received a Ph.D. with Distinction in 2003, a master of philosophy in Sociomedical Sciences (Anthropology) from Columbia University in 2000, and a master of arts with honors from the New School University in 1999. She is an associate professor at Queens College and the Graduate Center, City University of New York. Since 2004 she has been the director of the Immigration and Health Initiative, a program aimed at sponsoring research, teaching, and advocacy on the health issues of immigrant populations in the United States and abroad (http://www.immigration andhealthinitiative.org).

PAOLA ZACCARIA is an activist, former president of the Italian Society of Literary Women, and professor of Literary and Visual Anglo-American Culture at Bari University, Italy. She has published books and essays on twentieth-century Anglo-American avant-gardes, poetry, feminist criticism, Latina and African American literature, border and diaspora studies, transnationalism, interculturality, translations/transpositions/transcodifications, and literary and film theory. She is the Italian translator and editor of *Borderlands/La Frontera* (Bari 2000). She interviewed Anzaldúa in 1998 (published by «Acoma»), and she has written about Anzaldúa's work in many book chapters and journal articles. She directed a documentary on Gloria Anzaldúa that was shot in spring 2008 in California and Texas.

KELLI ZAYTOUN is director of Women's Studies and associate professor of English at Wright State University. Her work focuses on identity and cultural issues in the psychology of self-concept, cognition, and social consciousness. Other interests include Latina and multiracial U.S. feminist theories and memoirs and the women's movement and women's literature in Brazil. Her publications on Anzaldúa's work include "New Pathways to Understanding Self, Relationship, and Cognition: Anzaldúan Re(visions) for Developmental Psychology" in *Entre-Mundos/Among Worlds: New Perspectives on Gloria E. Anzaldúa* (2005) and "Theorizing at the Borders: Considering Social Location in Rethinking Self and Psychological Development" in *NWSA Journal* (Summer 2006).

LEI ZHANG received her bachelor's degree in English from Sichuan University, China, and her master's in Journalism from the University of North Texas. She is currently working on her Ph.D. in Rhetoric at Texas Woman's University. Her scholarly interests include feminist rhetoric, Chinese rhetoric, and composition and pedagogy.

Index

abjection, 211, 213, 222
academy, 147–152; conflicts, 48; disciplines, 5, 142, 145; job market, 97–98; and the spiritual, 46. *See also* disciplinolatry; graduate school; nepantla; tenure process; *and names of individual universities*
activism, 163, 164, 200, 206
Adorno, Theodor, 82
aesthetics, 133; hybrid, 131
affinity, 14, 15
Africa, 173
age, 4, 88, 220. *See also* identity: categories
Agee, James, 137–138
agency, 14–15; spiritual, 177
Alarcón, Norma, 49
Albania, 127–128
Alexander, Jacqui, 152
ALLGO, 3–4, 231n5
alliance making, 202–204, 217; global, 7. *See also* El Mundo Zurdo; new tribalism
American Sociological Association (ASA), 236
American Studies, 3, 7, 136, 147. *See also* "Transforming American Studies"
American Studies Association, 138–139, 141
analytical testimonio, 213, 239n4

Andric, Ivo, 130
anger, 20, 41–42, 70, 159, 199–200, 208; Anzaldúa's, 109, 229
Anglo-American Culture Studies, 3, 7
anglos. *See* "whiteness"
anthologies, making, 4; politics of, 112. *See also* Making Face, Making Soul/Haciendo Caras; This Bridge Called My Back; this bridge we call home
anthropology, 3, 7, 103, 108
Anzaldúa, Gloria, 132–133; activism, 2; as archeologist of knowledge, 166; as bridge, 2; childhood, 1; death, 3–4, 47–48, 49–50, 58–59, 113, 132, 195–196, 219, 225, 227; diabetes, 193–194; experimental style, 6; father's death, 1; health, 1; on identity, 12, 142, 195, 228; impact on readers, 11, 104–106, 109; impact on social sciences, 170–171; influence on writers, 7, 172–173; interactions with others, 56–57; later writings, 195; legacy, 4–5, 47–48, 58; menstruation, 1, 54, 193; mestiza feminist politics, 192; methodology, 169; as nepantlera, 73, 141; and occult knowledge, 231n11; optimism, 196; poetics, 133–135; reception in Mexico, 68–69; relationship to academy, 143–144;

Chicana(s)/Chicano(s), 237n2; culture, 121, 138; literature, 71, 73; nationalism, 176; students, 57–58
chilango-centrism, 68, 70, 71
Chile, 3, 6
China, 3, 6, 86–87
chronic illness, 191–192. *See also* diabetes; health care
Cihuacóatl, 122
citizenship, planetary, 12. *See also* immigration
class, 37, 71, 120, 222. *See also* identity: categories
coalition(s), 36
coalition-building, 12, 14, 108–109. *See also* solidarity
Coatlalopeuh, 121, 122, 192
Coatlicue, 122, 166, 168–169, 233n4, 242. *See also* Coatlicue state; serpent(s)
Coatlicue state, 41–42, 66, 95–96, 125, 166, 169, 193, 206, 207–208, 231n7, 242. *See also* conocimiento
Cobb, John, 146
code-switching. See *Borderlands/La Frontera;* language(s)
cognitive development, 205. *See also* developmental psychology
colonialization, 87, 131, 134
Colón-Otero, Sebastián José, 7, 8
colorism, 7, 35, 38; in Mexico, 70
"The coming of el mundo surdo," 232n15
commonalities, 24–25, 124, 126, 145; humanity, 88. *See also* El Mundo Zurdo; nepantlera(s); nos/otras; spiritual activism
Comparative Literature, 3, 7
complicity, 103, 107–108, 116
composition studies. *See* Rhetoric and Writing Studies
Conference on College Composition and Rhetoric, 183, 184–185
connectionist thinking, 86, 89, 146, 152, 242; defined, 144–145,
conocimiento(s), 1, 6, 10, 123, 126,

129, 231n3; applied, 40–44, 131; as Anzaldúa's journey, 11; and autohistoria-teoría, 19; defined, 205, 242; facultad of, 24; as multidimensional process, 100; seven stages of, 156, 206–207, 238n2; as spiritual practice, 55–56; and tenure process, 6, 92–100; theory of, 19–20, 40, 135. *See also* desconocimiento(s); Coatlicue state; spiritual activism
consciousness, 205; Chicana, 26; split, 122. *See also* binary thinking; conocimiento(s); desconocimiento(s); epistemology; mestiza consciousness
Cooley, Charles Horton, 235n4
Coyolxauhqui, 42–43, 100, 166, 242. *See also* conocimiento(s)
Coyolxauhqui imperative, 171, 208, 242; as methodology, 6
Cuba, 3, 6, 78–79, 165
cultural studies, 176
curandera(s), 40
Curiel, Enriqueta Valdez, 177

Dalai Lama, 30
dalit, 198, 238n1
Daly, Harman, 146
death, 30. *See also* Anzaldúa, Gloria
DeGuzmán, María, 7
Delgado-Gaitán, Concha, 237n1
depression, 60, 216–217. *See also* Coatlicue state
Derrida, Jacques, 67, 85, 192
desconocimiento(s), 95–96. *See also* conocimiento(s); oppression
developmental psychology, 205, 238n2
Dewey, John, 113
diabetes, 1, 59, 69, 193–194, 226
Dickinson, Emily, 15
difference(s), 12–13, 82, 83, 126, 129, 132, 175–176; among women, 113–114. *See also* commonalities; El Mundo Zurdo; new tribalism; nos/otras

Iran, 3, 7
Italy, 3, 7, 127

Jacobs, Glenn, 6
Jewish, 118; literature, 140
Joysmith, Claire, 7, 232nn2–4
Jung, Carl, 166, 168, 213, 215

Keating, AnaLouise, 2, 3, 7, 53–
54, 79, 91, 180, 231n4, 231n11,
232n12, 233n5; on nepantla,
237n6; and nos/otras, 90, 232n13
kindness, 56–60
Kleisath, Michelle, 7
knowledge(s), subjugated, 171. *See
also* academy; conocimiento(s);
epistemology
Koshy, Kavitha, 2, 6, 7, 236n6

labels, 54–55, 143. *See also* identity;
stereotypes
Lacan, Jacques, 15, 158
language(s), 133–134; dialect, 183,
186; home, 186–187; Spanish, 3,
134–135; vernacular, 132. *See also*
code-switching; linguistic terrorism; translation
"La Prieta," 14, 197–198, 220,
235n1
Lara, Irene, 40
Latin American Studies, 3, 7
latina(s)/latino(s), 37, 156; in Canada, 22–24, in higher education, 178–180; stereotyped, 34;
"white," 34
Latina/o Studies, 3, 7, 155–157,
211, 217
Latinidad, 23–24, 36, 37
"Let us be the healing of the wound,"
68, 72
LGBTQ Studies, 147, 151–152, 217.
See also academy
liberation, 7, 59, 125, 133, 150;
Third World, 151
liminality, 118, 119, 121, 123,
197, 198, 201. *See also* nepantla;
nepantlera(s)

linguistic terrorism, 45, 46, 183, 185
listening, 78, 88–90, 108
Llorona, La, 122, 168, 211–212,
213, 239n3, 243
Lorenz, Helene Shulman, 148–149
love, 55–56, 69, 162–163
Lunsford, Andrea, 7, 8

Machado, Antonio, 98
magic, 192
*Making Face, Making Soul/Haciendo
Caras,* 144, 210, 211
Malcolm X, 228
Malinche/La Chingada, 55, 122,
168, 243
Manicheanism, 125
Manifest Destiny, 28, 68
Mannheim, Karl, 221, 239n3
marginalization, 19, 95
Marx, Karl, 15, 158, 166, 167, 220
masculinity, 82
Mayan teachings, 68–69
media, 87, 199
meditation, 47
melancholia, 216–217
mestiza consciousness, 1, 36, 122–
123, 124–125, 140, 165, 170,
178, 180–181, 192–193, 230; in
Chicana feminist sociology, 181;
and conocimiento(s), 242; defined, 243; as methodology, 161;
and scientific spirit, 220–221; and
spiritual activism, 180. *See also*
conocimiento(s); mestizaje
mestizaje, 140, 242
methodology, 196; Anzaldúan,
166–171
Mexico, 3, 7, 160; (c)overt racism-
sexism, 68. *See also* borderlands;
chilango-centrism
migrant status, 81–82
migration, 83, 160–163; transnational, 181
migration studies, 36–37, 169
Mills, C. Wright, 222
mind/body/spirit split, 44, 92
mitá y mitá, 66

mixed-race, 36, 39
Miranda, Deborah, 227
Moraga, Cherríe, 26, 157, 229
Morales, Aurora Levins, 40
Morrison, Toni, 140
Mundo Zurdo. *See* El Mundo Zurdo

naguala, 207, 208, 243
nationalism, 128. *See also* new
 tribalism
National Association of Chicano
 Studies (NACS), 45
National Women's Studies Association
 (NWSA), 144
neoliberalism, 119
nepantilism, 124, 213–215
nepantla, 10, 35, 66, 79, 166, 181,
 200–203, 216, 227–228, 231n7,
 237n6; and academic life, 92, 94–
 95; and conocimiento(s), 206; and
 immigration, 35–36; defined, 4,
 143, 243–244; as methodology,
 6; threshold, 169; and twenty-
 first century, 11–12; as a type of
 Coatlicue state; and white women,
 108–109
nepantlera-activism, 200
nepantlera acts, 152, 200, 236n6
nepantlera(s), 44, 147, 200–203,
 207; Anzaldúa as nepantlera, 73,
 141, 143–144; defined, 143, 144,
 243. *See also* conocimiento
new mestiza, 36, 169–170, 244; as
 dialectical synthesis, 167; theory of
 self, 156–157
new tribalism, 12, 77–78, 84, 150;
 defined, 244; and multiplex self,
 122–123
Nicaragua, 165
nonbinariness, 198–203
nonduality. *See* conocimiento(s); spiritual activism
nos/otras, 8, 12, 67, 85, 88–90, 186;
 defined, 13, 244; and healing, 13;
 "now let us shift. . . . the path of
 conocimiento . . . inner work, public acts," 1, 11, 59–60, 134–135,

209; reactions to 40–41; transforming dualisms, 85–86. *See also*
 conocimiento(s)

objectification, 88–98. *See also* nos/
 otras
objectivity, 20, 52. *See also* epistemology
Ochún, 66, 122, 124
Olsen, Tillie, 137
O'Neill, Eugene, 60–61
oppositional consciousness, 36, 75,
 151, 200
oppression, 84, 89, 110, 125–126,
 224; hierarchies of, 199, 238n3.
 See also Coatlicue state; privilege;
 racism; resistance; sexism
Oppression Olympics, 199, 238n3
Ortega, Mariana, 8
Ortiz, Fernando, 119, 235n2

pacifist movement, 128
pain, 7, 59, 231n3; of borders, 136.
 See also Coatlicue state; nepantla
Pan American University, 51–52,
 143
Pardo, Mary, 237n1
patriarchy, 196, 201, 212, 223; capitalist, 198, 238n2
peace, 75, 76, 79, 132, 208
people of color, 12
perception, 19–20. *See also* conoci-
 miento(s); epistemology; facultad,
 la; nepantla
Peterson, Carla, 139
phenomenological sociological research, 222
Philosophy, 3, 7
pigmentocracy, 7
plastic surgery, 86–87
poet(s), 26, 28, 172–173, 174
politics, coalitional, 37, 215; of openness, 195; oppositional, 14, 151;
 of spirit, 9. *See also* identity politics; spiritual activism
Poniatowska, Elena, 72
postcolonial, 233n1

postcolonial inferiority complex, 15, 85–86, 87; and dualistic thinking, 88
postmodernism, 167, 205
poverty, 1, 228
Powell, Timothy, 151–152
privilege, 37, 111, 115–116, 126; academic, 95–96, 98; white, 103, 107–108
psychoanalysis, 166
psychology, 7
Puerto Rican(s), 66
Puerto Rico, 3, 7

qualitative research: in sociology, 6
queer(s), 12, 113, 114, 178, 198, 214; imagination, 82, 83; *See also* identity; Queer Studies
Queer Studies, 83, 146, 147, 210; Anzaldúa's contributions to, 81. *See also* LGBTQ Studies
Quintanales, Mirtha, 47

race, 71, 81, 220, 228. *See also* identity: categories; "whiteness"
racism, 1, 47, 140; in classrooms, 74–75; horizontal, 87–88, 90; internalized, 43–44. *See also* colorism; oppression
Ratcliffe, Krista, 185
rational thought, 92. *See also* epistemology
religion, 8–9, 76, 80, 168–169, 227, 235n3; distinguished from spirituality, 76, 120. *See also* Buddhism; Catholicism; identity; Santería
representation, ethics of, 119–120
research, polydiscursive method, 135
resistance, 133, 239n5
rhetoric and writing studies, 3, 7, 183–187
Rio Grande Valley, 50–51
risking the personal, 7, 13, 15, 200–203; defined, 2; and identity categories, 11, 13. *See also* self-disclosure
robello, ariel, 7
Robinson, Lillian, 139

Ross, Christine, 216
Royster, Jacqueline Jones, 187
Rowley, Michelle, 147
Rubin-Dorsky, Jeffery, 139, 140

Saint Teresa of Avila, 193
Saldívar-Hull, Sonia, xi–xii, 181, 237n7
Sandoval, Chela, 36
Santa Cruz, CA, 52, 59, 60
Santería, 118–120, 122–125, 234–235n1
Sedgwick, Eve, 84
Segura, Denise A., 6, 15
self-care, 97
self-change, 1, 2; and social change, 170, 220–221, 225. *See also* conocimiento(s); spiritual activism
self-disclosure, 52–54, 202. *See also* risking the personal
self-reflection, 120–121, 148; and transformation, 2; *See also* conocimiento(s); spiritual activism
September 11, 2001, 68, 73, 76. *See also* "Let us be the healing of the wound"
serpent(s), 213; *See also* Coatlicue
sex, 80. *See also* identity
sexism, 1, 140; in classrooms, 74–75; in Santería, 125. *See also* oppression
sexuality, 37, 81, 213, 214, 222; in Mexican society, 6, 96–98. *See also* identity: categories
Shadow self, 213–217. *See also* Coatlicue state; Jung, Carl
silence, 88, 94. *See also* listening
Sisters of Color United for Education (SISTERS), 178, 180, 237n3
Shildrick, Margaret, 194
slavery, 30, 172
Smitherman, Geneva, 187
Smuckler, Linda, 238n3, 239n6
social activism, 197, 199
social change, 78–79, 208, 215. *See also* conocimiento(s); self-change; spiritual activism
social justice, 12, 14, 37, 44, 53, 56–

Lightning Source UK Ltd.
Milton Keynes UK
UKHW012026150722
405892UK00010B/238